Riting Myth, Mythic Writing

Riting Myth, Mythic Writing

Plotting Your Personal Story

Dennis Patrick Slattery, Ph.D.

fisher king press

COPYRIGHT

Riting Myth, Mythic Writing:
Plotting Your Personal Story
Copyright © 2012 by Dennis Patrick Slattery
All rights reserved.
First Edition
ISBN 978-1-926715-77-3

Published simultaneously in Canada, the United Kingdom, and the United States of America by Fisher King Press. For information on obtaining permission for use of material from this work, submit a written request to:

permissions@fisherkingpress.com

Fisher King Press
PO Box 222321
Carmel, CA 93922
www.fisherkingpress.com
fisherking@fisherkingpress.com
+1-831-238-7799

Many thanks to all who have directly or indirectly provided permission to quote their works. Every effort has been made to trace all copyright holders. However, if any have been overlooked, the author will be pleased to make the necessary arrangements at the first opportunity.

Front cover image, *Baggin' the Dragon* © is a painting by Mel Mathews.

INCIPIT

Naturally, I thought about the significance of what I was doing, and asked myself, "Now, really, what are you about? You are building a small town, and doing it as if it were a rite!" I had no answer to my question, only the inner certainty that I was on the way to discovering my own myth.

—C. G. Jung, *Memories, Dreams, Reflections*

ACKNOWLEDGEMENTS

To all my mythological studies students and to all participants in my Riting Retreats in the United States and Europe. You all helped to nourish this book into being.

To Mel Mathews of Fisher King Press and to Kate Babbitt, who put all the parts in the right order. My deep gratitude.

"Pandora's Cabala" reprinted by permission of Stephanie Pope.

Spiral images reprinted by permission of Dover Publications.

Excerpt from "Flower Herding on Mount Monadnock" from A NEW SELECTED POEMS by Galway Kinnell. Copyright © 1964, renewed 1992 by Galway Kinnell. Reprinted by permission of Houghton Mifflin Harcourt Publishing Company. All rights reserved.

"Sometimes a Man Stands Up During Supper" from SELECTED POEMS OF RAINER MARIA RILKE, A TRANSLATION FROM THE GERMAN AND COMMENTARY by ROBERT BLY. Copyright © 1981 by Robert Bly. Reprinted by permission of HarperCollins Publishers.

CONTENTS

FOREWORD

Imagine sitting in an Irish pub, drinking ale and listening to the bard weave stories about so many different things, or perhaps captivated by the glow of an outdoor fire while listening to an elder telling stories about history, traditions, and ways to navigate the different life portals that each and every one of us will have to enter at some time. And then—there are stories about destiny, that illusive, mercurial something that catches hold of us at the beginning of life and never seems to want to let go. La forza di destino!! These are the experiences one has in knowing and working with Dr. Dennis Slattery. Whether sharing a pizza and beer or having the luxury of attending one of his lectures or classes, one is privileged to experience an authentic "elder" who, in the tradition of all those wise ones who came before him, has the gift of bringing the world of myth and imagination to life and showing us that indeed these are as real as anything we can touch and hold in our hands.

Dr. Slattery reminds us that myths teach us about all aspects of life, from birth to death, and through the weavings of these eternal stories not only help us recognize the presence of these universal and archetypal patterns but also shows us ways to approach the transcendent.

With more than thirty years of teaching and working with myth, Slattery's newest work, entitled *Riting Myth, Mythic Writing,* is a bold adventure in that it asks the reader to actively engage in the mythic tradition, who is asked to take on the role of bard and allow the soul to tell its story. While he opens the book in reminding us of the perennial wisdom contained in myth, he extends this work by inviting the reader to speak with Self and soul and, in a mythopoetic way, engage psyche as experienced in one's own symptoms, fears, hopes, and joys.

Unless one understands inherent profundity contained and revealed in myths and legends, it may be difficult to grasp the challenge inherent in Dr. Slattery's latest work. He wants his readers not only to know these perennial stories but to assume a certain authorship in the mythic process. His hope is that through this process of "Mythic Writing," the individual will cultivate a meaningful relationship with those transpersonal forces which guide the life process.

There are far too many workshops dealing with myth, legend, and personal writing experiences where individual narratives are somehow elevated to the domain of archetypal, mythic stories. Personal narratives are temporal, whereas myths are eternal and exist as the universal bedrock upon which each new experience is built. The "prima materia" of the soul's experience may not easily accommodate personal narratives, which tend to override, dominate, and ignore those eternal processes that represent the gold of myths. In this journey between the personal and eternal, we sail between Scylla and Charybdis, a journey of two worlds. One is the world of the ego and the whims, needs, and illusions of an egoic world whose actions are often purely secular, despite its protest of caring for soul. Then there is the world of the transcendent. This is the domain Jung spoke of as Soul and Psyche and Rabbi Herschel calls the "Ineffable." Once the realm of transcendence is touched, ego dominance and the supremacy of conscious intentions must, by necessity, take a back seat. Constructionism, narrative therapy, and the illusion that every piece of personal writing is a magnum opus of the soul must be humbled by all that is truly profound. We all know how important it is for parents to believe that whatever their child produces is sacred, and to some extent it is, even when it involves peanut butter, tomato sauce, sesame oil, and chocolate over noodles. But there comes a point when pasta and steak dinner and a really great bottle of wine really does sound and taste so much better than our child's culinary creative expressions. For anyone who partakes of the joys of gastronomical wonders, a moment of reckoning and humbling will someday come when we have to say that my cooking just does not match up with what I know is truly delicious. After more than fifty years of working side by side with many of my own families' cooks, learning the tradition of "La Cucina Povera," there are still some foods I still can't make as well as my aunts and grandfather have done for decades.

Slattery knows and fully appreciates great food and wines and knows where to find the pubs serving the finest brews in Ireland. He knows and loves tradition and has an eye for beauty, originality, and the dialect of Self. Now the question remains if he can inspire these same sensibilities in his students and readers.

His work is that of a bridge builder, a "mediatore," one who connects, and in this book he points to a realm where the universal and eternal can be approached through the personal. In doing so, he shows us the relationship between those myths that have guided humanity since the beginning of time and those very tender and personal moments when we begin to write our own story, tell a tale, and hope to God that our story is a telling of something that still connects our life to the life of all those who came before us and that bridges the ego to the transcendent and archetypal. Writing from the ego can be—well, the story of the ego, while the work of myths is a telling of the eternal, the story of soul and a wisdom that far transcends conscious understanding. These are two very different approaches to myth and story.

It is in this work of making connections between ego and soul that Dennis Slattery is a master. From his many years of working with these eternal motifs, he can easily distinguish when the story is created for the benefit of aggrandizing the ego, from those moments where Self and pure inspiration eclipses the wishes of ego. Two different worlds, two different sensibilities, and each requires the deft hand of a master to sail through these waters, in which one wrong turn will land you against the rocky shore. On the other hand, we also experience those moments when sailor and sea are one, and at those times one has access to those vistas reserved for seekers of—of what?—of wisdom, of knowledge, of a way of life that far transcends the limitation of their personal ego?

So dear Dr. Slattery, navigate well with these sojourners. Teach them the ways of ancient mariners, of the shoals that have stranded sailors since the beginning of time and those stretches of open water that allow for endless journeys across the deep blue sea.

Michael Conforti,
Founder and Director of The Assisi Institute
Brattleboro, Vermont

INTRODUCTION

PERSONAL MYTH: THE SOUL'S CENTRAL STATION

> Why write, if this too easy activity of pushing a pen across paper is not given a certain bull-fighting risk and we do not approach dangerous, agile, and two-horned topics?[1]

Mythic Voice

Several years ago in the parking lot of Pacifica Graduate Institute in Carpinteria, California, where I have been teaching for almost twenty years, I experienced a moment where a shard, an important shard, of my own myth surfaced through a voice within me but *other* than me. It was early morning. I like to set up my wares in the classroom an hour prior to the course's beginning. Teaching days at Pacifica are eight hours in length, so one had better be prepared with a full day's cache of material.

My own habit was to bring books that might be of interest to the students, my own texts to deploy in the class, folders stuffed with notes both hand-written and typed, perhaps a newspaper or magazine article I had snagged along the way to emphasize a point or idea I wanted to develop. I also shared texts that had influenced my own thinking and writing. So, as always, my groaning two-wheeled case with an extended handle was overburdened with options and bulging to the point that the clasps had long ago ruptured, victims of my ambitious desire to widen the contours of the class material. I found myself asking, as I rolled this mass across the driveway, why I had once more brought as much as three times the amount of material I could ever traverse, even in 16 hours. The response, at 7:30 a.m., startled me and stopped me in my tracks. From some wise source within I heard a responsive assertion which consisted of three succinct words: "Excess is Access."

I paused and smiled at this revelation, and humbly offered thanks to the primal source that helped me understand my behavior. I believe now that the voice's genesis uncoiled from the core of my personal myth. It did not arise from my ego; it came from a deeper, more

---

1 José Ortega y Gasset, quoted in James Hillman, *Re-Visioning Psychology* (1975; repr., New York: HarperPerennial, 1992), pp. xv-xvi.

resonant place in me, the soul and source of who I am. It carried an impersonal or, better said, objective quality about it so that I knew it was in me but not of me. Myths, I considered, even if personal, maintain their own autonomy but often let us in on their patterns if we are open and receptive to receive them. This last observation defines the purpose of the book that follows.

I felt great comfort in this pronouncement. I continued to the classroom equipped with some sense of myself that carried far beyond the amount of material for class; it went so far as to designate a world view, a way of being in the world and of relating to the material that contributed importantly to my life substance and texture both as professor and as person. The pronouncement gave voice to the mythic dimension of who and what I am. It was part of my narrative, but it had its origin much deeper, more in tune with a pattern in my soul, an arrangement of scarcity, of not having enough, of needing more, to come to an agreeable equilibrium. Excess opened up possibilities that I did not feel I had access to without the "too muchness" of my goods. Having "enough" was not "good enough." Too much was for me indeed enough. The myth within showed how it organized my behavior into a patterned meaning that carried the voice of soul within it; it enacted in language what I was behaving bodily and divulged, as if in a mysterious revelation, what I *was* as much as *who* I incarnated.

I am not so much questioning how mythos, or, for the Greeks, *muthos*, means story or narrative. It is simply not enough, or does not penetrate sufficiently into the energy field that myths inhabit. There is the pattern again, one I am in the service of. Our stories that we plot are often unconscious; nonetheless, they comprise ways of seeing, or to say it another way, mythopoetic modes of knowing and discerning through particular imaginal constructs that are first of all, embodied paradigms. It relies as much on a method or a way of seeing as it does on the content of those perceptions and fantasies. They need only be true for me. In addition, only I am in a position to tell my story. Others relating my narrative is little more than hearsay. What is important for the structure of this book is that each person who participates in its riting meditations has the opportunity to tell her own story, as unedited as one wishes to risk and in their own authentic voice as they understand that authenticity.

A myth, I began to discern, is a manner, and even a style of being present to the world's matter as well as to interior ideas and thoughts. A myth is like a fulcrum balancing two realities: the external world I meet day-to-day, and the inner psychic world that has its own objective nature, not needing me to exist but is rather working itself through me and that I must come to a fuller awareness of to have a fuller knowledge of what I am.

A myth includes a way, a *via* or roadway, a path, that allows things of the world to present themselves to me in a particular style of intellectual and emotional presence. One of its means of expression is through ritual behavior, as my lugging all those tomes within my roller suitcase advanced its expression and allowed it to emerge on that particular morning as a revelatory presencing. It was my way of ritualizing the teaching day, of giving it props and form, and certainly formatting how I wanted learning to progress: with abundance. Perhaps it took the shape of excess, but that line may be a fine, and even a shifting one. One person's excess is another's abundance or even another's scarcity! Shaping the contours of one or another along mythic lines may be a matter of attitude and disposition, to say nothing of style. Myths dispose us to inflect the world in one or more variant lines that often, but not need, converge. I may react conservatively to one life situation or idea and liberally to another. We each are polluted constellations of both tendencies. Discovering personal myth's changing and shifting contours is a life's work and indispensable to self-knowledge. Few tasks in life are more critical than exploring and realizing the terms of one's personal myth, as C. G. Jung's quote that comprises the *incipit* of this volume confirms.

My personal myth, then, is in large measure the consequence of how I structure my images of reality based on patterns that I have developed from my life experiences as well as deeper preexisting arrays embedded in the psyche of all of us. Further, lurking behind these patterns I believe are energy fields of the psyche that are unique to me and yet transcend me because they participate in a much larger cosmos than my own micro-world is capable of holding. However, I am able to participate in this larger cosmos. To study the contours of one's personal myth, which is the intention of this book through both a variety of sources on the subject and related disciplines as well as numerous writing meditations, is to begin to discern the patterns in the prose of our lives, in the poetics of the way of our knowing and shaping reality to conform at least in part to the inner terrain or landscape of our being. The more each of us is able to discern the formats and energies as well as the persons that inhabit and shape our fantasies, day dreams, night narratives, modes of perception, what attracts and interests us, what repels us, what is distasteful, boring, ugly, beautiful, where and what we distort, disturb and deflect, and to see within those patterns the energy flow of invisible presences, is to glimpse the outlines of the plot of our lives. Moreover, the more honestly and fully we comprehend the deep tap roots of our narratives as well as the elaborate fictions we are and continue to shape and be shaped by, the more our plot complexity reveals itself.

As he worked dream images and narratives in a group setting, the Swiss psychologist C.G. Jung would pay close attention to the emergence of patterns that rose up from the unconscious as clues to making sense of the dream.[2] Patterns of images, narratives and energies seemed to comprise the psychic scaffolding of a life, both consciously and unconsciously negotiated, and always without intermissions. I reference once more Jung's observation that begins this book: "I had no answer to my question, only the inner certainty that I was on the way to discovering my own myth." The key word here is *discovering*. It sets the landscape for the meditations that populate the journey through these meditations.

The avenues or corridors that I plan to implement in moving us into the (w)riting meditations throughout the chapters include the following: 1) the image of the spiral; 2) psychic energy as outlined by C. G. Jung; 3) the mythic energy involved in making something affectively present, a term developed by the cultural anthropologist, Robert Plant Armstrong; 4) the fields out of which one's personal myth arises and from which it has its genesis; 5) the patterns that reside behind and beneath the narratives that instill in our lives meaning and coherence, even within its multiple structures and impulses; 6) the force and power of ritual as enactment and as frame for the work of soul-making to reveal the contours of one's personal myth; 7) writing as a ritual enactment of remembrance of psyche's embodied motion and intentions.

I believe that by tracking and recording these areas we can develop inroads into the dynamic and unique energy that comprises our mythology, make it *more conscious*, as well as discern ways to change what is no longer operative yet remains obstinate hindrances in and to our growth as unique persons. Writing primarily, but not exclusively, will be the most dominant activity of the imagination to unfurl into these areas. Others will include "authentic movement" as outlined by Joan Chodorow and others, as well as drawing and painting to give non-verbal image and body to some of the meditations. Some of these writings will lead into pockets of darkness and obscurity, areas that may frighten us into turning the other face to resist gazing into that imposing and unnerving darkness. Whatever level of the pilgrimage you, the participant, wish to take without harming yourself is your decision. Each of you is encouraged to draw your boundary lines for this work and to work

---

2 C. G. Jung, *Dream Analysis: Notes of the Seminar Given in 1928-1930*, ed. William McGuire, Bollingen Series XCIX (Princeton, N.J.: Princeton University Press, 1984), pp. 99-101.

within a realm that is challenging but not debilitating, at times difficult but not disarming, for the richness lies in the depth of the treasures of insight you dig deep enough to garner.

Structure of the Chapters

The roads one could take into the mythos that lives within each of us and that we at the same time live outside in the world we inhabit, are infinite. Choosing certain fields to enter while stepping around others was challenging, until I was able to relinquish trying to control which should be included and instead simply listened to what might be most fruitful. The results include the following: "Introduction: The Soul's Central Station" allows me to outline in broad strokes the method and the manner of this exploratory pilgrimage; Chapter 1, "Meditations on Myth and Mythic Consciousness," discerns the broad contours of mythos and its implications for a richer, more nuanced, and consciously-lived life; Chapter 2, "Engaging the Myth That Rites You," explores the power and mystery of those numinous presences that help to shape the contours of our character and our callings; Chapter 3, "The (W)riting Self," engages the act of writing as a way to ritualize a conversation with and within the deepest layers of ourselves, as well as between personal and collective; Chapter 4, "Riting the Aesthetic Self: Mythopoesis," invites us to journey into the shaping or making quality of the soul, which is constantly, it seems, whether in waking life, in dream or reverie or sleep, in fantasies and aspirations, always in process of poetically and aesthetically offering imaginative form to our plot patterns; Chapter 5, "Riting the Wounded Self," opens to our afflictions, infections, even our *afflixations*, a word I coin to capture the sense of fixations within our afflictions. They can have the numbing capacity to fixate us in an arrested place in our lives, but can also allow us a new freedom, and to beckon us to a shifting narrative, to dissolve parts of that story in order to heal some part of us that may have been scabbed over for decades; Chapter 6, "Riting Through the Embodied Self," returns us again to our enfleshed being and becoming by urging us to reclaim our conscious embodied selves; Chapter 7, "Riting the Self as/and Other," asks that we consider the unitary presence of ourselves through the Otherness of the world; Chapter 8, "Riting the Spiritual Self," emphasizes that we are each spiritually psychological or psychologically spiritual because the soul is inspirited and enfleshed; Chapter 9, "Reviewing and Riting the Patterned Self," spirals back in an ancient geometric pattern that is retrospective, recursive, and re-collective as we review and grasp what patterns or motifs, what mythic themes seem to recur to restrain, resist, or renew our prose. The spiral is a geometry of retrieval that offers us a way back without duplicating where we have been. In the more innate and ancient triple spiral, for instance, that appears at the great Entrance Stone of Newgrange in Ireland, wisdom has it that it marks "the place where past and future collide in a miraculous present, where darkness transforms itself into renewing light."[3]

Each writing meditation will allow some uncovering as well as occasional moments of revelation, insight, observation, and revaluing within the cauldron of our life's ingredients, even its gradients of importance and value. Writing may be best understood as a ritual which includes moments of revaluing, renewing and perhaps resuscitating what might continue to serve both our development and our retreats back into earlier persistent patterns of thought and behavior as well as point out what might be best relinquished at this moment in our lives. Our personal myth, like all living myths, is organic: it grows, sheds, renews, shrivels, attacks parts of itself, restores others, ages, ripens, molts and renews. Holding on desperately to our myth can create an encrusted ideology out of the mythology such that all life energy end-stops. Riting meditations are thus exploratory to find and perhaps choose to excise what is keeping us from a full and joyful life. We can only imagine what is waiting to be let into our story if we give it space and an invitation to enter.

A good therapist friend suggested to me that sometimes the most important aspects of our lives is on the margins of it, and that writing may be a way to write those margins into fuller consciousness. Marginal matters in our lives may become most meaningful through writing of them in a meditative way. Our peripheral vision picks up shards of our myth and highlights them in consciousness: fragments from dreams, parts of conversations, a film that particularly stirred us, an overheard conversation, for instance.[4] Not main events but more minor experiences can yield the greatest insights by meditation and writing.

Modes of Knowing

For the past dozen years I have given one-, three-, and four-day "Riting One's Personal Myth" retreats across the United States, in Canada, and in Switzerland. In all cases, I have

---

3 Patricia Monaghan, "Foreword," in Frank MacEowen, *The Spiral of Memory and Belonging: A Celtic Path of Soul and Kinship* (Novato, Calif.: New World Library, 2004), pp. xii-xiii.

4 Dr. Charles Asher, Jungian analyst, personal communication, December 20, 2011.

been astonished by what participants create out of these "psychological prompts" that allow for a spiraling down into their particular histories to excavate at the deepest levels of their being what guides, informs, and helps shape their lives through twistings, distortions, woundings, and idealizations as well as through the persons and places that comprise the imaginal landscape we inhabit. For in each of our personal biographies are patterns of energy that guide, twist, distort and disassemble us, along with gifts of genius that create us into the being we are destined to become. But such a journey requires immense courage as well as a conviction that this voyage takes a lifetime to accomplish.

Many of the meditations I have used in these riting retreats will be included here; others more currently crafted for this text will also find their way into the chapters. It is almost impossible to gauge which meditations will work best, which will have less energy and thus must be abandoned, without first trying them out. Again, the test and the surprise is in what participants produce through these prompts. Therein abides the real story as well as the excitement that clusters around crafting this book together. This text is completed only with your participation as ritual writers of your narrative history and destiny.

Spiral, Presence, Pattern, and Energy Field will be our primary street signs. Imagination and intuition instead of reason and analysis will comprise our guiding modes of inquiry; the intent is to reclaim a poetics of myth rather than an analysis of mythology. Hence, mythos will be claimed over logos as a mode of knowing. Its tension is claimed in those realms of what is imagined as our fiction and what is remembered as our history. My hope is that this book will allow and encourage a deeper penetration into the self as it relates to the world than simply recording as in a diary, bits and pieces of our daily plot, the broken shards of our becoming. Its intention is to retrieve what we are through the poetics of depth and archetypal psychology and by means of the shaping and forming instincts of the soul. Attitude and angle of vision will take precedence over information and recollecting past events as simply the literal plot of our dramatic emergence. Inviting a fuller and deeper consciousness through imaginative writing will trump data-processing or information-herding. In it all I have a fundamental trust in the soul of each of us to reveal what is necessary to contemplate, not analyze, to confront and not flee from, to recognize as part of our own shadowed and illuminated being, the darkness and light of our soul's ambience.

We will resist both analysis and certainty; the ritual of writing is a manner of being present in what has been called "liminal space," where we give up control, seek not confirmation, and rest in the rite of space "neither here nor there; they are betwixt and between the positions assigned and arrayed by law, custom, convention and ceremonial. . . . Thus liminality is frequently likened to death, to being in the womb, to invisibility, to darkness . . . to the wilderness and to an eclipse of the sun or moon," writes ritual expert Victor Turner.[5] In our writing meditations we will indeed experience death along with renewal, not once but many times, for in the ritual process, some parts of our secure skin will be sloughed off, new skin gleaned and a fuller comprehension of our entire galaxy beckoned. Such is the exciting segment of how our personal myth enlightens and darkens who we are.

---

5 Victor Turner, *The Ritual Process: Structure and Anti-Structure* (New York: Aldine de Gruyter, 1995), p. 95.

1

MEDITATIONS ON MYTH AND MYTHIC CONSCIOUSNESS

You stumble—blunder, there is the treasure. One plows a field; the plow snags on something; one digs down—finds a ring; hoists the ring and finds a cave full of jewels.[6]

In preparation for a recent radio interview on the nature of mythology, I continued to wonder where myths originate and what they are guided and goaded by.[7] One idea that surfaced is that there exists a deep connection between psychic energy and its patterned expressions, rhythms, repetitions, imitations, analogies, metaphors, symbols, and styles. They each take part in a conspiracy to access deeper and more complex layers of one's fictional fabric, one which denies nothing in our imaginations. I thought too of how speaking of myths as stories is perfectly legitimate and yet somehow incomplete, for behind the story is a structure, behind the structure is an archetypal pattern and behind the archetypal pattern is an energy field that powers and shapes perception, imagination, memory and our particular form of constructing via intuition the events of our lives into coherent, if finally fragmented, experiences.[8]

If this insight is even partially valid, then myth may be likened to a gerund, as a way of seeing rather than a content of perception, although I do not wish to split these two parts of consciousness. But as an example, the heroic manner of being in the world, for instance, in which ego consciousness dominates, is one in which the person seeks to be in constant control, where order and prediction, conquest and mastery, operate the engines of that personal myth. All of these stances comprise potent yet limited parts of what remains a complex way of being and behaving. My point is that the heroic is a way or style of

---

6 Joseph Campbell, *An Open Life: Joseph Campbell in Conversation with Michael Toms*, foreword by Jean Erdman Campbell (Burdett, N.Y.: Larson Publications, 1988), p. 6.

7 Philip Lynch, interview of Dennis Patrick Slattery, November 3, 2009, *In Touch with Carl Jung*, blogtalkradio.com/carljung.

8 Susan P. Rowland, *C. G. Jung in the Humanities: Taking the Soul's Path* (New Orleans, La.: Spring Journal Books, 2010), p. 23.

constituting the world along a particular patterned and energy-laden groove. We want to avoid such a heroic stance in our work here but use the illustration of myth as a manner of perception that matters profoundly in how we envision and fabricate the world.

Out of such an observation, I suggest that a myth, then, is a patterned manner of imagining, a style of being present to the world. The way the world presents itself to me is no hodgepodge or accident; rather, it follows some invisible force, a particular muse-laden manner of presence. Many people are unaware that this is occurring; they assume that they are the creators of such a complex plot. This term *presence* I will entertain more fully later. Here, however, I suggest that when something attracts our attention in its present-ness, our personal myth is startled into full play on the stage of perception and interpretation; it seeks to know what is presenting itself in its full-bodied affective state.

What, I have often wondered, is at play in the field of myth that gives it energy or siphons energy from it? We can feel the depletion when we awaken from a night's sleep and have little or no energy, no interest in the world and little desire to arise. On the other hand, when do aspects of the world hold a powerful attraction for me and when does that attraction fade into indifference or otherwise become invalid for me because the energy that once (em)powered it has dissipated or shifted to other interests? Answering these questions touches on the changing, protean and elastic nature of myth if it is organically alive. As neuroscience points with plenty of evidence to the brain's plasticity, namely, its ability to change, so too with myth. Myth has a plasticity and an elasticity; otherwise we might be arrested in one way of living if the myth could not metamorphosis into new venues or mutate into new areas of attraction.

Such a thought led me to consider the way in which myths are a form of a method; I created the neologism *mythodology* to suggest that the manner of my interpreting the world carries simultaneously both a myth and a method in it—a mythic method aligned or in consort with the world's matter. Out of such a conversation between a "tension of opposites" arises a third thing, a *tertium quid,* that aligns the first two with a meaningful third.[9] It is *as if* all our perceptions are imaginal acts of consciousness in that they always engage a sense of metaphor, the creation of a third reality out of two conjoined, even if, and perhaps especially if, they are in-tense opposition. From it grows a significance based or resting on

---

9 The term "tertium quid" appears in *Alchemical Studies*, vol. 13 of *The Collected Works of C. G. Jung*, trans. R. F. C. Hull (Princeton, N.J.: Princeton University Press, 1983), ¶ 199.

the relation or equation of a to b and c to d in relationship with one another.[10] The mythologist Joseph Campbell suggests that "metaphor is the native tongue of myth." Metaphor reveals a presence of likeness within obvious difference; from its presence, a third possibility is borne out in the tension of likeness with difference. The third is what we carry with us as new knowledge within the rubric of the first two terms.[11]

I want us to entertain what is revealed if we think of a metaphor as an energy field that is instrumental in accessing unconscious contents in the same way that the energy of a drill bit can bore down and into dimensions of the earth not available without such a vertical force bearing down and in it. So, for instance, reading a classic work of literature or listening to a Bach Fugue invites the creation of a metaphor between my own mythos and the myth inherent in the poem or music's composition so that *some turbulence* arises between the two, to break open what is set in place to allow for insight in both the imaginative creation and my own mythopoetic self. An opening occurs between conscious and unconscious forces or presences through the poem or music as I experience and interpret it. Out of that engagement a third thing appears, which may be a newly-formed conscious way of grasping or apprehending what before was unknown. It may in fact be that all art accesses this energy of tension in likeness/difference with itself and within ourselves that nourishes us with a new way of apprehension. Something emerges as an intuition, a felt insight, even a vision of something true. Such a moment of presence is precisely what we are after in the riting meditations.[12]

In the imaginal act of reading, then, a collision often accompanied by a collusion, emerges between two mythologies that promotes a greater self understanding by means of the fiction I am journeying through. Metaphors as myths serve as transport vehicles to move us from one arena to another, from a visible reality into the terrain of invisible presences; it links what is known with what cannot be known directly, but only by way of analogy,

---

10 One of Joseph Campbell's favorite quotations from Immanuel Kant on the syllogism that comprises the structure of metaphor. See Joseph Campbell, *The Inner Reaches of Outer Space: Metaphor as Myth and as Religion* (Novato, Calif.: New World Library, 2002), pp. 29-30.

11 Campbell goes on to claim that "the life of a mythology springs from and depends on the metaphoric vigor of its symbols." Joseph Campbell, *Thou Art That: Transforming Religious Metaphor* (Novato, Calif.: New World Library, 2001), p. 6.

12 In a discussion on what it is that unites the opposites, C. G. Jung claims that "here only the symbol helps, for, in accordance with its paradoxical nature, it represents the 'tertium' that in logic does not exist but which in reality is the living truth." Jung, *Alchemical Studies*, ¶ 199.

through metaphor, that is, by likeness. Through the window of likeness, something new on the horizon of consciousness introduces itself. Myth powers this new perception.[13]

Similar musings have led me to believe that the psyche is fundamentally poetic, analogic, metaphoric, symbolic in its field-creating and pattern-producing proclivities. Its inherent and abiding impulse is to fabricate fictions—by which I do not mean lies or untruths, but authentic images and stories of the soul's life. The soul has a poetic existence that it uses to create its own elaborate fictions. Impulses[14] for such story-making arise from both conscious and unconscious forces. A mythology is in part a crafted aesthetic form that emerges as an infant from its mother's body. The mother is the myth and the child is the mythology that grows from such a maternal enwombing. Both carry their own energy fields, their own powers of presence; both have a persuasive force when they are affectively present in relation to others.[15]

Patterned presences witness and expose the imprint of the archetypes, which are energy fields in themselves. Moreover, as C. G. Jung reminds us, "an archetypal content expresses itself first and foremost, in metaphors."[16] Regarding the reality of myths, then, archetypes contain and entertain life energy, the libidinal force that makes meaning and significance in the realities we construct through perception and behaviors. Just as important to consider is the manner in which metaphors as energy fields bridge a range of qualities between conscious and unconscious contents as well as body-psyche. In so doing, metaphors convey

---

13 In her discussion of literary genres—lyric, tragedy, comedy, and epic—literary critic Louise Cowan develops the qualities and characteristics of these poetic universes through mimesis and analogy: "Such a generic territory is ruled by its own laws, analogically related to life yet different from daily experience." Louise Cowan, *The Terrain of Comedy* (Dallas, Tex.: The Dallas Institute of Humanities and Culture, 1984), p. 8.

14 James Hillman, *Re-Visioning Psychology* (1975; repr., New York: HarperPerennial, 1992), p. 18.

15 Armstrong is very emphatic about the personhood of a work. He writes, for example: "If the presence of the work is such that the work is treated after the fashion of a human person, then it also follows that such powers as the work owns must be very like those owned by human persons." Robert Plant Armstrong, *The Powers of Presence: Consciousness, Myth, and Affecting Presence* (Philadelphia: University of Pennsylvania Press, 1981), p. 16.

16 This quote is one of the central cores of depth psychology, in part because Jung goes on to reveal that metaphors and similes reveal not one or the other "but the unknown third thing that finds more or less adequate expression in all these similes." C. G. Jung, *Archetypes and the Collective Unconscious*, vol. 9, part I of *The Collected Works of C. G. Jung*, ed. and trans. R. F. C. Hull and Gerhard Adler (Princeton, N.J.: Princeton University Press, 1971), ¶ 267.

their own form of knowing through fundamental patterns. At times they can dehydrate, lose their vitality, their *élan vital* and so become anemic, drained of their gravitational pull on us. No energy is left in them; they dry out and can in turn become brittle responses to life. Recognizing these shards of ourselves that need to be jettisoned is part of becoming more fully conscious of what we are.

An individual may discover with dismaying clarity that each day is "same ole, same ole" in a deadening repetition where no imagination informs the day's events, no life energy is present, no soul life deepens and animates the ordinary. Joy is no longer an operative experience or feeling. Perhaps one signal of wisdom's presence occurs in knowing when to relinquish what feeds like a tapeworm in one's life, devouring all the erotic fuel from one's system. Not to do so is to invite in and even begin to worship dogmatic assertions, rigid beliefs, stern prejudices, unnamed resentments. Even more critical is the loss of the symbolic order of being which myths put us in touch with, in order to deepen our consciousness of ourselves in relation to our world. Symbols also help to organize experience, offer diverse responses to what without them might leave only one routine response; they allow for ambiguity and even paradox in life and keep intact the mysterious reality of being. Without the symbolic order and the accompanying energy that symbols carry to revitalize us by pointing us to invisible presences within the phenomenal world, life becomes colorless, reduced to a sparse number of adjectives that allow for limited unique qualities, differentiation and a paucity of joy.

We each can plateau at a stage of stasis in which symbolic thinking is not even recognized or engaged, which is to relinquish some fundamental vitality in the individual or in a larger orbit, in a culture or a civilization. Manifestations of literalism in the form of set and certain beliefs that entertain no others then proliferate become excessive to fill in the gaps, the black holes in an impoverished soul. Out of such darkness all forms of literalisms and absolute certainties emerge to plague the fertile soil of the imaginal as well as the fecundity of the soul's possibilities. Addictions can take many forms. One of the most arresting is a world view in which all vitality has dissolved, leaving one with a clichéd life, full of empty prose and a life of simple sentences that spark no variety, boast no adjectives, invite little complexity. If one's world view can fit on a bumper sticker, it may be a sign of life's limited possibilities.

One compelling antidote to such a futile condition is to retrieve the mythopoetic sense of life, its creativity and vital energic inflection, where what seems so familiar takes on a different caste because seen again for the first time, where perception once more imagines some new quality within familiarity. Such a spiralic form can shape personal biography or a more inclusive history into a poetic utterance; such mythic thinking encourages it to become what was before an unformed, frightening ordeal, now affectively present. Worth pondering is C. G. Jung's observation during a dream analysis seminar in 1929 in which he remarked: "One of the fundamental laws of natural development is that it moves in a spiral and the true law of nature is always reached after the labyrinth has been traveled. . . . Psychologically you develop in a spiral, you always come over the same point where you have been before, but it is never exactly the same, it is either above or below."[17]

This primal or primordial spiralic action is part of the ritual imagination; it fosters presence in a ritual act which coalesces what was before unloosed and unformed because unseen. All perception becomes at this point a work of art and an act of remembrance; it can be the occasion for an aesthetic response. Meditating on specific writing questions can release parts of the multi-volumed self with its episodic plot to reclaim the larger complexity of who we are. Poetic knowing has tight cords connected to a mythic form of discernment which I believe we can cultivate and strengthen through writing. Writing is an ordering action that can reveal patterns where one never expected them to be present. Let's begin then with a meditation that coaxes a part of our personal myth upward and outward.

Writing Meditation: Assumptions that Frame Me

Within the self swirl dozens, if not hundreds, of assumptions that help to frame as well as form our way of experiencing and modulating our world. They can certainly in-form our way of imagining a self-world dialogue that goes on even when we move through parts of our day below the threshold of awareness. Within assumptions the self-world dialogue can burrow into solitude, take a vertical turn underground and speak in whispers rather than fully-voiced utterances. Assumptions shape the sense of our world in an "as if" mode of

---

17 C. G. Jung, *Dream Analysis: Notes of the Seminar Given in 1928-1930*, ed. William McGuire, Bollingen Series XCIX (Princeton, N.J.: Princeton University Press, 1984), p. 100.

perception. What I assume about myself and others I then think and behave "as if" it were true.[18]

These same assumptions, or many of them, may have an expiration date stamped on them that we have overlooked. Even so, they can still exert strong pulls on us, structuring our styles of awareness as well as our behavior. What we assume becomes a daily part of our on-going narrative: our personal mythos. Further, these same assumptions may reveal where our perceptions are distorted, excessive, deficient, a bit twisted and where we are deformed in our knowing. They may at the same time, reveal the most interesting qualities about us. As carriers or cargo holds for the fantasies we harbor, we in turn protect and feed them regularly because their importance underscores how we define our essential self. At one point they were conscious beliefs that over time have become shop-worn and glazed into knee-jerk modes of thought and action. Assumptions witness how we imagine the world, even if we are only partly conscious in and of the process.

Part I

Describe an assumption that helps to get you out of bed in the morning. This assumption gives you energy and a purpose for getting up and plunging into your day with enthusiasm. For instance, "Today will have meaning for me," or "I can make a difference," or "I may discover something new today." The assumption you choose to write about is constructive, beneficent, benevolent and challenges you as a person to participate in the world in an engaging way.

Writers' Responses

There is an excitement about life, a wonderful curiosity inside of me.

---

18 C. G. Jung understood this "as if" or "als ob" mode of images central to depth psychology: "Every interpretation necessarily remains an 'as-if.'" Jung, *Archetypes and the Collective Unconscious*, ¶ 265. He writes in another volume of psyche's metaphoric sense when he addresses the symbolic quality of dreams and cautions against taking dreams too literally: "These 'shocking' surprises, of which there is certainly no lack in dreams, should always be taken 'as-if', even though they clothe themselves in sensual imagery that stops at no scurrility and no obscenity." C. G. Jung, *Aion: Researches into the Phenomenology of the Self*, vol. 9, part II of *The Collected Works of C. G. Jung*, trans. R. F. C. Hull, 2nd ed. (Princeton, N.J.: Princeton University Press, 1970), ¶ 315.

I want to taste life, I want to experience the beauty of life.

There is a "wonder," an "awe" inside of me about all this beauty, this earthly life.

Curiosity is what life has in store for me and that is the "treasure" I am going after every single day.

I know that there is so much more in store for me, so many gifts and blessings to come, already on their way, that I can't wait to open my eyes to a new dawn, and rising of the sun. (Birgit Krohn)

I must maintain the status quo, keep working, stay in our house, because the four kids still depend on me. I must keep working to pay family expenses, especially health insurance, until my children are in the position to take care of their own financial needs. In the meantime, I can plan, research, and prepare for the time that they no longer need my financial support. (Sara Sornson)

Part II

Describe an assumption that arrests you, or curtails your life or holds you back or takes the arresting form of an albatross around your neck, constantly pulling you down by constricting your options for understanding or tolerance. For instance, "I am unable to do X and always have been unable to do it" or "when I see X, I will not be able to express myself adequately." This assumption still guides you in a destructive way, but to date you have not been able to rid yourself of it, so stubbornly does it hold you back. Engaging this initial meditation is a way of setting you up for the terms of personal myth that follow. I also think it is of enormous benefit throughout this book to offer, when available, a few examples of how previous participants responded to many of the Writing Meditations. Here are a few from Part II of this foundational meditation:

Writers' Responses

If people really knew me, they would be disgusted.

I can hide forever.

Following my heart is dangerous and stupid.

Most of my assumptions are self-destructive. My reality is not spiralic, but cyclic. One assumption feeds the next. A beer, a cigarette, a man's arms around me. It's intoxicating, exhausting, and it's based on an old story, an expired carton of milk, a pair of shoes that are too small, yet I insist on wearing.

My nails dig below the surface, bleeding.

Who says that this is truth?

I have allowed others to create my identity, my assumptions have invaded my garden.

I'm aware, but I'm drowning, the forces are heavy around me, plaguing me, pulling me back when I'm DYING to leap forward.

I'm a weed in my own garden; an assumption/ a skewed perception is tangled around my heart, and the knot is so tight.

I'm afraid that if it's loosened, I won't survive—and I'm right. (Sarah Colburn)

Guilty

Not charged

At least not by those who matter,

Those who paid attention,

Those who were there.

Guilty

I was there.

I heard the words.

Did not stop it,

Did not expect it, expected it not to happen.

Thought it was idle talk,

A threat with no substance.

Guilty

Unable to overcome it.

Unable to release the feelings:

Anger

Regret

Abandonment

Resentment

Responsibility . . .

Guilty

I let him down.

I let him rave.

I let him go.

Guilty, weak, living on. (Sara Sornson)

Attributes of Personal Myth

Approaching myth requires an embrace of paradox.[19]

It will be beneficial for the reader to orient him/herself with a few characteristics of the term personal myth. Throughout the book I will add to this list of qualities or elements that comprise it, but I do not believe the term will be happy to be pinned down in any absolute way; to do so would violate its presence through the savagery of a single defining phrase. I used to think, moreover, that our personal myth was comprised of a main story. Of course that still holds true; yet it is also true that each of us is an elaborate, multi-valent series of fictions, all overlapping and interlocking, all elaborate, conjoined that, over time, reveal patterns of awareness, beliefs, fears, dreams, uncertainties, gifts, memories and creative fantasies. Discovering the lineaments of one's personal myth through writing, speaking, dreaming, authentic body movement, poetry, and drawing will contribute as indicators of one's rich and always shifting, guiding mythos. My underlying assumption is that the ritual act of writing, which I will say more of later, is a way to clear a field, make a space, encourage a deepening movement down and through the terrain of our personal myth by encouraging a conversation between our conscious, ego-centered life and the deeper unconscious part of us that has a life of its own outside conscious awareness. C. G. Jung sensed that deeper than consciousness was a lower stratum, the unconscious: "Once the unconscious is included in

---

19 Dennis Patrick Slattery and Glen Slater, eds., *Varieties of Mythic Experience: Essays on Religion, Psyche and Culture* (Einsiedeln, Switzerland: Daimon Verlag, 2008), p. 19.

the calculation, everything gets a double bottom, as it were. We have to look at everything from two sides, whereas the old psychology was satisfied with the contents of consciousness."[20] For we are each peopled by a multitude of presences, personalities and purposes, as well as layers of psychic activity that the act of writing can stimulate into awareness. These layers and presences can often appear in competition with and sometimes in complement with one another. I therefore begin with these premises: a personal myth

- Is a loom on which we weave the raw materials of daily experience into a coherent story.[21]
- Organizes my experiences of the world and determines or influences by what categories I will engage the world's matter.
- Molds my life events according to categories of awareness.
- Draws to me what I imagine to be true.
- Frames the "als ob," or "as if" quality of the soul. The "as if" quality of my days expresses the mythic principles I live by.
- Reveals that what I believe about myself and the world will influence what I believe to be true.
- If vital and alive, is always evolving and continually assessing what is working and what is useless or abusive for me in my on-going self-definition.
- Is flexible, Protean and elastic so long as it remains organic and living.
- Can harden or calcify from an organic living thing into a rigid dogmatism that is closer to a cadaver than to a malleable life principle.
- Is a mode of perceiving which may be more important to its health and growth than the subjects and objects of perception.
- Is a way into the aesthetics, poetics, mystical, and transcendent qualities of my being.
- Is always in process of constructing a model of reality, a guiding set of values and twistings of the normative.
- Is related intimately to my organic bodily being and emanates in part from my incarnated substance.
- Is an inner shaman, a guiding guru that can open me to larger forces in both my interior world and the larger reality I am enshrouded in daily.
- Is comprised of energy fields of consciousness that shift, intensify, diminish to allow for certain elements to enter, others to be denied ingress.

---

20 C. G. Jung, "Depth Psychology and Self-Knowledge," in *The Symbolic Life: Miscellaneous Writings*, vol. 18 of *The Collected Works of C. G. Jung*, trans. R. F. C. Hull (Princeton, N.J.: Princeton University Press, 1976), pp. 811-821.

21 David Feinstein and Stanley Krippner, *The Mythic Path: Discovering the Guiding Stories of Your Past—Creating a Vision for Your Future* (New York: Jeremy Tarcher/Putnam Books, 1997), p. 20.

- Embodies a quest and every quest harbors a question or is motivated by a central question. Each of us must find that question on our own journey, not someone else's travels.
- Has a vitality that is measured in large part by its capacity to and for change.
- Is actively engaged in the formation, de-formation and re-formation of my personal identity, which may be the central task of our adult years.
- Is always related and defines the epistemology I function within to process what events occur to me to fit them into a story that has coherence and continuity.

Let this initial list of characteristics be the starting point for our journey. More will be added as we begin to engage through a wide variety of writing meditations the contours and boundaries of the myth that guides us.

Meditations on Writing

What voices are liberated by writing that reaches out to the *whole psyche?*[22]

I used to feel that writing was painful, humbling, even humiliating and, finally, never complete, never good enough. Over the years my perspective has shifted dramatically. I do not know if there exists a more powerful way to access the deepest layers of our being than writing, even more so than speaking. Writing has its own ritual gradient, its own energy field. In riting retreats I make some claims about this imaginal and mythic act of consciousness wherein one can think, discover, recover, and thus deepen a sense of self in relation to a larger world and to one another. By writing I mean here script, cursive, or long-hand writing, not keyboard typing. The only technology engaged is the pen. The slow looping and curving of the letters "in one's own hand" is essential to slowing and often thereby deepening the quality of expression. More on this shortly. For now, here are a few observations on this mysterious and fruitful act of consciousness I want to engage more deeply. Writing

- Is a form of sustained meditation. It is a powerful way to foster and deepen the reflective process.

---

22 Susan P. Rowland, *C. G. Jung in the Humanities: Taking the Soul's Path* (New Orleans, La.: Spring Journal Books, 2010), p. 23, Rowland's italics.

- Is a form of discovery. Inherent in anything we wish to contemplate is an inner form that energizes and organizes the experience.

- Is a way of revealing oneself to oneself as Other. Otherness that is us emerges in the act of writing that is unique to this form of knowing.

- Is another form of spiritual contemplation, a willed openness to mystery, to the transcendent, to the personal and collective unconscious,[23] to the soul's moods, lexicon and atmosphere.

- Is a means of drawing into presence my faculties of perception, remembrance, imaginings, as an embodied action.

- Is a bearing witness to an event, a memory, a dream, a trauma, a moment of joy wherein some formed reality seeks voice in a particular style of expression.

- Is the act of a dilettante, namely, one who delights in things contemplated in an unfettered spirit of free play.

- Ramps up the act of contemplation; it focuses attention and opens to the unconscious reservoir of narratives, images, and ideas to make porous for a time the divide between conscious and unconscious contents.

- Allows me to break something down into edible parts so I can digest it, recycle it, spiral back to it, remember it, retrieve it, revision it, anew.

- Evokes a rite of passage from the known to the unknown and a return to what is now strangely familiar. It is the rhetorical equivalent of the Hero's Journey.

- Is the occasion for surprise, for joy, for revelation and insight as well as for self-revision and renewal.

- Embodies my thinking and thinks through my body; my imagination is stirred in an incarnate way in writing long hand.

- Evokes, invokes, provokes and unfolds or unfurls what is not yet fully conscious.

- Brings shards of my personal myth into greater conscious presence and into a larger field of meaning through midwifery.

- Evokes energy and this same energy force stirs the deeper roilings of the soul.

- Is a unique form of remembrance; without the act of writing, some parts of our narrative will not be retrieved and perhaps never known.

- Liberates, frees, unleashes what has been imprisoned by not forcing solutions but rather inspires mystery's presence.

---

23 Jung is clear about the distinction between a personal and a deeper and more shared collective unconscious: "But this personal unconscious rests upon a deeper layer, which does not derive from personal experience is not a personal acquisition but is inborn. This deeper layer I call the collective unconscious. . . . This part of the unconscious is not individual but universal." Jung, *Archetypes and the Collective Unconscious*, ¶ 3.

Guides on the Path

Fundamental and necessary guides in this study which will help to establish the perspective and point of view for burrowing into and befriending one's personal myth through an assortment of riting visitations into our past in order to see it anew are the works and insights of Dante Alighieri, C. G. Jung, James Hillman, Joseph Campbell, Jill Purce, Robert Plant Armstrong, Elaine Scarry, Marie-Louise von Franz, Theodore Andrea Cook, D'Arcy Thompson, Susan Rowland, and Johann Wolfgang von Goethe. Other voices will join in. Motion and movement seem to be the soul's intention and constant—a making or shaping and seeking analogies to reform and redefine itself throughout a life.

2

ENGAGING THE MYTH THAT RITES YOU

Thus it is that I have now undertaken, in my 83rd year, to tell my personal myth. I can only make direct statements, only "tell stories." Whether or not the stories are "true" is not the problem. The only question is whether what I tell is *my* fable, *my* truth.[24]

> Tell all the Truth but tell it slant—
>
> Success in circuit lies
>
> Too bright for our infirm Delight
>
> The Truth's superb surprise.[25]

The two quotes above, each poetic in its own right, point us to the truth of our experience that is enwombed in the myth we live daily in our perceptions and fantasies and nightly in our dreamscapes. We keep in mind as we move into the field of writing meditations that a personal myth incorporates, in part: 1. a psychic energy field; 2. a way of perception; 3. categories by which I gain greater consciousness; 4. a spiralic path; 5. psychic energy flow; 6. a meandering by means of analogies and associations and "as if" constructions, to name a few. Guiding the mythic imagination are a few categories that I want to clarify at the outset.

I know that readers may feel at this stage a bit impatient with my approach because it may seem that I am being too indirect, taking Emily Dickinson's poetic lines above too literally. I want to acknowledge that reality and to underscore the idea that while myths are indeed narratives, stories, fictions, fabrications which point us closer to what is true rather than pulling us further from it, behind and beneath the stories are objective structures that are not only part of psyche's necessary scaffolding but the larger world's as well. To these I turn now for brief descriptions.

---

24 C. G. Jung, *Memories, Dreams, Reflections*, trans. Richard and Clara Winston, ed. Aniela Jaffé (New York: Pantheon Books, 1963), p. 3.

25 Emily Dickinson, *The Complete Poems of Emily Dickinson*, ed. Thomas H. Johnson (Boston: Little, Brown and Co., 1960), pp. 506-507.

Terza Rima as Spiralic Knowing

At the outset I suggest that the *terza rima* is an archetype of transformation; to be transformed is predicated on being in motion. Terza rima is both a noun and a verb.[26]

I became most interested in the memorial/imaginal quality of the spiral through a rhyme scheme that the 14th century poet Dante Alighieri invented to give shape and consistency to the personal journey engaged by Dante the pilgrim, who later crafts his experience into a little more than 14,000 lines in a poetic remembrance of that pilgrimage of the self. He called it the *terza rima,* which means "third rhyme." Here is what it looks like in the Italian in the beginning of *Inferno,* the first of three canticas that comprise the poem. The other two are *Purgatorio* and *Paradiso.* I quote the poem's beginning:

Nel mezzo del cammin di nostra vita (A)

Me ritrovai per una selva oscura, (B)

Che la dirritta via era smarrita. (A)

Ahi quanto a dir qual era e cosa dura (B)

Esta seva selvaggia e aspra e forte (C)

Che nel pensier rinova la paura! (B)

When I had journeyed half of our life's way,

I found myself within a shadowed forest,

For I had lost the path that does not stray.

Ah, it is hard to speak of what it was,

That savage forest, dense and difficult,

Which even in recall renews my fear.[27]

I believe his genius in inventing such a rhyme scheme reveals the motion of memory and imagination as it circles, or better, spirals, back to where it was—almost. For in the geometry of the spiral, it never really lands back at its origin; rather, it returns, but always above or below its point of origin. It returns a bit off the initial track so that the spiral remains open-

---

26 Dennis Patrick Slattery, "Dante's *Terza Rima* in *The Divine Comedy:* The Road of Therapy," *International Journal of Transpersonal Studies* 27 (2008): 85.

27 Dante Alighieri, *Inferno: First Book of The Divine Comedy*, trans. Allen Mandelbaum (New York: Random House, 1981), 1.1-6.

ended, a bit diffuse, not stuck in the same space, and expanding both outwardly and inwardly at once. I want us to grasp the poetic geometry of the soul as Dante outlines it here, for it is a primal pattern of mythic memory itself that guides this entire pilgrimage we are entering. I sense that the *terza rima* is psyche's path, its method, its schema, for the act of becoming more conscious, which is what mythic awareness embodies. We live, I suspect in a *terza rimic* way all the time, but perhaps have not recognized its structure before; it is a form of the spiral, which I want to address in a moment. But for now, let's stay with Dante's own discovery and apply it to the way each of us forms meaning within our memories, out of the miasma of the events that occur each day.

The *terza rima* is a patterned structure and a methodology of becoming more conscious about the story and its invisible patterns guiding its genesis and development. *Terza rima* is a duplicative knowing wherein some insight is mirrored both backward and forward and gains in the motion a texture and profundity that rests on imitation and remembrance.[28] It is a recapitulation into newness, grounded in what has been, returned to, and recalibrated into a new insight. Let's look at the rhyme scheme more closely: consider first the forward motion of the journey: from A to B.

But at this step in the pilgrimage forward, something happens to return one to A that in the word that ends the line at the same instant rhymes with but is not *identical to*, or an exact copy of, the original A. Not a repetition or a photograph of the original A is achieved, but a retreat, a return to something familiar that carries in its structure something new, something unfamiliar, and just beyond what is known. What is crucial to notice is the simultaneous motion into the familiar and unfamiliar. The familiar becomes new; it is unfamiliar because of the step from A, then B, then back to A, not to its double, but to its approximation, to its loose equivalent. The paradox is that the action of the journey is a return to the new, which rests completely on the memory of what was, initially. The middle term's presence does not allow an exact return to the original A. Consciousness arises and increases precisely because memory does not return to the exact same place from whence it began. If it did, there would be no discovery of what is new but not yet realized, only a copy of what was.

Here Dante's genius as a psychologist and mythologist as well as poet reveals itself: between the forward movements—a two-step—and the backward motion—a one-step,

---

28 Dennis Patrick Slattery, "Introduction," in Slattery, *Day-to-Day Dante: Exploring Personal Myth through the Divine Comedy* (Bloomington: iUniverse, 2011), p. 4.

temporality in the form of *history* itself that erupts into presence as a specific modality of temporality, both in the motion of the body's movements in the pilgrimage and in the motion of the poem's movement in rhymed language. History itself becomes a way of knowing, and my contention for our pilgrimage in this book is that the ritual act of writing allows that history in the form of our individual biographies, to emerge with a greater clarity than remembering by itself is able to offer. Memory arises on an individual level as well as history on a collective level, both as a structure for understanding the great patterns that often appear to govern human life generally, and as the specific cultural history of our own contemporary world. In one way, then, to recollect our own biography is at the same time to remember in ways not previously available. Perhaps the collective world and world view we are unfolding from and consistently enfolding back into is made apparent for the first time. If so, then when Dante finds himself at the journey's beginning, in a dark wood, he is awakening from a deep slumber of self-ignorance and ready to begin the journey to self-awareness. He will accomplish this through writing his *Divine Comedy*. Writing sharpens our remembrances and gives them a more permanent shape and structure in a creative poetic act; we can return to these written expressions over time and both renew and revise at that moment what we can now see. But the process must be continuous if the myth we are unfolding is organic and vital. I think we can discern from this brief summary that remembering is as much an act of imagination as it is of recollection. Out of that matrix we can detect many of the large patterns of our own personal mythology. We could say that the patterns emerge in the form of our remembering as well as in the actual fabric of the world's patterns that are shared, universal and timeless. C. G. Jung calls these constructions archetypes, which are patterns inherent in the psyche and form the template of "*a living and lived myth.*"[29]

One more piece of the amazing puzzle needs to be mentioned before we move on. We have been discussing the first step, or *terza rima* motion of the first three lines. Now I want to connect it to the next one to see what happens psychologically to the past as it is given a transfusion through the present while at the same time the present is resuscitated through

---

29 In the same quote, Jung observes that "psychology therefore translates the archaic speech of myth into a modern mythologem—not yet, of course, recognized as such—which constitutes one element of the myth 'science.'" Quoted in Greg Mogenson, *Northern Gnosis: Thor, Balor, and the Volsungs in the Thought of Freud and Jung* (New Orleans: Spring Journal Books, 2005), p. xi.

the past; without this continuum in consciousness, we cannot grow more aware of the patterns so persistent in the plot of our lives.

Here is the structure:

A—B—A

to

B—C—B

So that, to return to the original Italian, the first B (oscura), the middle term of the first *terza rima*, becomes

B (dura)—C (forte)—B (paura!)

The middle term of the preceding *terza rima* metamorphoses into the first and last rhymes of the next *terza rima*. In that transformation, what can we discern and experience as readers not just of the poem but of our own lives as we follow by analogy the contours of this pattern as well as the psychic energy that emanates from them?[30]

Memory herself, depicted in the figure of the Greek goddess Mnemosyne, stirs the heart's vessel of forward motion, of breaking new ground, or seeing anew by means of what has just passed. Now the past is retrieved (even redeemed?) into new envisionings. Writing, I contend, is one ritual that promotes and encourages such a motion. If we pull back the lens for just a moment in the poem, we as pilgrim-readers can sense that the first *terza rima* deals with the past—"I found," "I had lost"—the next with the present—"it is hard to speak of what it was"—as it unfolds, unfurls, uncurls or spirals back into the past—"which even in recall renews my fear" (che nel pensier rinova la paura!)—and the third envelops the future —"But to retell the good discovered there / I'll also tell the other things I saw"—which wraps past/present/future into a tightly corded knot of omni-temporal meaning. Writing is an imaginal ritual that can make this pattern evident in our own experiences.

My own sense is that in any authentic motion of healing, all three dimensions of our embodied temporal-spatial self must be engaged, made operative, imagined, provoked, invoked as a holistic entity, so that the entire person is present in his/her past-present-future becoming. With such engagement, one's personal myth may be made present first in shards

---

30 Slattery, "Dante's Terza Rima in *The Divine Comedy*," p. 86.

of bits and pieces at a time, and then, over time and meditation, into a larger mosaic of coherence.

Spiralic Structure of Consciousness

> The geometric representation of forward motion which is at the same time recapitulatory is the spiral.[31]

Dante's terza rima structure is a rhetorical version of the dual spiralic motion of pushing out and returning, but, as I have mentioned, not as an exact duplication of what has been. More accurately, it is closer to a replication into newness. Such is the spiral's powerful psychological force of consciousness as well as the genius of memory herself, the essential act of which, especially when written in long hand and not on a computer, captures something of the sense of ourselves in embodied memorial motion. One writer who has studied spirals in world mythologies, rightly claims, with compelling persuasion, that "each stage of growth occurs in a spiral."[32] I do not believe that our own stories, or stories generally, prescribe a circle; rather, the structure of story itself is spiralic. The personal and collective myth we are embedded in gives the energy as well as the shape to the spiral, an ancient pattern in nature, which some writers claim, is perhaps the oldest known.

While ostensibly we live in a linear fashion with time moving from past—present—future, we also live, and more deeply, in a mythic geography, wherein the motion of myth unfolds and enfolds back on itself spiralically and recursively. At times we spiral down, pulled deeply into a life event, while at other times we spiral up, pushed beyond ourselves to moments of clearer vision and a sharpened understanding. Stories themselves move spiralically rather than in circles, although at times we may feel that our own life fiction is caught in "a vicious circle," as often happens with addictions and in periods of paralysis that can take a host of forms. When, for example, we read a narrative, we read forward across the page as well as imaginatively/spirally back into what has already occurred. Dementia,

---

31 John Freccero, *Dante: The Poetics of Conversion*, ed. Rachel Jacoff (Cambridge, Mass.: Harvard University Press, 1986), p. 263.
32 Jill Purce, *The Mystic Spiral: The Journey of the Soul* (London: Thames and Hudson, 1980), p. viii.

Alzheimer's, and amnesia shatter that continuity of folding back in a spiral motion; we lose the thread of our life's coherence when the spiral is no longer active in remembrance. The flow of our lives is then end-stopped. When memory disintegrates, we can no longer inhabit the pattern of the spiral and may move through each day like a rudderless ship in which everything is new. Such a condition can overwhelm and discourage us from continuing.

I suggest that the spiral is the geometry of the psyche and the basic structure of memory/imagination. The growth of human consciousness is the continual refining of its own organizing, the ordering principle guiding us from the microcosm of our individual life, to the mesocosm of the social matrix we are immersed in, to the macrocosm of the larger world and cosmic terrain.[33]

The spiral is also at the heart of a motion that seems essentially analogical and metaphoric, which is to say, mythic. The soul seeks analogies of itself, but not literal duplications of what it is as a unique identity. That movement or *search and discovery* is part of the impulse of our personal myth. We are in constant motion, spiraling out to the world and others as well as in to our own interior cosmos where meaning is generated, discovered, and fashioned. Increased awareness of who and what we are as well as the destiny we are each to fulfill occurs through this spiralic consciousness. C. G. Jung offers further validity to this notion when he writes: "Analogy formation is a law which to a large extent governs the psyche."[34] The guiding action of psyche is to seek resemblances, similarities, likenesses and further forms of itself by means of analogy's power and to make them present as confirmations of its essential nature. Writing assists that search by ritualizing meditations that will lead to deeper levels of awareness of our life patterns.

Some of the best biological observations on the structure of the created order claim that the spiral is the key structural element because it reveals "diversity in similarity and extends to the diversity of our mental character and our physical structure."[35] Nature herself seems bereft of straight lines and more revelatory of an endless variety of curves and spirals, from the elaborate and aesthetically engaging single-celled shell to the structure of the Pleiades

---

33 Joseph Campbell, *The Hero with a Thousand Faces*, Bollingen Series XVII (Princeton, N.J.: Princeton University Press, 1973), pp. 37-38.

34 C. G. Jung, *Aion: Researches into the Phenomenology of the Self*, vol. 9, part II of *The Collected Works of C. G. Jung*, 2nd. ed., trans. R. F. C. Hull (Princeton, N.J.: Princeton University Press, 1970), ¶ 414.

35 Theodore Andrea Cook, *The Curves of Life* (1914; repr., New York: Dover, 1979), p. 4.

and Milky Way. From the seedbed of physical nature to the imaginal garden of the human psyche, asserts physicist David Bohm, the curving, spiraling, folding, unfolding and enfolding of both the explicate order of nature and the implicate order of the human being reveal a patterned prose of the grand story of creation. Our own personal myth is always engaging such action as it struggles to complete such a magnificent epic story.[36] Theodore Cook observes that universal laws seem to govern spiralic or similar circular formations in various organic and inorganic phenomena.[37]

No less is this true of writing our personal myth. "By chance," which I enjoy writing because of its false claim—for chance seems more a purpose disguised as a casual accident —I came across a writer on C. G. Jung's writing. It was a startling and welcome moment of synchronicity, a meaningful occurrence that resides outside of what we normally label cause-effect. In her writing, teacher of literature and depth psychology, Susan Rowland discovers in Jung's rhetorical style an alchemical spiral that imitates the content of his writing.[38] Her claim is that in his prose style, especially obvious in *Modern Man in Search of a Soul,* Jung "makes the reader experience the *creative immanence of the imagination* as an essential component of a portrait of *the whole psyche.*" Her next image is worth repeating for our work on personal myth. She plays with the spiralic image in the act of writing by suggesting that the "evocation of the 'hole' in the spiral essay form that is the 'whole' of the ineffable unconscious"[39] is a rich metaphor that brings into communion the gaps of our stories with the wholeness of our being that creates a compendium of our personal myth. Our own stories carry and mirror the structure of one of the most predominant natural geometries, the spiral. Our story structure then links us intimately to the structure of nature.

At the center of the spiralic geometry that we embody in our storied lives rests a still, tranquil air gap, an open space in the spiral that allows for change even as it keeps the entire spiralic motion in tension with itself. It also appears to offer a place to return to, not unlike Dante's schema outlined above; always a gap, a slight round fissure, entertains slippage, for

---

36 See especially David Bohm, "Quantum Theory as an Indication of a New Order in Physics. Part B: Implicate and Explicate Order in Physical Law," in Bohm, *Wholeness and the Implicate Order* (New York: Routledge, 1998), pp. 140-157.

37 Cook, *The Curves of Life,* pp. 4, 11.

38 Susan Rowland, *Jung as a Writer* (New York: Routledge, 2005), p. 43.

39 Rowland, *Jung as a Writer,* p. 43, Rowland's italics.

motion, for further iteration, without concern for making "an airtight case." No breathing room is allowed in the logos of the latter configuration.

The power of the spiral's wholeness and shape rests in the tension it creates between its wholeness and its holeness, even, perhaps, in its holiness? For the spiral is a sacred geometry that attends the vital motion of a life mythically lived and reflected upon; at its center is a mysterious playfulness we never want to lose in these meditations, for the play in the spiral's center space is like the playfulness in our lives that promotes joy, a willingness to change and be affected by our relations with others, including the orders of nature, spirit, soul and body, along with all that we co-habitate with daily.

As an illustration, and as a first meditation, let's return to what I hope was a good experience for you in elementary school when you were assigned practicing writing the various letters of the alphabet in cursive. In this method of learning to write that most of us were subjected to, we were given paper with thick blue lines at the top and bottom, with a more pale line in the middle, which was to serve as a canopy where we were to keep many of the lower case letters in bounds. But now if we were to return to those early formations, we can feel how much of the Arabic alphabet, in long hand writing, engages the spiral, the curve, the sweeping back at the letter to create an entire series of curving shapes. Printing cancels this effect out, as does typing. Perhaps there exists a deep psychological, even mythic magic in these cursive letters.

Riting Meditation

Your meditation at this juncture is to write out the upper and lower cases of the alphabet. Don't hurry or be hasty but rather, with as much presence as you can, feel into each letter, both upper and lower case versions, to sense first through your hand gripping the pen, and then the motion through your body, for the psyche is an embodied presence, even an opportunity to make present what normally hides in the background, out of sight.

In slow meditative practice, in a ritual attitude of making something present that has been so familiar over the years, but perhaps is now fading with the advent of technology that privileges typing over writing, form these ancient letters in both upper and lower case. Sense the curving, even spiralic or partially spiralic contour of each letter, both upper and lower case. Think for a moment, too, what a delight it is to receive a card in the mail from someone with his/her own handwriting offering expressions of friendship, sympathy, support, or crucial news for you. They are treasures because they are expressed in the person's "own hand." Or think of buying a book at a used bookstore, which happened to me recently, in which the author had, with great affection, inscribed it for another. To think that the author had handled and written in it in his own cursive style gave the book a magical quality that would not be present without the presentness of the trace, the memory of that person touching the book, marking its face, adding value through the power of affective presence. We are also aware of what a signed copy by a famous writer does to the price tag of that edition. It emblazons on the book a presence of subjectivity, of person hood and of a moment in time, that is absent without the inscription. Writing makes subjectively present some quality of numinosity; it lifts the book above the ordinary. So is it true of the writing meditations in this book.

Give yourself as much time as needed to write out the letters. Pay particular attention to the way they feel under the slow drag of the pen, the way the hand moves in large and small circles, in spirals, in curves and flows of lines that are never straight, always bending, bowing back on itself and, in words, to one another in creating a psychological and emotional field of relevance. Such is the power of the letters in their mythic dimensions. To feel their motion is to enter their own mythos, for they too have a history, an etymology and a cultural/historical reality almost like persons who inhabit and shape our ideas in words, one letter at a time. Your own style of making these letters reveals aspects of yourself as well, as handwriting analysis can confirm. But that is not our concern here.

C. G. Jung, one of the architects of this book, noted of his own writing: "My writing must be equivocal, ambiguous, to do justice to psychic nature, with its double aspect. I strive consciously and deliberately for ambiguous expression because it is superior to unequivocalness and corresponds to the nature of being."[40]

Susan Rowland, mentioned above, well-versed in the study of Jung's style of prose, observes that "Jung's spiral essays wind around their themes, going deeper and wider into historical origins and cultural analogies." And then this important insight for our pilgrimage: "The reader is given a *process* captured in ideas and images, more than a definitive statement or conceptual argument. . . . The spiral essay works more through the rhetorical arts of

---

40 C. G. Jung, *The Red Book: Liber Novus*, ed. Sonu Shamdasani, trans. Mark Kyburz, John Peck, and Sonu Shamdasani (New York: W. W. Norton, 2009), p. 244.

persuasion by analogy and metaphor than through the logical methods of amassing evidence to 'prove' a thesis."[41] My intention here is to reveal how from the formation of a letter, to writing, to the structure of an essay, the spiral is the controlling geometry of our personal narrative as well as the path of the energy flow that vitalizes our lives.

As I write these words, I am looking at two spirals: one is of a shell I picked up years ago on a beach in Santa Barbara, California. Its configuration is whole and perfect, with a magnificently balanced spiral that curls into itself, its center comprised of a darker calcium than the rest of its exterior. In all it is about half the size of my fist. I find that while looking at it, I feel a soothing sense of things through its portal. I can feel its tension that is less a conflict than a formed energy presence which it has held since its initial formation. I can feel its ingeniously efficient and economical aesthetic. When I turn it over in my hand and feel its spacious interior as it turns in grace in its cavernous portal, I sense the smooth skin of its other life, a texture as unblemished as new skin, or as silky as the slippery movement of water. Its outer shell is wrinkled, not unlike the texture of elephant skin. The two realities, rough and smooth, comprise its elegant curved surfaces and shape. Both rough and smooth are necessary for its created wholeness.

The other image, which I purchased from a flea market vendor in a small Texas town, is of a Fossil Squid (Orthoceras); the note with it tells me it was taken from the Sahara Desert in Morocco. It is dated within the Devonion Period and, get this: it is estimated to be between 345-395 million years old! Its dark grey, almost black exterior has been burnished and buffed to glisten like a newly-polished bowling ball. Its base is its natural rough-hewed light grey. Its spiralic outside is so deep that, when set on its side, it could serve as a miniature ashtray or a tiny reservoir for holding a few thimblefuls of water for thirsty hummingbirds to hover and drink from. Its textured mottled surface reminds me of the barnacled face of a humpback whale often seen in the Santa Barbara Channel in the summer months.

As I gaze at both of these magnificent bodies of motion in still life, I feel connected to the ancientness of the earth, the sea, the hard-shelled sheen on the mind itself and, to some deeper, more invisible reality that is the very origin of mythic and narrative consciousness. These images are the frozen replicas of stories themselves that insist we continue to fold

---

41 Susan Rowland, *Jung in the Humanities: Taking the Soul's Path* (New Orleans: Spring Journal Books, 2010), p. 32.

back on what has already occurred in the plot, and to pull it forward in spiralic fashion, to make meaning out of otherwise discrete series of events that comprise the more linear motion of our lives, but that also hide a spiralic pattern or form that, through writing, we can more consciously deepen into greater discernment. The spiral is then the meaning-making geometry of our soul and the life force or energy field of our lives that embody significance. The spiral helps me to create meaning and purpose out of events and to see the larger formed structure of the narrative.

As such is true of writing, it is no less valid for reading, which will also be part of this enterprise and is indeed present right now as you journey across these corridors of letters.

Psychic Energy's Field of Myth

> Fields may be viewed in this respect as the medium through which archetypes incarnate into matter.[42]

> What energy field was created, which destroyed, when two commercial 737 jet liners hit and brought to collapse the twin towers of world commerce in New York's World Trade Center in 2001?[43]

These introductory pages, prior to entering a field of writing meditations, wish to get behind the notion of myth as narrative to an earlier genesis, where psychic energy, a spiral geometry and fields of convergence and divergence are operative, and out of which emerges a particular narrative at a specific juncture in one's life. All of these terrains must be included in a study of personal myth so that the backroom forces are acknowledged as personages that give rise to the front room story.

The connection of energy to narrative finds an important source in the work of one writer who has worked on the idea of *mimesis* in the Greek philosopher, Aristotle's, fine brief theoretical text, *The Poetics*. In his exploration of the nature of narrative as an imitation of an

---

42 Michael Conforti, *Field, Form, and Fate: Patterns in Mind, Nature and Psyche* (New Orleans: Spring Journal Books, 2003), p. 57.

43 Dennis Patrick Slattery, "Psychic Energy's Portal to Presence in Myth, Poetry and Culture," in *Eranos Yearbook: 2006/2007/2008*, ed. John van Praag and Riccardo Bernardini (Einsiedeln, Switzerland: Daimon-Verlag, 2010), p. 439.

action of the soul that the story taps into through its particular and formidable plot structure, S. H. Butcher suggests that "the praxis that art seeks to reproduce is mainly a *psychic energy* working outwards."[44] When we consider such a dynamic within the field of personal myth, we notice that stories themselves are comprised, in part, of energy fields, plotted and configured psychic energy that is not the same as the dynamic energy we use to get out of bed in the morning and perform our daily round of tasks. It is more, in keeping with C. G. Jung's thought, a *libidinal* energy, aroused in the process of being attracted to something; some object, idea, image, person, notion grabs hold of us and we move towards it with an innate desire to know; psychic energy gathers at this instant to hold or fix our attention.

I want to introduce this idea for it bears directly on what in the world draws us to it, what kinds of movies, books, food, music, people, enterprises, ideas, prejudices, disharmonies—because some "quantum" of psychic energy is active within the myth we are in, operating continually to give it shape and direction. It is also the key ingredient in the menu of unconscious contents seeking more conversation with consciousness. Jung's own work focused on the "energic approach to psychic events."[45] I sense the importance of this idea because it relates to the way that a metaphor, a symbol, or some other form of analogy gathers around energy, actually creates and channels it to guide us to certain things in their attractiveness or, alternatively, we greet with indifference. There does exist in the poetic ground of the psyche "a relation of equivalence . . . between physical and psychic energy. . . . So let us call our hypothetical life energy Libido, so it is distinguished from a universal energy."[46]

The metaphors we live by, therefore, are bridges between psyche-soma and the world; in other words, they reveal by analogy a relationship of body and psyche that is indispensable to understanding. Myths themselves, as metaphorical alternatives to a more logic or rational-oriented way of understanding, serve also as bridges on this same level of psychic energy and body energetics. I believe the above is a modest inroad into the ways that stories excite us, make us want to hear or read them again, extract our own stories from us when we hear

---

44 S. H. Butcher, *Aristotle's Theory of Poetry and Fine Art*, 3rd ed. (New York: Hill and Wang, 1902), p. 8, my italics.

45 C. G. Jung, "On Psychic Energy," in *The Structure and Dynamics of the Psyche*, vol. 8 of *The Collected Works of C. G. Jung*, trans. R. F. C. Hull (New York: Pantheon Books, 1960), ¶ 17.

46 Jung, "On Psychic Energy," ¶¶ 26-32.

one, for story energy is a poetics of libidinal energy that can create powerful fields around us as individuals as well as surround, even hold captive, or liberate, entire nations. Humankind has in the past gathered around the story of a superior race, of the narrative of weapons of mass destruction, or of the story of a redeemer, a savior, a messiah, with such a ferocity that it has brought on cataclysmic wars and destruction as well as hope and security for hundreds of millions of individuals. Such is the intrinsically powerful and destructive potential of myth. A myth has the power to create or destroy entire nations.

Story is the vehicle by which the intense psychic energy has a place to sit, to ride inside the narrative, feeding it, stoking its fires, energizing the souls of people, organizing thought patterns, delineating values, confirming long-held views, as well as confronting old habits of mind, at times bringing them to the ground and allowing them to fragment under the weight of their massive but energy-less void.

By analogy, I understand one's personal myth as akin to a text to be reread and even revised over a lifetime as more of its contours become known to one within it, where the energy flows, becomes blocked, reverses course, creates new tributaries, channels itself into new pathways, swirls back on itself in small eddies, grows stagnant and rancid, or dries up in some of its chapters. The field of myth is an affective one—resonant, challenging, energizing—inviting a ritual enactment to formalize its presence and to finalize an action, a thought, an image, to bring it home to rest and to revitalize us, all perhaps in a single action. The ritual itself sets up an affective field. Our main ritual in this exploration is that of writing longhand as a ceremonial enactment that allows a more meditative, meandering, spiraling back, down and into the story, to the energy that provides its life force, so to animate its design and discern its shape and focus of interest.[47] As best we can, we recognize and develop a style of mythic consciousness that does not allow the ego's ideas to reign by excluding all other persons within us that comprise a diverse totality of characters that in their diversity may aim towards unity, but not an enclosed exclusivity. Our task within the

---

47 This energy, an invisible force from which derives the form of something in the act of writing, has a dramatic analogue in the natural order of spirals. The biologist D'Arcy Wentworth Thompson observes that "the majority of spiral forms . . . are plane or discoid spirals, and we may take it that in these cases some force has exercised a controlling influence, so as to keep all the chambers in a plane." D'Arcy Wentworth, *On Growth and Form* (Cambridge: Cambridge University Press, 1992), p. 195. The deeper connection between the spirals of Arabic letters, the spiral in nature, and the spiral in psyche calls for further exploration.

ritual field we will create is to reclaim what psychologist James Hillman believes has been lost, along with a mythic sensibility: the ability to personify, that is, to imagine both the inner cosmos of who we are and the outer terrain that we move within, while not permitting the impulse to personalize everything into our narrow container, to override our capacity to personify the myth we are and are within: "The mythic perspective toward myself and my existence can begin right in psychopathology: my own person with all its personal passions and experiences can evaporate. It does not depend on 'me.'"[48]

Our search for the terms of our myth is a paradoxical journey: on the one hand, we do not wish to become locked into MY STORY as if I owned and exclusively scripted it. We don't. On the other hand, by remembering and imagining our past and our present, and at times our presentness through our past and our past through what we hope for, we significantly collapse the linear stranglehold that limits rather than expands the possibilities in our story as well as the plot of our possibilities. Part of our success here will be in the way we can create a field of our own vulnerabilities as well as what I am willing to risk in the enterprise of self-exploration that is at once about me and yet goes beyond me to tap into larger archetypal patterns and energy fields that guide me, even when I think I am the only hand on the rudder.[49]

Do you remember the very popular film from a few years ago, *Field of Dreams*, starring Kevin Costner? Based on W. P. Kinsella's novel *Shoeless Joe*, it provocatively illustrates creating a mythic field that has the energy and force to draw hundreds to it, as shrines and holy sites have succeeded in doing for millennia around the world; in such a place is a power that, while invisible, is no less mythic, metaphoric and at times, miraculous by means of the values it holds, the healing it accomplishes or invites, and the restoration it affords, as in a vessel like the grail cup itself. The power of the novel is that it affords us an insight into how powerful a vision can be to shift the trajectory of an entire life.

After his initial revelation, the narrator of the story remembers: "The vision of the baseball park lingered—swimming, swaying, seeming to be made of red steam, though perhaps it was only the sunset. And there was a vision within the vision: one of Shoeless Joe Jackson playing left field."[50] That was enough to intensify the narrator's current mythos, to

---

48 James Hillman, *Re-Visioning Psychology* (1975; repr., New York: HarperPerennial, 1992), p. 49.

49 Hillman, *Re-Visioning Psychology*, p. 48.

50 W. P. Kinsella, *Shoeless Joe: A Novel* (Boston: Houghton Mifflin, 1982), p. 7.

shift it in the fashion an earthquake moves an entire city in an instant, and sets him on his life's work. Such is the Power of Myth to invest a life anew.

Myths Evoke the Powers of Presence

> The details of a life are themselves to be opened out so we can feel the archetypes playing under them.[51]

> The presence achieved in a work is the sum total of all the powers that excited it, quickening it from its core to its flanks, charging it with significant perusals, the affirmation and interrogations—of consciousness.[52]

We are seeking through this contemplative pilgrimage of writing meditations to feel our way back into remythologized thought, a way of imagining that has been lost with the rise of surface glitter, the survey, the opinion poll, the sound bite, the tweet and the twitter—all of which may end-stop reflection in favor of the gut response based often on nothing more than a prejudice or a knee-jerk resentment.

Robert Plant Armstrong's pioneering work as a cultural anthropologist is one of the wisdom ancestors in this pilgrimage we have undertaken. As he studied the masks and statuary of the African Yoruba people, he found their work inspirational for thinking about art in a wider orbit through the power of ritual's relation to these living vital images of the African tribe. I find in his musings many rich parallels to personal myth and ways to make many of its elements present.

Armstrong early in his study muses over how, for instance, a tribal mask, wrapped carefully in cloth and set in a box in an attic of a home has no or very limited power. But that same mask, when taken out of its container and unwrapped, then brought into a ritual circle of its Yoruba people and donned by one of the tribal elders, becomes infused with power and affective presence.[53] It also assumes the presence of its own subjectivity and

---

51 Joseph Campbell, *Mythic Worlds, Modern Words: On the Art of James Joyce*, ed. Edmund L. Epstein (Novato, Calif.: New World Library, 2003), p. 10.

52 Robert Plant Armstrong, *The Powers of Presence: Consciousness, Myth, and Affecting Presence* (Philadelphia: University of Pennsylvania Press, 1981), pp. 15-16.

53 Armstrong, *The Powers of Presence*, p. 11.

should therefore be treated as a person as well as a thing; in the tension of these two qualities of being a power arises: "It is in the energy of such interplay that a fundamental 'power'—or energy—of the work of affecting presence is to be found."[54]

I want to draw an important analogy here. For just as parts of our lives enwrapped in our personal myth may remain swaddled in cloth and removed to an attic, out of the light and fresh air of consciousness, so may the ritual act of writing be akin to bringing those parts of the myth that have no power when static and hidden, suddenly back into an animated flow of energy and their own power when they emerge from under the words we use to remember them in a ritual act of expression. Those events become transformed into mythos through the logos of riting; they gain mythic power and even authority when invoked by language. They gain such power because of *(w)rites of passage*. Even more: the passages written assume a patterned structure in prose when gathered, for in the assembly of illustrations, the patterns are invited to emerge and converge into a coherent prose plot from out of the memory onto the page.

Our project then is to engage in this riting retreat on personal myth the power of our own presence through the corridor of writing meditations. We are most interested in this ritual action because it allows us to recognize and acknowledge the qualities of internal significance in what Armstrong refers to as an "aesthetics of virtuosity."[55] This work of virtuosity is crucial to our own mythic project because it contains the presence of the sacred. Power inhabits it and lifts it from profane existence to sacred meaning in presence. It is one of ritual's rights.

So too is it the case in the writing ritual. Here too, the degree and depth of meditation—what level it is you wish to engage the writing meditation on—will yield a level of Presence that can be profound, memorable and life-altering. One may then see one's mythos in a new light, through a dark ray, one of a deepening consciousness. The insights can be both affective and extremely effective in stirring one to a larger, more infused wholeness of one's self. Rituals empower, offer power, invoke energy, strengthen memory, embody recollections, and incarnate what has been under a blanket of our consciousness.

Here is what I believe happens in writing one's personal myth: the ritual act of writing evokes levels of energy, which gives what we write Affect. Myth is what makes present "the

---

54 Armstrong, *The Powers of Presence*, p. 6.
55 Armstrong, *The Powers of Presence*, p. 10.

power of the analogic"[56] with such persuasive poignancy that what I write takes on an "as if" quality of a life, its fiction, its fabrication and its fabled existence. Writing has this capacity because of its own power to evoke energy fields of awareness: what was lost, forgotten, discarded or, as a colleague of mine writes, "is left on the side of the road,"[57] suddenly appears like an enfleshed apparition that enhances our human condition. Each of these memories participate in the larger patterned plot of our work as lived.

Personal Myth as Subject/Object Reality of a Remembered Life

But who should live your life if you do not live it?[58]

The question is whether or not there can ever be a recovery of the mythological, mystical realization of the miracle of life of which human beings are a manifestation.[59]

Writing into and through and then out of one's personal myth requires an authentic desire to make something of one's self *for* oneself *through* one's self. To make something present is crucial. It allows the soul to make itself in the world. Eros, the presence of life's energy, is part of the enterprise of self-recovery. My hope is that the various meditations quicken something in you, unwrap an image from the attic, allow it to breathe and speak within the wider circle of your story and of your own tribe of people, and invite it to enhance its significance through questioning its parts while affirming its wholeness. If we move into a more mythic consciousness, we can then witness the parts of ourselves not readily remembered in the past, welcome them into the unfolding of self-discovery in the present and even allow them, like ancestors, to guide us into the future. We may give them the same claim to reality as Armstrong allows for the presencing power of what affects us; he reveals through a few illustrations what I believe writing does to animate properties of ourselves we wish to re-member into the tribal arena of our complex narrative.

---

56 Armstrong, *The Powers of Presence*, p. 25.

57 Robert Romanyshyn, presentation at Pacifica Graduate Institute, Carpinteria, California, February 11, 2011.

58 Jung, *The Red Book*, p. 249.

59 Joseph Campbell, *Myths of Light* (Novato, Calif.: New World Library, 2003), p. xviii.

For instance, in a kind of psychic animism, "we might readily suppose that the rock which augmented the lethal efficacy of ancient's man's hand shared the affect accompanying the attack in which it was used."[60] In this mythic presencing of an object, it becomes a person, just as the remembered parts of our own heritage—personal and collective—augments these moments into life forms—personal and personable. Or, as Armstrong develops it further with another example, "Can we not also imagine that the arrow loosed in flight might have taken to itself a little of the anticipations which flew with it toward the prey it was directed to kill?"[61] Embedded in his illustrations is the experience of being witnessed by another; the rock and the arrow becoming living presences that carry the mythos, the intention, the aspirations, the desires, the destructiveness of the hand that throws it or the bow that zings it. There is present and manifested not only a power of subjectivity but a power of the mythic and of particularity.[62] The mythic imagination may just be what allows us to see the subjectivity, the personhood, in what we normally perceive as objects.

As writers, we note that the pen we use is also a co-conspirator and co-creator of our words that capture presences in order to help us see the patterned realities we nurture, protect, worship, conjure and at times even congratulate. We too become, through the act of writing, a "work of affective presence," for in writing we re-present ourselves in lights we have not before shone on our story. Armstrong calls this act an aesthetic response and labels it more particularly "the power of the syndetic."[63] It is the first projection, he believes, in which the human being "first projected his psychic forces into the world beyond his body; now the world exists beyond himself."[64]

So it is with writing as well, for in that aesthetic ritual action something of ourselves reaches out of us and beyond ourselves to another plane of being, external and in some sense eternal, permanent. I know that from my own decades as a writer, I exist in the world differently when I write and when I have written, for a different field of being has been enacted in the process of creating both prose and poetry. To project myself outward in

---

60 Armstrong, *The Powers of Presence*, p. 25.

61 Armstrong, *The Powers of Presence*, p. 25.

62 Armstrong, *The Powers of Presence*, p. 27.

63 Armstrong, *The Powers of Presence*, p. 22.

64 Armstrong, *The Powers of Presence*, p. 23.

words transforms how I inhabit those memories, images, desires, pathologies and perversions that comprise me. But now I have a perch other than the one within to envision who and what I am and may be.

Riting one's personal myth is a conspiracy. In the act it conspires to free oneself from what has not been conscious while embracing it at the same time, but with a field now constructed to make those memories manageable, in the sense that they do not any longer have the devouring power they did when left alone to chew on us little by little, for good or ill. To reiterate with some change, an important distinction drawn by Armstrong: in the act of writing, I become less interested in the thing itself as a stand-alone reality and more enchanted with "the thing-in-presence."[65]

In the presences that life affords and that our personal myth gravitates towards as part of its migration into the fullness of who we are, we discern the patterned energy fields that comprise our own uniqueness along the limited but unique boundaries of our own style. That style grows out of a unique subjectivity; far from being too arbitrary or without value, our subjectivity is not only "spiritual" but can include "the very center of our root activities, the source of the super-existence of knowledge and the super-existence of love."[66]

---

65 Armstrong, *The Powers of Presence*, p. 27.

66 Jacques Maritain, "Poetic Experience," *Review of Politics* 6, no. 4 (1944): 387-402, available at
  http://maritain.nd.edu/jmc/jm3301.htm.

3

THE (W)RITING SELF

The more writing succeeds as narrative by being detailed, organized, compelling, vivid, lucid, the more health and emotional benefits are derived from writing.[67]

Let's begin with our writing to see if we can construct through it a space of ritual where we create a field that opens us to a reality that is at once connected to but a bit unfamiliar, where the imagination through the ritual of writing is given an opportunity to roam, to deepen, and to spiral into the interior terrain of our lives without losing touch with the world that enwombs us at every moment. Here we plant the seed that will develop through the soil of our prose.

I want to caution you at the outset: take these prompts for meditation as far as you wish to go, but protect yourself at the same time. I have found in riting retreats that material from participants' pasts are reactivated either in the writing itself and/or in reading what one has written to the large group or to small pods of 3-4 individuals. I underscore in the retreats that no one will ever be called on to read; what I want to avoid in every instance is a feeling on the part of those engaged in the meditations that they need to write in a manner that anticipates they will be called upon to share with others.

That feeling can destroy the entire purpose of self-exploration through the mediated act of writing, a strange place to be situated because at the same instant writing allows for a deeper intimacy with one's self as it conveys some space or distance to one at the same time. I believe writing engages another voice, an Other part of who we are, and that far from fearing it, I ask that you embrace this new or re-newed connection with yourself. For instance, when I write in my journal each morning, between 4 and 4:30 a.m., because that is the time of most extreme openness and porosity for me, I discover that I do not know what I think about an idea, or an event from yesterday or two days earlier, or of something that surfaces from when I was 11 years old, until I begin writing it out; writing becomes a

---

67 Louise DeSalvo, *Writing as a Way of Healing: How Telling Our Stories Transforms Our Lives* (Boston: Beacon Press, 2000), p. 19.

ritualized form of remembering and imagining, both discovery and invention at once. It is a ritual shaping into a formed experience of meaning what before had remained disconnected and without shape. This act of shaping our past into a coherent presence is itself a mythopoetic act of imagination.

So engage writing as a gift of discovery. Work the meditations that most engage you; at the same time, pay attention to those you wish to avoid. The latter may be the important ones to face when the time is right. Resistance is often a clue to something present that one wishes to sidestep. Instead, head up, head right for it.

Imagine, before you begin, if you have not already, a ritualizing practice for your writing, what you might craft to make the writing experience as intense and enjoyable as possible. For instance, before writing in the morning, which is when I am most active with words and thoughts—be it journaling, working on a poem, crafting a letter, writing notes from my reading, drafting a book review, a talk, an essay for publication, a book chapter or a full manuscript, I:

- Light a candle to the Muses, whose mother is Mnemosyne, the divine figure of Memory herself. The candle illuminates my capacity to recollect.
- Light a stick of incense. I keep my study well-stocked with packets of varied fragrances. The olfactory stimulation is immensely helpful in moving me into a new space that is very different from the space of reading or of responding to emails, for instance.
- Have a fresh cup of coffee, tea, or other beverage that helps to relax me.
- Use the bathroom if needed; interruptions I try to keep to a minimum in both body and soul.
- Have files or notes or books around me so I don't continue jumping up and going to the shelves. If I do not have them I make notes in the writing to insert them later.
- Do not respond to phone calls or the doorbell.
- Sometimes put on aftershave lotion or cologne. The added aromas assist my creative process.
- Keep a recently published piece out and in view. For instance, in writing this book, I keep in front of me a recent published book on exploring personal myth through Dante's Divine Comedy.[68] My intention here is to feed off of previous achievements, to gain strength from it as a booster to the current project. These creative works from our past carry immense

---

68 In the Introduction I touch on the power of personal myth in writing that in reading literary classics "both the poetic work and each of us inhabit a particular mythos; as such, the poem and we ourselves are organically changing as the mythology we are in develops and deepens organically." Dennis Patrick Slattery, *Day-to-Day Dante: Exploring Personal Myth through the Divine Comedy* (Bloomington, Ind.: iUniverse, 2011), p. 1.

energy and reveal what we can achieve. They can also help one enter the field of energy that writing requires. If you have no work of your own, be it a cross-stitch, a painting, pottery, place one of your favorite books or other objects by you as a friend to encourage you in your creations.

- All these are rituals that embody a right rite, a righting ritual to balance me and to move me into the strange, surprising, frustrating and ultimately privileged enjoyment of crafting something that has never existed before into a coherent and enticing form for others to share and use to push further into their own thinking. They comprise the seeds that bore fruit.
- Rituals engage presence; they make what is peripheral or on the margins affectively present.

Writing Meditation: The Image of Myself as a Writer

Each of us carries an image of ourselves as a writer. It is a fantasy that some carry with great frequency and intensity, while for others it is an idea whose time has not yet ripened. So many of us carry a book or a short story or an original idea in us; some realize the project. Others get started but wane in the process. Others do not. Regardless, entertain the following questions:

- What is the image of myself as a writer? Include here a few ideas that you assume about yourself as a writer.
- Have I a writer's voice that is different from my speaking voice, or even my reading voice?
- What is my earliest memory of writing? Was it pleasurable, deplorable, painful but rewarding, frustrating, revelatory?
- What is my most vivid memory of writing?
- What is it right now in my life that stirs my soul to write?
- Do I have or wish to begin a writing practice today that I nourish and cultivate regularly?
- Have I written much that was not assigned, not part of a course, a project, a retreat?
- Which do I enjoy most: the thought of writing? The act of writing? The feeling of having written? Allow these some ranking and then reflect on each of them. Keep the number small.
- Do I write regularly, even daily, in a journal? If so, in what way does it serve my life narrative?
- Have I desired to begin a journal and to remain faithful to it as a way of crafting my life into words? Use this present text as an occasion to begin.

Writers' Responses

As a writer I have a split personality—or perhaps more accurately, I have a proficiency and a deficiency. My proficiency is in analytical writing, as in technical writing and intellectual pursuit of the structure and function of psyche. I'm comfortable with my proficiency. It has been the source of sustenance and well-being for as long as I can remember. I am not at all comfortable with my deficient side, and I find myself now much more interested in exploring the deficiency. By the way, I imagine my deficiency as the domain of writing that is poetic, narrative, fictional, imaginative, and adventurous.

My two assumptions about myself as a writer come directly out of the image I just described. Assumption one is that my imagination is bound up, locked, defensive, self-protective—wounded, perhaps—when it comes to "creative" writing, which I think means to me, writing about real people in real life with real passions, problems, joys, and sorrows.

The other assumption I have is that I am an intellectual writer, but even as an intellectual writer I'm also somewhat wounded. I sometimes imagine my "wound" as if it were a "trick knee" that collapses whenever too much pressure is applied—whenever it is called upon to function well in a difficult situation. As I write I hear myself saying that I am a fraud in my writing and that I cover it up with intellect and analysis. (Annemarie St. John)

The word "desire" comes to mind first, a somewhat frustrated desire to write. I've often remembered the time when I was eight or nine and I bought a Big Chief tablet, planning to fill it up with great imaginings. I revisit that memory often because I never wrote anything in that tablet. I can't remember exactly why those pages remained blank—other interests intervened, sports in particular, probably intervened—but I do carry the memory of that initial unfulfilled desire. So that image now cautions me to fill up the pages, to keep writing despite an impulse to back away from the page, to avoid what Faulkner called "the agony and the sweat" that characterizes the writing process.

A second assumption or image of myself as a writer stands in direct opposition to the first image of that blank Big Chief tablet: the times when I have written, the pleasure and satisfaction of getting it down on the page. In contrast to that impulse to back away, I've always had the sense that I can get "it" down successfully. Where did that confidence originate? Two Athenas, my godmother aunt and a great-aunt, made sure that I read the good stuff. Then, I had teachers, friends, even students, who encouraged me. Some very minor writing successes have helped keep the fires of my writing desires burning.

So desire, then guiding voices, formed my image of myself as a writer, but even more significantly in this formation are those occasions that sparked me to write, moments when something lighted the creative fires. Occasions, moments, points of ignition seem to be very important, and here in the last month of 2009 I look for those occasions, worried a bit that the sparks to light the desire to write may be harder to find, searching for the motivating voices to fill up the page and for the courage to take my desiring fire and make something worthy on the blankness of the page. (Mike Crivello)

He watches. Listens. Observes. Doesn't participate much. Just sucks it in. Not all of it. Selective sucking, this. Spits out anything too bitter. Or too sweet. And simply ignores anything bland. He likes rough, funky, edgy, startling, big, spicy . . . and a lot of similar qualities. He doesn't like slick, smooth . . . you know the rest. He's a scholar, but he doesn't remember much. What he does remember, he distorts to suit his purposes. "Forgetting everything he knows until the next line comes along." Or trying to. Not an easy task.

Maybe Foreman and Gertrude Stein were on to something. Begin again.

He watches. Listens. Tastes. He savors. And he cooks, children, sometimes, he cooks. (Jack Halstead)

Know me

the weaver

teller of story

I am the dancer

dances upon page

spreading sound

into song

melody like honey

the river of one's life

I am the one

who shows up

my feet to the fire
the Sayer of Truth
the voice of the All
slow beating the drum
from the simmering
of hearts

I say "yes"
I tell story
that ye may know truth
under illusion
one voice
the voice of the all
who weaves into loom
rich loam of the earth
plowing seeds into mystery
unfolding into light
to take root
into reason
spread limbs of knowing
branching into rhythm
dancing story into flight

I come to the table
talk into the night
past dawn
and back into dark
spin out diamonds
the gold into wonder

I wander the page
give birth to the knowing
hatching the egg

grabbing the gut

bleeding into the pain

the jugular of truth

Blood red

the story, the singing, the drum,

dancing the night

screaming to be heard

we gathered round fire

through eons of time

I, teller of story

grab lightning

stab the dark

to the depths of one's being

I give story to be told

in the lair and the den

brought the pen to the

book, set the page

afire

I sink into fold of the grist

to the angst

past the roar of the wave to the dark bed of the sea

I am story

Know me as fire

the teller of truth. (Cassandra Christenson)

Who Am I As Writer? I am wild I am loose I am messy. I write it real now as I feel it. I describe to you the dead crow road kill on the way here. That will unleash a murder of crows I saw last week when my dear nephew was here.... I am flexible, unfolding layers going hither and thither, reeling it back and forth. Coming up empty. Coming up full.

I am motion of Ink. I am hand cramping. I am unschooled, non-degreed, unpublished. I am a whispering shout. Timid and Fearful to express real thoughts if others will Judge and Package me. My writing is facile. I link story to story. I am Baird Siveau (the Bird's Eye View) the See-er Witness-er. Tell it like it is. Call the shots. Let Others be the Judge.

I am undisciplined. I have worlds of adventures, levels of life lived. I want to stop wasting time and spew it out. All of it. I am a young girl in a middle-aged woman's body. I am a series of ancient souls moving "her" pen. Whose pen? The pen. I am soul expressed. Yet if no one reads it how will it touch others' souls? Lonely soul express stuff connect with other. Possibly soothe, comfort and enlighten other.

Too long a wannabe novelist. "Oh I've lived so many lives."

The monster sits with his fat bottom on my head, I struggle to breathe to force a little air in and out and squeak and I realize I am that silent scream in a nightmare I am having where I am napping and can't wake up. Dreamer dreaming. Multicellular every layer. . . . (Katy Mollie)

Writing Meditation: My Life as Parts of Speech

Tell X that speech is not dirty silence

Clarified. It is silence made still dirtier

It is more than an imitation for the ear.[69]

The parts of speech we engage to write and to read are more than structural-grammatical necessities. They each embody psychological realities as well as create energy fields that can move, persuade, dissuade, influence, emotionally charge, bore, or stifle both writer and reader. Parts of speech create dynamic discourses that shape our thinking as we use them to give form to our ideas, images and beliefs. All of these comprise bits and pieces of our personal myth. The energy of a preposition is much different than the energy of a verb, for instance. When these words gather, the energy can increase markedly or decrease to an unpersuasive dribble.

Give your life specific parts of speech that serve as shorthand, in part, of who you are.

• List five verbs that describe you.

---

69 Wallace Stevens, "The Creation of Sound," in *Wallace Stevens: Collected Poetry and Prose* (New York: The Library of America, 1997), pp. 274-275.

- List 5 nouns that describe you.
- List 5 adverbs that describe you.
- List 5 adjectives that describe you.
- List 5 prepositions that describe you.
- List 4-5 of these parts of speech that you wish to rid yourself of.
- What parts of speech might you replace them with?

If needed, look up these parts of speech on the Internet for a quick review.

After you have done so, create 5 sentences using any of the above to begin to structure a narrative line of who you are currently. These parts of speech have the capacity to shift, some dropping off, others coming on line in your life to keep the organic quality of your personal myth from becoming stale and untrue to your sustained changes.

Writing Meditation: Fiction and/or Poetry Writing

From talking to many people about writing, almost without fail, each brings up a topic on writing that one wishes to engage "creatively." I think all writing is creative but it may assume different forms; "creative" seems to have gathered around works of fiction most predominantly. Such an urge is within each of us to create, shape, make whole and share a formed fiction which has deep analogies in us. It is another form of telling our own story by connecting our particularity with the more universal narratives that already exist in the world. Let's let go of the fiction/non-fiction duality and assume that whatever we write is in part a fictional display.

- Describe a story that you would like to write or poetry that you would enjoy creating.
- Can you describe where that creative energy pocket resides in you?
- Does it have its own voice, its own demands, even a nagging force that is always playing on you and in you?
- Have you already followed that voice, that imperative, that may feel like some Other presence?
- What would it take for you to enter into such a project?
- What is it that stifles your beginning, or continuing, that project?
- How might a writing life change the way you currently live?
- What would it add and what might it make less possible to do that you engage now?

Writing Meditation: Your Current Writing Life

> Any lived story is therefore exceedingly old, yet ever young, exceedingly limited, yet somehow unlimited.[70]

Many of you who engage this book are and have been writing for various periods of time. I am one of those people as well. Writing is not something I choose to do; it has been chosen for me and is using me for some purpose. Several years ago I ceased fighting its urges and manifestos and even stopped choosing what to write about; those topics are given to me as cursive commands to write. Some of these topics feel indeed like curses. I can, of course, as you well know, refuse the call and simply not answer these promptings. Or I can continue to yield to them and create as best as I am able, given all the constraints that can deflect the projected prose.

- As a writer, what would most change in your life if you could no longer write?
- What does writing nourish in you?
- What do you feed the daemon of writing? Daemon is not a demon or a devil; it is a guiding voice or force in you.
- What do you find is unveiled or uncovered in you by writing?
- Describe any rituals you perform that aids you in preparing body, mind and soul for the journey of writing, your own pilgrimage in prose.
- What depletes you most about writing?
- If the ritual act of writing is a necessity for you, not a casual pass time, then it is intimately a part of your personal myth. Can you muse on what it is in the myth that you are living within that has made writing such an imperative?
- What part of your lived writing life is yet unlived but that you sense must be lived out, however imperfectly, at some time?
- What are you being called to write right now?

---

70 Lois Parker, *Mythopoesis and the Crisis of Postmodernism: Toward Integrating Image and Story* (New York: Brandon House, 1988), p. 38.

Writing Meditation: Reveries on Writing

How would I write *A Thousand Acres* now? The fact is, I probably wouldn't.[71]

I want to present a handful of observations on writing and ask that you take up one or two of them in response, or as prompts for you to push into your own thoughts on writing. See what surfaces.

- Writing is a form of contemplation.
- Writing is a ritualized form of a distinct act of remembering.
- Writing is an act of prayer, a willed openness to mystery, to something that both transcends me and is immanently a part of who/what I am.
- Writing is a personal and intense form of bearing witness.
- Writing is a form of myth-making.
- Writing connects me to a larger history than just my personal memories.
- Words both reflect and shape me at the same time.
- Writing carries its own unique form of psychic energy that I can feel when I begin to write or even think about writing.
- Writing makes my subject matter more affectively present than does speaking it.
- Writing is a form of meditation and is akin to a spiritual act.
- Writing is a languaged form of intuiting, discovering, and shaping something into being that has not existed before.
- In writing, language itself remembers me as I remember to use and organize it in specific ways.
- Writing places me in the tenuous liminal space between control and chaos, between order and disorder, between certainty and ambiguity.
- Writing is a ritual enactment in which the border between my conscious and unconscious life becomes more permeable, porous and permissive.
- Writing is an imaginal act of accommodation, conciliation, re-conciliation, even forgiveness.

Simply go with whatever one of the above, or one that grows out from one of them, takes hold of you. Write without planning ahead; simply write what wants to be heard.

---

71 Jane Smiley, "Taking It All Back," in *The Writing Life: Writers on How They Think and Work*, ed. Marie Arana (New York: Public Affairs, 2003), p. 391.

Writers' Responses

My first memory of writing, of being a writer, of learning to write? I look back, feel back and do not come up with an answer, with a memory. What seems to happen for me in writing is that I feel as if I am simply a tool through which the words express themselves, somewhat like this pen. And perhaps this lake is also whetting my creative juices as it has whet the inky tip of the pen so that it could write & so now we are both writing, the pen & I. I feel as if we are creating together our first memory as a writer. I do not feel that the words are mine—more like they come thru me. I have journaled in the past & always felt dissatisfied with what I wrote, very rarely wanting to ever read it again. Perhaps that process of writing & re-writing that I experienced in college in the writing class, seemed so tedious to me. What I wrote was good, and yet it just seemed so over-worked—it took so much time. It's as if I just want to get it out, let it through and be done with it, not go over & over & over. If that is writing I do not want to do it. Or do I? I particularly like it when it comes, fully formed out of my head, like the goddess Athena from the Head of Zeus. (Kristine Haugh)

As a writing self I'm someone who lets go with ease but never forgets the joy of holding hands; someone who is in touch with his feelings and is able to set boundaries when necessary; someone who has learned how to fall without too much trepidation; someone willing to wait and trust in the possibilities of the moment—believing all the pregnant possibilities will present themselves in time if only I wait; someone who sees the possibilities in the tear, the story in the stone, the hope in the star, the faith in the chair, the cold in the gun, the poem in the truck stop. And someone who has learned to kiss and be kissed and to keep the seat down. Quite accomplished, actually. (Chuck Lustig)

Writing Meditation: Riting to Heal

The more I wrote, the more of a human being I became.[72]

Writing has the capacity to mend some tear in the fabric of our fiction, the storied self that is always plotting its course both within and without. By exposing to the open air of prose

---

72 Henry Miller, quoted in DeSalvo, *Writing as a Way of Healing*, p. 4.

what afflicts, wounds, emblazons the scar tissue of resentments, hurts, slights, wrongs, wrong paths chosen, one has the opportunity to close the gap or the gape in the soul-holes of one's being.

I don't think these next meditations are easy, nor should they be. But they are necessary for our sense of personal freedom and authenticity. Every wounding carries within it a narrative; every scar that covers a wound is a storied memory that should not be erased or effaced, but rather directly faced in speech. Where the wound resides there are words that can honor its presence without allowing it to twist your life to it.

Where right now do you still carry a wound, an affliction, a hurt or an infection that gnaws at you with the sharp teeth of resentment, self-pity, or self-destructive thoughts? It may be important to recognize that in our pathologies reside some of the strongest delineations of our mythology. Our wounds carry specific pathologies that alter our world view and in this regard they are mythic matters. James Hillman suggests that "The psyche does not exist without pathologizing."[73] Writing allows prose to produce the pathology and then to claim it on a different level, not by curing it or dissolving it, but by integrating it into the soul fabric of our daily life.

Describe or narrate, as in a story, a wound that continues to afflict you from years ago or as recently as yesterday.

- Another approach: enter into a dialogue with it by personifying it as a person.[74] Ask it what it wants from you, for example, or what it is doing still inhabiting your life.
- Let the wound fester in prose by allowing it a voice, a platform, from which to speak.
- See if in its language it has changed, transformed or grown in stature or diminished over the years.
- See if it has anything to ask or say to you.
- What are its terms for survival and even for flourishing?
- What contract or compact can you make with it to shift its position of importance or devouring presence in your life?
- You are wanting to make it present in prose on a more mythical level than simply a literal wounding of body, emotion, intellect, or self-esteem. What do you associate with it?

---

73 James Hillman, *Re-Visioning Psychology* (1975; repr., New York: HarperPerennial, 1992), p. 70.

74 James Hillman beautifully designates the realm of personifying in the following way: "Personifying not only aids discrimination; it also offers another avenue of loving, of imagining things in a personal form so that we can find access to them with our hearts." Hillman, *Re-Visioning Psychology*, p. 14.

- Write a poem to it or about it, including your own feelings that attend it.
- Write this contact/confrontation/conversation out until it seems to be spent/satisfied/satiated in language.

Writing Meditation: Where to Write.: Finding a New Home Space

> What is that deep longing for home? Is it the desire to find a place of love and acceptance? Is it an eternal search for our center, for the place where we feel whole?[75]

When I think back on when I began writing little cultural vignettes for newspapers in Dallas and San Antonio, and later in local and national magazines, I recall that I wrote most of them in coffee shops, in stores, while doing laundry at a public Laundromat, or in vacant classrooms on university campuses. I discovered that writing in a new space, away from all my possessions except the journal I kept with me and my favorite writing pens, shifted my imagination into new soil.

I wrote pieces, for example, on my sons playing with burning sticks of wood at a campsite in East Texas; of watching a woman load her soiled laundry into a clothes dryer, then returning an hour later enraged that her clothes were not clean; of riding my bicycle in Santa Barbara along the path close to the runners carrying the Olympic torch through the city; of becoming a grandfather twelve years ago when our granddaughter was born; or riding a motorcycle with 300 others to Mission Santa Barbara for an annual "Blessing of the Bikes" with the very popular Franciscan priest, Father Virgil Cordano. These and others were my attempts to capture something simple but meaningful as an experience that, couched in the right language, could be enjoyed by a diverse audience.

The point here is that I wrote them all not at home but in a park, sitting at a picnic table, or any of the other language places that induced better writing than what might have spilled out at home. The familiar bred both content and contentment. I recently read Winifred Gallagher's book on Place. Early on she observes an important move she made to an old house: "Along with sharpening the awareness of how a 'change of scene,' as we often put it,

---

75 Charles Asher, *Soundings: Seventy-Five Reflections on Love and Romance, Personal Development and the Search for Meaning* (Santa Barbara, Calif.: Desert Springs Publications, 1988), p. 47.

makes one feel like 'a new person,' country life aroused my interest in some peculiarities of the unseen order."[76] Place carries power, energy and vitality that can surround and open us to new ways of thought and prose. Move about a bit in your writing.

- Explore where you live for other venues for writing away from home.
- If you have already done so, describe what and where you found a space more conducive to writing.
- If you are exploring writing space options for the first time, write something at that place that includes something about it.
- What do you detect is different about the prose as it relates to place? My belief is that each place carries its own energy field that will affect one's writing if one fully enters its landscape.
- Was the writing more difficult?
- Were the distractions greater or less?
- Was it easier to write or harder by changing the milieu?
- If you have done this not once but in several locations, recall what it was that brought you back to a space, perhaps for years.
- Compare if you can the difference each writing space offers you that is not present in the others. Play with this space of crafting your subject matter with prose in different terrains.

---

76 Winifred Gallagher, *The Power of Place: How Our Surroundings Shape Our Thoughts, Emotions, and Actions* (New York: Poseidon Press, 1993), p. 21.

4

RITING THE AESTHETIC SELF: MYTHOPOESIS

Each quality in the psyche represents a certain energic value, and if you declare an energic value to be non-existent, a devil appears instead.[77]

Poetry is knowledge, knowledge of form. This means there is an organic relation between all the disparate parts of the poem.[78]

My underlying conviction here and throughout this book is that the soul is always in poetic, metaphoric, symbolic motion towards meaning, which it seeks through the power of analogy. It is analogic by design, spiralic by temperament and energic by impulse. All of what attracts us, enchants us, pulls us to it, uncovering where our interests lie, is comprised of energy fields that shape and prescribe the movement of our personal myth. Lying below all of the above, like an aesthetic base line, is the place of the imagination as the shaping, cohering force in the fabric of our existence. We are in large measure fabricated fictions, not lies, but narrative identities, plotted persons, storied selves.

The presence of aesthetics in one's personal myth opens to psyche's work in the vicinity of beauty. The word "aesthetics" has its origin or etymology in the act of "showing forth" or "a revealing." Beauty and revelation are interwoven and gather energy around them both when something intensely attracts us. Aesthetics is a form of being present or a making present. In this chapter we will uncover some aesthetic moments in our lives that have exercised a significant effect in our developing mythos.

When C. G. Jung spoke of the soul, he chose to use the word "anima" as an animating principle of being and understood it as feminine. When he was asked how it was that the anima had such power as carrier of our most profound fantasies, he responded: "because we undervalue the importance of imagination." [79]

------

77 C. G. Jung, *Dream Analysis: Notes of the Seminar Given in 1928-1930,* ed. William McGuire. Bollingen Series XCIX (Princeton, N.J.: Princeton University Press, 1984), p. 53.

78 Louise Cowan, "Poetic Knowledge and Poetic Form," lecture at the University of Dallas, Irving, Texas, April 15, 2007.

79 Jung, *Dream Analysis*, p. 53.

In his response he underscored the power of imagination to create worlds that, while historically unreal as factual events, are nonetheless psychologically valid and potent: "an imaginary fact is not a non-existent fact, but one of a different order."[80] Our personal myth is an imaginal construction that frequently has more power and influence over our lives than the events themselves. This idea means little to nothing until we submit them to the imaginal way we make meaning, which is in large measure a mythic move, not one based largely on reason or cause-effect logic. The paradox here is that we often believe we are making "rational" decisions, but in truth we are imagining them into being first, then giving them a label after the fact. Mythic thinking is based more on an intuitive knowing, a being present to the truth of an experience or object that does not slide along the causeway of causality.

To amplify Jung's notion, we are exploring our personal myth, which one might claim from a more rationalistic stance, is non-existent or only a figment of our imaginations. I agree with both of the above, which is why our personal myth is so powerful and persuasive in the daily acts of our lives, wherein we make decisions based on values, prejudices, likes and dislikes, memories of past experience, feelings, moods, ideas, fantasies, fabrications, habits—none of which is false but rather fantasy expressions of a different level of attunement. The purpose of our writing meditations is to evoke some of these areas of our consciousness into presence before rational explanation has a chance to get its foot in the door. My hope is to both roil and rally our unconscious material as well, so we can shadow ourselves into depths of consciousness not formerly available to us.

Our imaginal life is a symbolic life, one that works best by relationships, by seeing the poetic sense in things and people and by becoming more conscious of who they are, more than why they are, and to create relationships with these OTHER presences that are indeed, "twat tam asi," what Joseph Campbell often quotes as "thou art that."[81] Imaginally, I am indeed the Other. We are, I believe, metaphors for one another; often what I have decided is non-existent in me becomes exactly what I see in the other. We poeticize one another regularly and rhythmically. The aesthetic self is deeply connected to the metaphoric self.

---

80 Jung, *Dream Analysis*, p. 52.

81 Joseph Campbell, *Thou Art That: Transforming Religious Metaphor* (Novato, Calif.: New World Library, 2001), p. 84.

Moreover, a metaphor might be understood as a created complex with a nuclear element within it and a large number of secondarily constellated associations.[82]

In its structure, a metaphor can mirror or duplicate a complex as well as a complexity of relationships to reveal within the psyche a web of complications in new and surprising ways. We are: storied souls, patterned persons, fictional figures, imaginal individuals, energic entities, mimetic membranes, poetic personas—and more. Under-girding and framing all the above is our personal myth—the framing figure of our fictions as well as the imaginal scaffolding of our original and unique designs. Joseph Campbell helps to galvanize some of these ideas when he writes: "When you are in the act of creating, there is an implicit form that is going to ask to be brought forth, and you have to know how to recognize it."[83] Part of the scaffolding involved in this bringing forth form is one's personal myth, itself an informing principle which has its own patterned way of knowing.

Writing Meditation: Arrested by Aesthesis

I want to make one of my own assumptions here: each of us has been arrested, enchanted, stopped in our tracks, or made breathless and infused with *a sense of wonder* by:

A book
A film
A painting
A poem
A piece of music
A natural setting
Another person
A statue, a sculpture
An image or atmosphere in the natural order
Add your own here.

---

82 C. G. Jung, "On Psychic Energy," in *The Structure and Dynamics of the Psyche*, vol. 8 of *The Collected Works of C. G. Jung*, trans. R. F. C. Hull (New York: Pantheon Books, 1960), ¶ 18.

83 Joseph Campbell, *The Mythic Dimension: Selected Essays, 1959-1987* (Novato; Calif.: New World Library, 2007), p. 183.

Such an arrest could be so powerful that it set your feet moving on a life course very different from the one you had been trodding, plodding or rushing through. I have met students who read a particular work, say by Joseph Campbell, Marie-Louise von Franz, or a novel by Fyodor Dostoevsky or an epic by Homer or a poem by Mary Oliver, and something major shifted inside them, like two tectonic plates rubbing against one another to create a new piece of ground that rises from the sea of one's desires. At such a moment, a revelation or an unveiling occurred which altered a life path by shifting the main plot of one's narrative.

- Describe in narrative form that moment of aesthetic arrest, where you were moved by the beautiful that had a major impact on your life.
- Describe an experience of listening, reading, or viewing a particular object, person or event that quickened something in your imaginal life, or revealed something gaping and unfulfilled in you that you were compelled to pursue.
- What was the effect, either immediately or long term, that you still carry with you?
- Conversely, did you feel a desire to engage another life, or a major change in the one you had been living, but decided to refuse the impulse, the call, the confirmation, or the witnessing?
- How is your life right now different from what it was before this presence abrupted into your landscape?

Writer's Response

Unknown Priestess

Greetings, unknown priestess,
Created from the dust of withered stars!
Not finished yet,
In between stages,
Or forgotten,
Crumbling down,
Before long
Washed away in the rivulet of time?
Speak to me,
Chant your sacred song into my heart,
For I see your beauty,
I hear your whispers,
Chimes of your soul echo through the universe,

Revealing your story.
Wounded
I see the hail of horrid dreams,
Cracked on the surface,
I wonder how deep the gapes cut
Into the depths of your being.
And yet,
Here you are standing,
Tall
Like a tree
Deep rooted in the ground beneath
Straight, statuesque,
Beautiful
In your simplicity and purity,
I recognize you
From eons ago.
What is it you are waiting for?
The arrival of another tide?[84]

The following meditation is an important one for me. As you have noticed, throughout the book there will be responses from Riting Myth participants from many different retreats and several countries. The following is my response:

> When I was 20 years old in the mid 1960s I worked as a deputy bailiff in a Municipal Court in Euclid, Ohio. I had just bought a new car, was attending a newly-founded Cuyahoga Community College in Cleveland, had an exciting social life and was dating a person I thought I would be happy marrying.
>
> At the same time, I met a fellow in one of my Sociology classes who worked for a Cleveland newspaper and was also earning his Associate Degree. After class we would go to a pub to drink a few beers and talk about our lives. We both admitted an overwhelming boredom and a desire to hit the road, to break out of the boundaries, out of our comfortable lethargy. Through some negotiating at the Cleveland Docks which welcomed ships from around the world, we were hired as crews' mess boys on the HMS Transamerica operated by Poseidon Lines out of Hamburg, Germany.

---

84 Brigit Langhammer, reflecting on Alberto Giacometti's sculpture *Large Standing Woman.*

On a breezy balmy summer evening in June 1966, my friend and I shipped out from the Cleveland harbor bound for Bremerhaven, Germany. The voyage up the St. Lawrence Seaway into the North Atlantic to Germany took 21 days. Eight of them were spent outside of all land except for large icebergs in the North Atlantic. When we arrived we hitchhiked and trained our way to Ireland, where we stayed with relatives in County Mayo.

After two months or more from the time of our departure, we flew from Shannon, Ireland home and hitchhiked from New York City to Cleveland. During the ship's voyage I wrote in my journal at the ship's aft each night, watched carefully by 10 seagulls that followed the ship across the Atlantic and ate the grub we threw overboard twice a day. The writing was my first real initiation into recording my story, the most important of my life. In these evenings I fell in love with finding words to describe both my interior as well as exterior life.

When I arrived home and continued my studies at Cleveland State University, I devoured every novel I could locate that dealt with the sea: all of Jack London, Joseph Conrad, Herman Melville, Richard Henry Dana, the Admiral Hornblower series and others. It was then that I vowed to devote my studies to literature, for the poets, I saw clearly, so supremely understood and gave voice to my feelings on board and on the sea. These classics, as much as the voyage itself—or their mysterious combination, gave rise to my life's work. Here I am now, 42 years teaching and still relishing these classics, several of which I continue to teach.

Now my personal myth was seeking a direction and the poetic utterances of giant imaginations led me to my work. Melville's *Moby-Dick,* however, was the great hook that caught hold and dug deep. I still delight in the delicious wound it gave me so many decades ago now. Its aesthetic ambergris still flows through my veins and informs the myth I am within, like being in the belly of the whale.

Writing Meditation: Allowing Beauty to Find You

The way we perceive beauty is a milestone in how and what we see. Take a walk in a favorite park, street, woods—some place that holds tranquility for you. It can also be a city street or your own neighborhood. Meander. Stroll. Linger. Be indirect and with no set purpose. Be open and porous for something to strike you, to be invited in, to become present: a sound, a sight, a smell, a taste of something new and unfamiliar, but perhaps now seen for the first time. *Don't work at it;* simply be present to what wishes to be known:

- Pause by it, linger around it, or simply sit somewhere and let what wishes to be known appear to you.
- Allow it to become present to you as you disarm yourself and invite it in.
- Then, when you feel you are ready, describe the experience of what arrested you.
- What stopped you in your tracks and drew you in, if even for an instant?
- What was it that made you curious?
- My sense is that psychic energy gathers around an object at this moment and gathered in you as a result of its presence.
- Ask if any memories are associated with what arrested you.[85]

Writers' Responses

The intent of the meditation was to take a walk and find something that drew my attention and spoke to me. As I walked down the path from Room G and passed the Barrett Center, I noticed four pylons/construction cones sitting on the landing between the first and second set of stairs. I wondered what was going on but continued to walk in my search for something beautiful for the aesthetic writing assignment. However, within two steps something in the back of my mine said: "you noticed it; write about it."

Part A: simply be present to its presence:

Primitive shapes: truncated cone, squat square

Usually gather with family/tribe instead of being alone

Molded quickly with hardened drips at its base

Scarred from the feet of others standing upon your base/shoulders

Hard for dirt to stick to you, but some still manages

Very plastic with your highly specular shine

Part B: record a dialogue with it:

Oh! profane object that normally gives much dread at your sight. With your simple structure we project your lack of consciousness invading the field. What brings you to the temple's steps where we go to raise consciousness? I would love to

---

85 The phrase "aesthetic arrest" Campbell takes from James Joyce's novel, *A Portrait of the Artist as a Young Man,* where Stephen Dedalus explains the qualities of art that do not seek the viewer to desire it but to be changed by it. "The mind is arrested and raised above desire and loathing," Stephen relates in the novel. Quoted in Campbell, *The Mythic Dimension,* p. 235.

have a conversation with you (you know the oaks can quote Shakespeare) but you seem to have nothing to say. Are you intimidated by the bushes and flowers? I would think with all your travels and what you have seen that you'd be able to tell stories all day and night. Why do you rebuff my requests for a dialogue? Are you stupid or a Zen master? Speak to me oh guru of the highways and byways. Maybe you don't think I am worthy of your sage advice. How can I convince you that I am ready to follow you to the ends of the earth to hear your words? (Joe Lohmar)

Artemis

My soul wants to fly

drink the nectar of flowers, wherever they are

take a bath in ripe mangos

speak without secrets

led by the goddess of the forest

Haiku

Septembermoon, full

nothwithstanding the cool wind

warms up my tired face (poems by Monika Rabenbauer)

Drawing Meditation: Giving Image to Words

Beauty sometimes gives rise to exact replication and other times to resemblances and still other times to things whose connection to the original site of inspiration is unrecognizable.[86]

Here we shift a bit from using words to draw forth a reality of beauty, an aesthetic instance, to drawing. You can use pen and pencil or crayon, pastels, or paint if you prefer. This meditation follows directly on the last one where you gave space for beauty to find you rather than you hunting it out.

---

86 Elaine Scarry, *On Beauty and On Being Just* (Princeton, N.J.: Princeton University Press, 1999), p. 3.

Many of you have exquisite talents in drawing and/or painting. The level of your skill is unimportant here, however. What you are seeking in this meditation is making

- The object that you encountered present through its image or
- A quality of it as an image or
- An image of your relationship with it or
- An impression it left you with or
- Something was revealed to you via the image.
- Use some language here, along with the image, if doing so will ripen your experience in your own imagination.

Keep in mind the quote that begins this meditation. When you are finished with what you wished to convey through image, move to the third part of this experience below.

Writer's Response

Desire to be bear foot within aesthetics purple sage flower nuzzling up against a large succulent with arresting center—that was the draw—it called me—come see— look! I'm here—but it's about the affectionate relationship of breeze—soft furry purple beaconing, wooing, resting, nuzzling—the unexpected the drawn to. Does the succulent *feel* this caress? Then separation I was first drawn—in-spiration by the unfolding center, the fresh, *healthy* new life readying to unfold its center only to find relationship. These kisses & licks & nuzzles of soft furry magenta-purple settling against one of the older succulent leaves—luminous green w/a red-yellow illuminated edge nuzzling a succulent leaf w/my toes—my caress making the whole succulent tremble. He likes being touched—by the caress of breeze, my toes & furry purple-magenta loves touch so much that he requested his strategic location right at the edge of the sidewalk & near the smoker's gazebo where I sat earlier in group context of letting go Turning my gaze away but still touching—my love of touching his rubbery, fleshy softness & bodily warmth purple-magenta furry back to nuzzling, my toes letting go, breeze wafting through seduction of sensuous experience—sun kissing, breeze, honey bee the succulent's trembling vibration from the soft breeze Does he want to say anything to me? Are words necessary? I lift my right arm in a flirtatious gesture as if at a bar & engaged making a soft fist to rest my head against

as I listen to our conversations of heartswell, exquisite surrender to the unfolding.
(Mary Fullwood)

Writing Meditation: A Possible Synthesis or Communion

Through two media you have given some form to your aesthetic experience. Now use the following to meditate on the two pieces you have constructed:

- Was there something presented in your drawing or painting that was not accessible for you to communicate in language?
- From the writing and the drawing, what was made or created that carried the most affective presence, an emotional reality of the experience, for you?
- Are there two separate realities created?
- One overarching reality or presence with two different emphases?
- From the communion of the two expressions, what might you say is a necessary condition for beauty to appear?
- What is the nature of beauty such that it appeared in the way it did for you?
- Beauty is in part a mythic experience because it taps into a patterned awareness or a form of consciousness that is metaphorical and symbolic at once. Make any observations on either the writing or the image drawn that leads you to some sense of your personal myth incarnated in either or both of these creations.

Writing Meditation: The Aesthetics of Home

The soul has always been associated with a reflective part in us or the reflective function.[87]

Closer to home, actually within it, is an aesthetic order and arrangement of each room, whether it be an apartment, a studio loft, a condo, a house, or a mobile home. We arrange our surroundings around values that may include a certain efficiency, but I think it has more to do with a desire to mirror the personal myth that we inhabit as domicile. Our arranging things in certain constellations is a poetic way of giving our subjectivity a home in matter,

---

87 James Hillman, *City and Soul*, vol. 2 of *The Uniform Edition of the Writings of James Hillman*, ed. Robert J. Leaver (Putnam, Conn.: Spring Publications, 2006), p. 21.

for what we live with and within matters immensely. How fascinating we find it to enter a person's living space for the first time and to notice what attracts us, what brings us into a quickening intimacy with the surroundings that quickly enwrap us. Then to reflect on how these objects—the colors of the walls, the texture of the carpet or rugs attracted the inhabitants—offers an aperture into qualities of the person we may have had no knowledge of previously.

Noticing is itself an aesthetic action,[88] wherein what wishes to present itself is not random; rather, it is adjusting to and following or being guided by a certain mythos in the soul, what I am calling a personal myth. In these imaginal moments, "the thing presents itself, displays its plumage, its underbelly, its promises and colorings, shadings, nuances, and, yes, its inherent contradictions."[89] So we not only notice through a personal myth, but we craft our homes to be a mimesis or an imitation or a representation through furniture, photos, fabrics, arrangement, order, pattern, geometry and form of how our interior lives are arranged. When I look at the order and arrangement of my study, for instance, with its hundreds of books crammed into so many varieties of large and small bookcases, paintings on the wall, my small altar where I burn incense when I write in the early hours of the day, the figures that populate that altar, some looking at me, others—porcelain and wood dragons, brass Buddhas, clay figurines, arrow heads, ancient shelled fossils millions of years old frozen in a piece of shale, dirt from monasteries or megalith sites in Ireland, pine cones from hiking paths around the United States, a vial with water from a Lake in Switzerland, stones with labyrinths carved into them, two rocks from the Terezin Ghetto 40 kilometers north of Prague—I realize the qualities, if not the patterns, of my own personal myth. Each of our rooms is in part a memory theater, as I have just enumerated the memorabilia of my little altar. Each of the books I have purchased over decades—at last count a crushing 7,000 volumes—has a history, a place and a purpose that at the time I thought was important to own it. I cannot give them up; each is a part of my own story, my own myth.

- Choose a room, or an area of a room in your home to notice with fresh eyes, as if you were a guest who entered it for the first time.

---

88 Hillman writes in the chapter "Segregation of Beauty" that "nothing stirs the heart, quickens the soul more than a moment of beauty. We stop. We flee. We gasp." Hillman, *City and Soul*, p. 188.

89 Dennis Patrick Slattery, "Toward an Aesthetic Psychology: A Review of James Hillman's *City and Soul*," *Jung Journal: Culture and Psyche* 2, no. 1 (2008): 52.

- Describe its order and arrangement.
- What strikes you about the order and/or the arrangement?
- Do you detect any pattern in the presence of things, in their juxtaposition? In the flow of space between objects?
- What is it in you that "gives it" order?
- When you decide to rearrange a room, what principle, pattern or purpose guides you, gives you direction?
- What new pattern or arrangement are you seeking?
- Are your decisions consciously made? Intuitively crafted? Logically mapped? A combination of them?
- Do you sense some other force or presence is also working your new arrangement or worked your old one into its present state or condition?
- Do you find that you re-arrange things at particular important moments or crossroads in your life?
- Has it been out of boredom, fatigue, feelings of exhaustion or low energy? Or out of excitement to try a new form to your belongings? Describe it.
- Ask yourself what you might be ritualizing or re-ritualizing in your reordering impulses.
- Notice that writing out your responses to the above is also a way of rearranging the furniture, items and stereo of your personal myth.

Writing Meditation: Spiralic Aesthetics

Growth under resistance is the chief cause of the spiral form assumed by living things.[90]

On the following pages two spiral shells offer another way of meditating on the aesthetics of form and pattern.[91] Some writers have suggested that the spiral may be older than the circle as a geometry of the soul, and the pattern of life itself as it unfolds forward, as I suggested earlier with the poet Dante's *terza rima* rhyme scheme.

---

90 This profound insight by the botanist James Hinton is quoted in Theodore Andrea Cook's *The Curves of Life* (1914; repr., New York: Dover, 1979), p. 14.

91 Ernst Haeckel (1834-1919), the artist who produced these two prints, was a German biologist, naturalist, philosopher, physician, professor, and artist. I wish to thank Lindsey Beaven, a Depth Psychology student at Pacifica Graduate Institute, for bringing this collection of images to my attention.

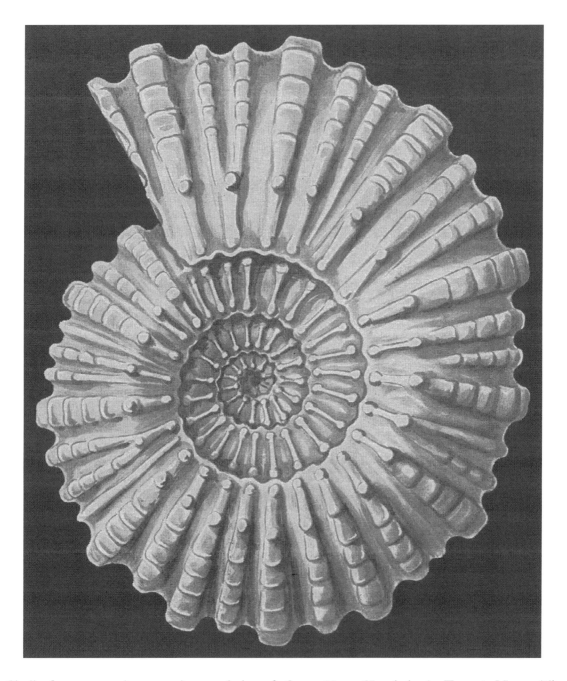

Shell of an ammonite, an extinct cephalopod. *Source*: Ernst Haeckel, *Art Forms in Nature: The Prints of Ernst Haeckel* (Mineola, N.Y.: Dover Publications, Inc. 2004).

Ammonite shell. *Source*: Ernst Haeckel, *Art Forms in Nature: The Prints of Ernst Haeckel* (Mineola, N.Y.: Dover Publications, Inc. 2004).

- Choose one of the spirals to notice closely.
- First, describe it as objectively as you can: what is it you see in its design?
- Note its details in as much particularity as you can. Stay with the shape and texture of the spiral as if you were describing its concrete presence to someone.
- Then, move to the second part of this meditation:
- Describe the spiral through its qualities: what it evokes in you.
- What does it make present for you?
- Do you discern anything of yourself, your own life, reflected in it?
- Does it awaken any feeling, image, thought, memory or idea in you?
- Are you able to see the spiral not as an object to be studied but more as a person or a subjectivity to be engaged?
- Is there any way in which the spiral's presence defines or describes your own being present towards it?

The observation above grows out of an insight suggested by Robert Armstrong regarding the aesthetic work, in which he writes: "the work's subjectivity participates in that generality of acknowledgement we think of as *myth,* which is a special font of aesthetic power . . . we are as likely to encounter the mythic in government as in art."[92]

My own belief is that the way in which a work of aesthetic presence appears to me mirrors back in its subjectivity qualities of my own mythic life, which patterns the way a subject purposely presents itself. Subjective and objective modes of being merge in the mythic enactment of becoming present. I become present in a particular way to what presents itself in its own way. Myths inhere in things of the world as well as in my own being. My everyday life is enwombed in metaphors that analogize my personal myth. This idea seems important to ponder because it suggests that I am formed and created by things of the world; they have impacts on me that I have yet to fully realize.

Writers' Responses

Spiraling Down

Spinning vision pulsing, repulsing

---

92 Robert Plant Armstrong, *The Powers of Presence: Consciousness, Myth, and Affecting Presence* (Philadelphia: University of Pennsylvania Press, 1981), p. 48.

Calling me in, pushing me out.

Tantalizing, terrifying.

Where am I held within its bars?

Is it prison or freedom?

Shadows move.

I jump.

Cover my ears, shield my eyes.

I try to resist its pull, excavating excuses:

It's not a good time

It's too early—too late.

I'm too busy, too tired.

I'm just not ready.

Simmering center smoldering, summoning.

Charcoal coaxing.

Sucks me in, convulsing, sliding

Down.

Can't breathe. Can't see.

So fast.

Moving imperceptibly between light and shadow.

Down.

I can't control my own movement.

I cry for help, to stop. To catch my breath.

The voice within calls out to me, urgently:

Keep moving, sinking, flying, rolling.

Keep going.

Back to where your soul lives, and

Where your heart is open, and

Where your spirit flies free.

Down. (Virginia Bobro)

The Spiral

Oh shell spiral

Cellular intensity

Season of waters

Beginnings of hands thrashing

Into new life

If I uncover your face

I shall find the Medusa

Strung up in sky

With these tears

I see the sparkling drop

The eye of knowing

Into the myth of new beginnings (Sheila Fugard)

Writing Meditation: The Poetics of Soul

Poems too have muscle and/often strong-arm a cherished/prejudice, slams it to/the table's top; the strain is/sufficient to change my belief/core.[93]

Some years back I noticed how powerfully reading poetry often evoked lines of verse in me, as if my aesthetic self wanted to begin a dialogue with the poem and was forming responses in my imagination to make the poem being read a much richer experience. It is as if the poem wanted to be remembered in a poetic way by my own imagination's conceiving a response to it. In this way both the poem and I become more consciously aware of ourselves. Poetry's gift rests in part in being able to increase my consciousness.

Only much later did I come on the term "active imagination" outlined by C. G. Jung that conveyed what in part, was taking place in me. Poems would seem to make us pregnant with bits and pieces or fully formed poems in response. Active Imagination implicates the voice

---

93 Dennis Patrick Slattery, "Poem's Pressure," in Dennis Patrick Slattery and Chris Paris, *The Beauty Between Words: Selected Poems* (Stormville, N.Y.: Water Forest Press, 2010), pp. 22-23.

of the unconscious and even invites it up to be heard and seen, allowing us in the process to become more intimate with its content.[94] It is, as an imaginative process, the "aesthetic way of formulation"[95] that runs counter to but still seems to complement a more scientific way of understanding. I find that it offers a way of witnessing on a deeper level, what might be termed a "hermeneutic of publicity." Before discovering Active Imagination as a method for encouraging presence on a deeper fuller level, I called my approach a "Mytho-Poetic Method" or "Evoked Poetic Presence."[96] Here are a small handful of ways to employ to facilitate entering a poem so that it may/will evoke poetic responses in you, evoked I believe, "by Muses hidden in the curtains of a poem being read aloud."[97] I will follow these suggestions by an example to make this evocative method more concrete:

- Enter a poem as you might enter a dream state, or a film, giving yourself over to it completely and not comparing it to or force it to align with your lived reality.
- Read it aloud. It is so important to activate the aesthetic field that the poem wishes to be witnessed through.
- Submit to it the way you submit to a film, to a painting or a piece of music, by withholding judgment and allowing yourself your fullest presence.
- Be aware of its silent hermitage and allow yourself a sensory presence to it.
- Be open and receptive to its analogies, its correspondences, and its associations.
- Let these associations emerge on their own without your forcing any part of it.
- Write them down next to the lines of the poem that evoked them.
- Allow yourself to enter the time of the poem, a time that could be understood as some midpoint between myth and dream, between intellectual understanding and imaginal presencing, between intellect and intuition.
- Let your visceral awareness also be present and allow it to guide you. Poems are felt in the body as well as grasped by the intellect through a visceral aesthetics.
- Feel the poem in your tendons, heart, ligaments and organs of the body.
- Trust what emerges for you through the poem; do not judge its contents or filter out any material, however dark or forbidding it might appear.

---

94 Joan Chodorow, ed., *Jung on Active Imagination* (Princeton, N.J.: Princeton University Press, 1997), p. 10.

95 Chodorow, *Jung on Active Imagination*, p. 12.

96 Dennis Patrick Slattery, *Just Below the Water Line: Selected Poems* (Winchester Canyon Press, 2004), pp. 156-159.

97 Slattery, *Just Below the Water Line*, p. 156.

- Do not entertain frustration. Simply remain attentive to the poem's words and the images that are birthed through them.
- Remain open, receptive, and porous.
- Do not judge what you write. You are not seeking correct answers, only authentic ones.
- Keep a sense of amusement about you. The muse of poetry is benevolent and will guide you if you are honest and open to the experience.[98]

One morning I am reading one of my favorite poets, Galway Kinnell. In his poem, "Flower Herding on Mount Monadnock,"[99] I read the following lines:

> The air is so still
> That as they go off through the trees
> The love songs of birds do not get any fainter.
>
> 3
>
> The last memory I have
> Is of a flower that cannot be touched,
> Through the bloom of which, all day,
> Fly crazed, missing bees.
>
> 4
>
> As I climb sweat gets up my nostrils,
> For an instant I think I am at the sea.
> One summer off Cape Ferrat we watched a black seagull
> Straining for the dawn, we stood in the surf. . . .

I try without forcing it, to center on the words in a non-willful way, as one would do in meditation, to listen to what they expose, but not push against or try to be too conscious or critical about what is heard. You can, with too much effort, strain yourself right out of the poetic experience.

In my response, the following words surfaced on their own:

---

98 This list is taken from Slattery and Paris, *The Beauty between Words*, pp. xxx-xxxi.

99 Galway Kinnell, "Flower Herding on Mount Monadnock," in Kinnell, *A New Selected Poems* (Boston: Houghton Mifflin, 2001), pp. 41-43.

When in the marigold of a memory
no cattle move, no rheumy noses run;
wind song takes on a purple hue
and dangles from the web
of a spider so still, its odor
is palpable.

I continue to read Kinnell's poem:

But at last in the thousand elegies
The dead rise in our hearts,
On the brink of our happiness we stop
Like someone on a drunk starting to weep.

After a moment of silence with these lines, I write:

I sense the call of spirit begin
In my legs inebriate and course
Upward, pulled by the
Gravity of heaven

Kinnell's poem continues:

6

I kneel at a pool,
I look through my face
At the bacteria I think
I see crawling through the moss.
My face sees me,
The water stirs, the face,
Looking preoccupied,
Gets knocked from its bones

Musing on these lines, I respond:

Narcissus reflects his fleshy image

off the sheen, the slick shine of my bones.

His gaze hides in my marrow.

Further verses from his poem and my response follow, but I think the above is sufficient for you to try your longhand response to a poem:

Pandora's Cabala

She is perfectly imagined
limitless and nothing that is

a precise cut in two. The making of two, a stitch
for holding together while gathering materium

throughout and through the poetries in you
this just-so neat incision—this stitch

like the latest rage she wears she were's
in slim-lined fashion sleek as skin-all skin, at first

but, inked, the web of looks de (re)inscribe her:
ain wets the etches with tattoo; sketches

the penultimate hide once set to hidings
her, the way you wanted her: maid

ready-made to wear, she where's nothing when she
comes (you'll catch that or you won't)

although insatiable contagion ornaments in air her dark
and bitch-made skin so virtual and real she *dis*appears

again . . . what wild nature glowing, always seeming
to be true surrounds now with embryon enmeshed

in hour of dark and skin-made bitch she hides
she hides! hiding ever more the skin she lives

living all the way in, in skin

under skinny, skin skin

while she there's three vales over no face
and you catch her unbecoming and you call that trace

a *mirror of under* and *ain soph* when you name her, but
when you name her, name her from her many names

because then you see, you are in her sac of chit
like a bit of chat as virtual as flesh spent spiny high

no backbone wears beyond that sky the way that she
will you; she's a re[(de)ma]teria material an *ain soph aur*

the primo prima, wet and nurse, an equally inured
but, equally some dark and morning light

do not name her as you name her
she is nothing she is[100]

- Create a response to any of the lines that arrest you, slow you down, make you pause and wonder for a moment, or bring to your awareness some shard of your world.
- Write your responses in poetic form next to the lines that drew your attention. My sense is that these lines conveyed something to the personal myth you are reading the poem through.
- Add one more set of lines—4-5 at the end of the poem.
- Try your hand at writing a poem back to this one in a brief poetic response.

Writing Meditation: A Poem's Completion

Poetic contemplation is as natural to the spirit as it is the return of the bird to its nest, and it is the entire world which returns with the spirit to the mysterious nest of the soul.[101]

---

100 Stephanie Pope, "Pandora's Cabala," *A Hudson View Poetry Digest* 1, no. 3 (2007): 21-22.

101 Jacques Maritain, "Poetic Experience," *The Review of Politics* 6, no. 4 (1944): 387-402, available at http://maritain.nd.edu/jmc/jm3301.htm.

Let's continue in this poetic vein for a short time. My observation is that whatever you write is coming from the imaginal field that the poem constructs as well as the mythic field that exists within and that patterns your life in a particular way. It is part of the reason why a bold, unforced and uncensored response to any of these meditations is essential.

In this next meditation, I offer a poem that has been truncated, its ending deleted:

> Can I trust what you tell me
> In the dark
> Even as wind slips below the door
> To lighten your words?
> Is darkness the deep space of
> Luminous prose, a black hole of
> Brilliance when you speak
> Of disease you clutch with
> Your left hand?
> The dark, now letting loose
> Itself for dawn to push it
> Back—
> Will now turn your words angle down
> Under the bed or to a dry shower
> Stall
> To forestall the light of a day
> That could right well[102]

Stay with the poem, reading it two or three times, until an extension or an amplification of it enters you; write it down. If more than one response calls to you, write them both out. The poem has instilled a motion in you, a movement that is aesthetic, psychological, personal, and mythic in design.

---

102 Dennis Patrick Slattery, "What You Tell Me In the Dark," in Slattery and Paris, *The Beauty Between Words,* pp. 70-71.

Writers' Responses

Come to Me

Come to me my child, my lost babe,
Heart of my Self, lost . . . abandoned,
left by the roadside as I headed off
for the glittering city on the hill.
Come to me, my darling infant,
I'll wrap you in soft, warm fleece,
Suckle you with the honeyed milk
I fed to the gods in the temple of gold.
Come to me, gift of my spirit,
Let me touch you with the tenderness
of Psyche's feather that brushed away
the cobwebs of my long, restless sleep.
Come to me my Beauty, my jewel
Your place is set—the candles lit,
Flowers scattered across a bright cloth,
Celebrating your return, marking my joy.
Come to me, my beloved,
I've cleared the branches and boulders
Along this unused path.
Please come back. (Joyceann Wycoff)

Poems Are the Leaves

Poems are the leaves
On the trees of one's life.
Notice in the autumn how they drift,
Fall in the gutters of drawers
Brilliant colored

On second look are brown,

Desiccated,

Compost.

Distinctive shapes remembered

In plastic, cloth and glass, useful,

Washed and put away.

Occasionally a new beauty in size or in color

Is found on the walkway

Unique in its intriguing detail,

Aching with ancient art,

Quietly dying. (pcraig)

Writing Meditations: Aesthetics of Therapy: Dante's *Divine Comedy*

A poem should shake us up out of our comfort and lethargy and conventional ways of seeing.[103]

Now we enter into three writing meditations, one for each of the three canticas, or territories of Dante's famous poem, written in the early years of the 14th century in Italy. It tells the story, in a little more than 14,000 lines, of the condition of one man, Dante himself, as a pilgrim, who one day wakes up in midlife out of what seems a sleep or period of extended unconsciousness, and wonders how he has somehow lost his way in the world. Not an uncommon occurrence.

He is then guided by a number of figures in the poem/pilgrimage into the realm of the afterlife, where individuals who have died are now, as shades, in their condition either for eternity, or, in the case of those in Purgatory, cleansing themselves to enter Paradise. So, practically the entire poem takes place in the state of these souls after death. The guides are, first the Roman poet Virgil, who guides Dante down spiraling to the left through the abysmal and unredeemed suffering of Hell, then up the spiralic path to the right that

---

103 Cowan, "Poetic Knowledge and Poetic Form."

comprises the road of Hope ascending Mount Purgatory. From there he is guided almost to the end of the poem, into Paradise, by a historical woman he knew and loved from afar in Florence, Beatrice Portinari. At this juncture Dante's journey ends with a vision of harmony and balance, of wholeness and peace. He has traveled, or pilgrimaged, as Helen Luke has written, from "a dark wood to a white rose."[104]

It occurred to me that his story offers in dramatically vivid and often horrific detail, his personal myth in storied form which captures qualities, conditions and situations that we all face on our own life's journey. I wrote a book on this process, of which three of the 365 pages—one for each day of the year— I offer here in order to bring the aesthetics of the poem in line with the biography/history of each of us. Through them we can journey in three installments with Dante on his pilgrimage which captures bits and pieces of our own sojourn through life.

Let us begin in Inferno, with an entry that, first of all, offers lines from the poem first, followed by a brief summary of what is taking place in this moment of the narrative. What follows is a brief meditation of mine on the more universal or archetypal action that the lines capture and detail out in very particular ways. The last part of each entry offers a writing meditation in which you, having been part of the poem's journey, reflect on your own life in light of Dante's changing situation, one in Hell, one in Purgatory and one in Paradise.

In the first entry, I have chosen the realm of the suicides that Dante and his guide, Virgil, have spiraled down into. It begins close to the start of the canto and describes the terrain that Dante poetically suggests mirrors the condition of one who has committed suicide. Notice closely the details of the terrain he and Virgil enter.

Entry 1: Hell

> No green leaves in that forest, only black;
> no branches straight and smooth, but knotted, gnarled;
> no fruits were there, but briers bearing poison. . . .
> This is the nesting place of the foul Harpies, . . .
> Their wings are wide, their necks and faces human;

---

104 Helen Luke, *Dark Wood to White Rose: Journey and Transformation in Dante's Divine Comedy*, 4th ed. (New York: Parabola Books, 2001).

their feet are taloned, their great bellies feathered;

they utter their laments on the strange trees.[105]

Dante and Virgil enter the Seventh Circle, the Violent against Themselves. The first inhabitants they encounter are the monstrous and mythic two-natured birds, the Harpies, who have faces of women and taloned feet as birds of prey. They perch on trees that are absent any life. Nothing grows in this realm of suicides and squanderers. The terms of the geography mirror with exacting horror the moral offense of the shades condemned to this realm. The strange birds historically soil what they land on. They are images of pollution and dirty what was valuable and good. Dante does not specify what laments they utter; perhaps he is unable to hear them clearly, so confused does he become in this region.

Dante's genius is to offer poetic and dramatic descriptions of the landscape that exactly mirror the nature of the soul's condition. We see through the analogy of geography what the terms of the soul's condition are and were. We are given a glimpse of what the interior geography of a suicide might look like if we could penetrate into the soul: nothing is straight or smooth; everything is knotted and gnarled, like the thought of a suicide as s/he contemplates self-murder within brambled calculations.

All life has ceased; nothing fruitful is present in one's life. Hope has been annihilated. Time stands still. The Harpies are the life force of the suicide: revengeful, pitiless, full of wrath and lamentation. Reason becomes gnarled, allowing one to rationalize one's way to self-destruction.

Riting Meditation

What situations in your life are gnarled and knotted, thus obliterating any clear path of action or direction?[106]

- Read the passage over a few times. You need not know the entire poem to work specific passages. Read over the reflection I offer and then turn to the Meditation.

---

105 Dante Alighieri, *The Divine Comedy*, trans. Allen Mandelbaum, intro. Eugenio Montale (New York: Alfred A. Knopf, 1995), *Inferno* 13.4-6; 10; 13-15. All passages from *The Divine Comedy* are from this translation.

106 Dennis Patrick Slattery, *Day-to-Day Dante: Exploring Personal Myth through the Divine Comedy* (Bloomington, Ind.: iUniverse, 2011), p. 51.

- Choose a situation or condition you are currently experiencing, or one you have been in and may still be living with, or one in which you have resolved or extricated yourself from.
- Pay attention to what is evoked in you by the powerful adjectives "knotted" and "gnarled."
- The poetic passage is a way into your own poetry, your own aesthetic narrative, there to reflect on it through the poem.

Writers' Responses

I get wound up in food and suicide, eating at times what may harm and kill me.

Why? That dream—no—longer ago than that—the witches—no—longer gone still—an early impulse—born, not born—back to creator. Who/what created and why?

There's no answer to that . . . it just is.

That gnarly place gets gummed up in the food, in the twisted nourishment spellbinding bound up thinking unable to say NO to the death impulse that lives so deep according to Freud and Kali.

Life springs forth through sinewy knots in aged trees who are deep rooted. (Pam Bjork)

My marriage of 39 years has aspects to it that are gnarled and knotted. Although I'm not sure that one can have a relationship for 39 years that does not have gnarled and knotted ways. My marriage is the first item of the twenty important life events. My marriage moved me from a family of "foul harpies" to a family of loving embrace. My family is my anchor—my husband, my two sons and their wives and my two grandchildren are veritable grounding elements in my life. I adore them all. They make me happy—they are all delightful to be with. However, in 39 years I have come to know myself better. I'm not the same person who married many years ago. What I first loved in Jim, I still love—but more and more I find myself individuating away from his ways—his ideas on religion clash with mine—his social nature clashes with my desire for introspection—lifestyle patterns are changing and how are we to negotiate this path?

"To what do you extend your arms in great affection?"

I extend my arms in great affection to my own loving family that I have created. I know too well what a family of harpies looks like and how destructive that family field can be. My husband's sweet nature has engendered my nourishing side and through our union we have created a special vessel of family. It nourishes me every day. I know it is there awaiting me whenever I want to reach out to any part of it, I will be welcomed. It is my life's blessing. (Dianne G. Light)

Living in a place where almost all of my friends and neighbors are retired, I often glimpse an inner world of other senior citizens that feels like the seventh circle. I hear that life essentially ceased when they stopped "doing" or "working." When introduced they ask each other who they used to be. The response is usually something along the lines of: "I was an accountant," or "I was a teacher."

There is an almost frantic effort to fill time in the "waiting room" with "fun." Frequently there is great lamentation about loss, malfunction or replacement of body parts, loneliness, illness, death, the awfulness of how the world has changed, and all the problems with grown children who have left, or won't leave, home.

Dread of the future, or lack of it, threatens to destroy the present. Self-destruction is accomplished by fear of change, fear of looking within and anger at the "unfairness" of age, pain, loss, and death.

It requires much effort to avoid being entangled in the knots of hectic fun used to hide painful emptiness. It is hard to jump into the void of change instead of clinging to the so-called safety of being one of the group.

Seductive words clutch at me, trying to pull me back into the barren wasteland of no hope—this is all there is—why fight it—it's too late to change anything. I have to armor myself against the offended and puzzled cries of my harpies: "Why on earth would you want to go back to school? I would rather be shot. What are you going to do with that degree at your age? You must be crazy! Are you that bored? No one in their right mind would do what you're doing."

I can tolerate being in this barren place only because I know the way out. I don't have to remain in this land of no change but that of physical deterioration. I can be empathetic about the fear that underlies the laments of the harpies. I know that the knots of taking the "easy" way out by living someone else's life cannot bind me unless I choose to not live my own life. (Julia Berg)

Entry 2: Purgatory

I threw myself devoutly at his holy

feet, asking him to open out of mercy;

> but first I beat three times upon my breast.
> Upon my forehead he traced seven P's
> with his sword's point and said: "When you have entered
> within, take care to wash away these wounds."[107]

Dante's act of humility before the angel guarding the large iron gates of Purgatory is necessary. Only he can reveal a right deposition to persuade the angel that he is amply calibrated to begin in earnest a pilgrimage of penitence leading to purification. He beats his breast three times, in recognition of the Trinity within him, before receiving the seven wounds of the sword that, in some translations, it is suggested that its point is broken off as a sign of mercy. The intention of the angel is not to maim Dante, but to mark him as an initiate into the inner sanctum of purification.

The intention of the penitential journey, then, is two-fold: to be marked first in penitence, and then to have each marking effaced in purgation. The angelic sword markings are a divine remembrance of what the hopeful pilgrim must erase before arriving at the earthly paradise where Beatrice awaits him.

In so many stories, the heroic must be wounded, deflated, or brought down to a level at which s/he might then make it through an opening to a new life. When we are marked and wounded, we feel more intensely our mortality and our heroic nature. Cleansing the soul is a necessary form of suffering, but in hope, not despair; now the suffering has as its intention erasing the stains of one's imperfections, to purify one's vision to see what the heavenly realm has to present to us in our quest for spiritual completion. The wound is a corridor into blessedness; both are necessary for increased knowing. Something larger in us than our sense of I is at stake. The totality of who one is, is implicated in this suffering.

Meditation

What part of your life has been marked or afflicted, which laid you open to a more profound level of knowing?

---

107 Dante, *Purgatorio*, 9.109-114.

- This passage from the second landscape of the poem places Dante and us in a world of hope, where possibilities for a future are alive in us after traversing the hopeless realm of Hell.
- Dante here is about to be permitted to enter through the large iron gates of Purgatory to begin his journey of renunciation as well as to receive the grace needed to complete his passage.
- Look through the description and reflection to where your own life has been scarred, marked, wounded and initiated into some other level of being.
- Write it out, referring if you like back to the passage to give you a compass bearing.

Entry 3: Paradise

> From that sphere which I noted as most precious,
>
> I saw a flame come forth with so much gladness
>
> that none it left behind had greater brightness;
>
> and that flame whirled three times round Beatrice
>
> while singing, so divine a song that my
>
> imagination cannot shape it for me.
>
> My pen leaps over it; I do not write:
>
> our fantasy and, all the more so, speech
>
> are far too gross for painting folds so deep.[108]

Failure and progress are not so much opposites as they are complementary movements of the soul in life as it struggles towards achievement. Memory fails, words buckle, imagination deflates—and the trade off is progress, motion, beyond where our abilities have defined limits.

In the force of these limits, St. Peter appears to quiz Dante on what he does or should know: the nature of Faith, the highest of the 3 cardinal virtues. He is thus placed between what he cannot express and what he can and must divulge. Speech will allow him to pass this first of 3 exit exams; yet speech is too crude to ingather the beauty of the song heard in heaven. Words reveal inadequacies—a hard realization for any of us to accept.

---

108 Dante, *Paradiso*, 24.19-27.

In a culture of achievement and near-hysterical obsession with success and improvement, there exists little space for failure. Where might failure be acknowledged? We hear in certain military or political or social arenas that "failure is not an option." It seems arrogant to utter such, for in pursuing something at all costs so that failure is kept out of the house, we can create more devastation when failure is not allowed to be one of the guests we accept. "Success" may be a major failing. Failing may be a way of wisdom in which what was set out to be achieved is seen as wrong or wrong-headed, a terrible error in judgment, as when a nation pursues a certain course of action hell-bent on success. So too in our own lives, when we deploy success as the only acceptable consequence of our actions, we have already failed, for we may have denied what we needed most.

Meditation

- When has admitting failure actually liberated you?
- When has failure turned out to be a form of improvement?
- Under what circumstances have you been so moved by beauty that you could not give it expression?

Each of these writing meditations on the journey of one soul, mirroring the experiences in part of all our pilgrimages, opens up a corridor and creates an energy field from which to work within. Aesthetics has its own portholes into our personal myth.

5

RITING THE WOUNDED SELF

A myth may make a cow sacred in one culture and hamburger meat in another.[109]

I am introducing the term pathologizing to mean the psyche's autonomous ability to create illness, morbidity, disorder, abnormality, and suffering in any aspect of its behavior and to experience and imagine life through this deformed and afflicted perspective.[110]

The energy of the soul can flow into a field of afflictions and become mired there in endless repetitions of playing back, in a vicious circle, the same hurts, resentments and wounds to itself and to others. Rather than rushing to efface and erase such woundedness, we will explore in this chapter what the hurt wishes to express. Where does the voice of the violence against me, and from me to others, reside? Can I make use of the ways the world wounds me to see into it something of the deeper complexities of my personal myth? I believe just such a possibility exists, but it is not easy to revisit, much less reclaim, these moments in memory and prose, for we quickly learn that enormous energy is still prevalent, circling the wounded fissures. Out of affliction, however, can emerge compassion for both self and for others who may be suffering the wounds of memory as well. One is not condemned to perpetual pain.

Most all of us have been arrested by and consequently been wrested from our more comfortable and familiar way of life and thrown into confusion and rage over wrongs slung at us.

I want to include here as well the experience of witnessing or learning of violence done to another and the destructive impact it can have on both the perpetrator and the victim. The closer we are in affection and familiarity with the other person, the more damaging that act toward them can have on us, as when we witness some cruelty leveled at one of our children, a spouse, a best friend, or a partner. Of course, this includes self-afflictions as well.

---

109 Sam Keen and Anne Valley-Fox, *Your Mythic Journey: Finding Meaning in Your Life through Writing and Storytelling* (New York: Jeremy Tarcher/Putnam, 1989), p. xi.

110 James Hillman, *Re-Visioning Psychology* (1975; repr., New York: HarperPerennial, 1992), p. 57.

More broadly, we can suffer with the injustices directed at a specific group of people or an entire nation. These too take their toll and open us to a vulnerability that may be almost impossible to cope with while foreclosing any sympathy for the others' plight.

I want to keep open with large boundaries what gathers in wounding the self, be it an individual or a collective self. For example, I have written elsewhere how retired people not on Medicare who are charged 2-3 times the insurance rate for drugs—sometimes averaging $1,500 per month. Or the current abysmal minimum wage of America today, 2012, is an obscenity and an act of violence against one's worth. Developers who move into an already densely-populated area and build hundreds of new homes, stressing further the infrastructures of sewage, sanitation, water, traffic and general quality of life. All of these constitute acts of violence against a community's basic well-being. More recently, the Wall Street financial theft and the predatory subprime lending practices, all laid out with persuasive and clever exactitude in the award-winning documentary, *Inside Job*, reveal the depths of fraud as acts of violence directed at an individual or an entire people that alters their lives immeasurably.[111] Others have claimed that these massive attacks on trust comprise a particular form of terrorism as well. Regardless, woundings assume many shapes and motives for inflicting them.

Healing from hurts—psychological, emotional, spiritual, physical or economic—can be opportunities for further insights into the personal myth we live within; in these moments of turmoil, we spin back on our history in the geometry of the spiral to reassess ourselves, our goals, our sense of self-worth, even our purpose for being.

These moments of wounding or repeated assaults on us, wherein we hold on to the negative charge that gnaws away our peace of mind in our waking life and then may appear in symbolic narratives in our dreams, comprises what one writer has labeled "impacted energy cysts."[112] More prosaically, such an inner presence has been called "one's inner hoodlum,"[113] a gangster that continues to terrorize one's interior world that then spills into the realm of behavior and more largely, into the crafting of an entire world view. In the

---

111 Dennis Patrick Slattery, "The Voice of Violence: Its Afflicted Utterance," in Slattery, *Harvesting Darkness: Essays on Literature, Myth, Film and Culture* (New York: iUniverse, 2006), p. 210.

112 John Upledger, quoted in Edward C. Whitmont, *The Alchemy of Healing: Psyche and Soma* (Berkeley, Calif.: North Atlantic Books, 1993), p. 10.

113 Whitmont, *The Alchemy of Healing*, p. 22.

process, our coveted beliefs can be dismantled, encouraging us to rethink the contours as well as the terms designated by our personal myth. If our personal myth begins to offer us a too-familiar and comfortable center of gravity, then lacerations, either self-inflicted or branded from outside, may throw us from that ordered world into new arenas of growth and awareness.

A writing ritual as an act of remembering can break into this impacted gnarled mass and begin to dissolve it through the cleansing agent of understanding and perhaps, eventually, forgiveness. Psychologist Robert Karen observes that "this ability to live with ambivalence—with both love and hate, but with love predominating—is what distinguishes the forgiving from the unforgiving personality."[114] His insight reveals that far from dissolving the reality of hate, one can learn to live within its presence and not be disfigured by it.

When these events become obsessive experiences, the terms of our personal myth, often lying dormant and undisturbed, are roiled and rise up; they may uncoil in pain and anguish, now to be grasped in tangible and often exaggerated ways. I see these moments of suffering as potential breakthrough opportunities, both painful and liberating at the same instant.

Writing Meditation: The Wound That Keeps on Giving

> To be wounded is to be opened to the world; it is to be pushed off the straight, fixed, and predictable path of certainty and thrown into ambiguity, or onto the circuitous path, and into the unseen and unforeseen.[115]

Like Pandora's box, which contains the mysteries of virtue and defeat, there are certain wounds that many of us continue to relish, often unconsciously, re-opening. We are a scarred and marked species. Wounds, with scars as their visible or invisible memories, dismemberments, crucifixions, riddle our being as we walk or run through life, or as we simply stop living. On a psychological level, C. G. Jung believed that "we all have to be

---

114 Robert Karen's excellent treatment of forgiveness beyond resentment in *The Forgiving Self: The Road from Resentment to Connection* is a strong affirmation of the power of generosity over suffering (New York: Anchor Books, 2003).

115 Dennis Patrick Slattery, *The Wounded Body: Remembering the Markings of Flesh* (Albany: State University of New York Press, 2000), p. 13.

'crucified with Christ,' i.e. suspended in a moral suffering equivalent to veritable crucifixion."[116]

- Describe a wound that, for whatever reasons, you continue to re-open, re-incise, re-evaluate, relive, re-member with obsessive accuracy and fierce fidelity. It can be a physical, emotional, psychological, or spiritual affliction.
- What is its origin? What is its power as you understand it?
- What is it you might need from the wound that now seeps out of you anew?
- Can you describe its voice, its tenor, its tone?
- Imagine being in a dialogue with it. Can you write out a conversation with it, listening to and recording it faithfully as you hear it?
- Can you draw or sketch its image? Here you might put a feeling into a concrete shape or design.
- What does the wound, the affliction, need or desire from you?
- Can you respond to it with sympathy and even love? Can you speak through compassion to the wound, that is as an archetypal reality, both you and Other at the same time? It has its own psychic laws and ways of being as an autonomous presence in the world.
- Give it a chance to speak and for you to speak back to it, not in the enclosed suffocating place of anger but in generous regard for its presence.
- If it helps, tell the hurt your story and let it suppurate in response.

Writer's Response

Clearcut

A verb

meant

perhaps

to sound surgical, precise.

I can tell you

it is anything but

---

116 C. G. Jung, *Psychology and Alchemy,* vol. 12 of *The Collected Works of C. G. Jung,* trans. R. F. C. Hull, ed. Herbert Read, Michael Fordham, Gerhard Adler, and R. F. C. Hull (Princeton, N.J.: Princeton University Press, 1968), ¶ 24.

without or within
on the land or
in the gut
the shredding of my own soulflesh
as the timberjack rips through
alder after greensweet alder
on a lush summer morn
the lushness of my mourning a
blood-rich agony

O dear God
i cannot support this grief, this
Knowing i
must bear witness
to the carnage
and that love
and care
and trust
were not enough to make a difference
that every second gesture
has only come to this:
death
without
regeneration
yet I must know
and know again
and yet again
the teeth of that great saw

its roaring screaming high whine
savaging my inner core
my very deepmost
heart of refuge

the whole forest community of unseen

sniffs and grunts, rustles, clicks and

subtle stirrings in the night

gone gone gone gone gone

nothing left but

the dry and lonely wind.

What does this wounding say to me? I am not ready to hear some

noble, sane words of sense-making or justification.

What it says is,

Yes

I am your despair.

As the light is upon the water,
I am here. (Madeleine Houston)

Writing Meditation: A Wound You Inflicted

> The details of a life are themselves to be opened out so we can feel the archetypes
> playing under them.[117]

Not just being the recipient of a wound, but ones that we ourselves have inflicted, can break loose dimensions of our personal myth when we spiral back in memory and shame to retrieve them.

Writing may be a form of ritual surgery that reestablishes the wound we inflicted within our life narrative. Writing can also be "an exercise to develop the quality of absorption" wherein we become more deeply immersed in our narrative. Writing can "quiet and calm us

---

117 Joseph Campbell, *Mythic Worlds, Modern Words: On the Art of James Joyce*, ed. Edmund L. Espstein (Novato, Calif.: New World Library, 2003), p. 10.

and engage us most deeply."[118] It is one powerful way to give shape and form to what otherwise might remain formless and thus more horrible in its destructive energy on our well-being.

- Painful as it may be, recollect and describe something you have done or thought to another in the past that still carries intense energy for you and within you when you remember it. Thoughts themselves can carry powerful haunting presences throughout our lives. So do not limit the remembrance to an actual physical deed. Wishes, desires, hopes, all imagined with great intensity can also wound, infect and infest our well-being and feelings of serenity and joy.
- It may be guilt, shame, remorse, or self-loathing that is aroused in you when you recount it.
- So two steps here: first recount it as a narrative with the most salient details that are aroused in the remembrance. In its particularities, its details, reside the elements of one's personal myth.
- Second, describe your feelings that gather around the remembrance. The feeling or affective state that is evoked is just as important as the memory itself.
- You may even wish to recount in writing the affect that surrounded you in carrying out the original event and then the feelings of remembrance that constellate around its recollection.
- The third part of this most important writing ritual is to make, if possible, some peace through reconciliation with the event as it exists now in your memory. That is the section of your life that can be redeemed; the event is done in the past but not finished in the present and not yet fully integrated to help align you with the future.
- Think of how you might express this act or thought by fitting it into your larger narrative.
- What part of your story does this act complete?
- What part of your narrative does this act dismantle?
- Give this remembrance a home; retrieve it from its orphan status in your story.
- Write a poem about it or to it.
- Narrate it as a fiction in the third person.
- Allow the wound to close around you. Let the stitches be made up of its story. Stories can stitch wounds closed so they are staunched from oozing further. They will not, however, disappear because the scar will remember it. Scars are wounds' stories recollected.
- Make a note to yourself to remember it again in a month within such a dedicated ritual.

---

118 Louise DeSalvo, *Writing as a Way of Healing: How Telling Our Stories Transforms Our Lives* (Boston: Beacon Press, 2000), p. 73.

Writing Meditation: Wounds By Oneself to One's Self

> It is unfortunate when our anxiety over what looks like personal confusion or dereliction blinds us to the forces of liberation at work.[119]

It is not difficult for us to understand how we can make ourselves into an Other. The prejudices, vitriol and anger towards or desire to harm or eradicate an Other may be those segments, persons and particles of ourselves we most wish to dismiss by continuing to ignore and deny by foisting that energy we feel towards this internal figure on to someone beyond ourselves.

Countless books and articles have been written in the last decade about the nature of the *Self as Other*. One of its most cogent thinkers has expressed it this way: "*Oneself as Another* suggests from the outset that the selfhood of oneself implies otherness to such an intimate degree that one cannot be thought of without the other, that instead one passes into the other."[120]

- Describe a wound that you received that you will not let go of, refuse to relinquish, or continue to build altars and even tabernacles to, so to house the treasured affliction.
- Describe a form of self-abuse you have ritualized over time, engage in often, find some relief in, or gain comfort as well as pain and suffering from.
- What feelings are associated with either one of the two above?
- In the process of remembrance, which is also a way of imagining the past as a fiction, can you detect and describe the origin of the self-infliction/self-infection?
- Describe a self-inflicted wound that serves you as a buffer zone, or a neutral landscape between you and yourself or you and the larger world you engage daily.
- Can you explore the above to see if there is any sense of what lies behind it, what habitually drives it, as well as who is benefiting from it besides you?
- Writing about it can serve as a small crawl space in the rafters between you and the self-inflicted's power to keep you in a particular place, frame of mind or emotional dungeon.
- Writing may help to liberate you from that crawl space.

---

119 Mary C. Richards, *Centering in Pottery, Poetry, and the Person* (Middleton, Conn.: Wesleyan University Press, 1964), p. 133.

120 Paul Ricoeur, *Oneself as Another,* trans. Kathleen Blamey (Chicago: University of Chicago Press, 1992), p. 3.

- It can also be a solid measuring device and aid in your moving, at least with this one self-infection, to a state of acceptance in self-affection.
- So ask: what would my feelings of myself be if I could reclaim some space to allow this self-infection to cohabit with a more authentic and sustained sense of self-affection? Here you build a new relationship with yourself in altering your personal myth.

Writing Meditation: The Power of Hate, Part I

Myth . . . is a projection in concrete and dramatic form of fears and desires undiscoverable and inexpressible in any other way.[121]

Everything human is relative, because everything rests on an inner polarity; for everything is a phenomenon of energy.[122]

What we hate, despise and recoil from is a patterned life response; thus, it resides within the purview of myth. Hate is a particularly powerful expression of our personal myth. Its power to destroy by making something or someone potently present is incalculable in the damage it can cause one who hates as well as the object of one's hate.

We do hear innocuous expressions of hate, as when one says "I hate it when it rains after I have just washed my car," or "I hate too much mustard on my hot dog" or "I hate people who show up late for meetings." We take the use of the word here with some salt.

But we also find that hate can be a patterned response to particular situations, people or life itself such that the psychic energy that gathers around such devastation can make us sick on several levels. We have all felt hate at such a deep level that we may have entertained murderous thoughts of annihilating the source of such vitriolic waste. What and who we hate points us to something deep living in our own lives, carrying our own shadow or inferior nature of ourselves; writing about it to get it into the air through a meditation can be healing by cultivating a more compassionate form of knowing.

- Choose a hateful situation from your life, perhaps one long-festering or recently acquired.
- Describe its origin. Tell the story of the onset of hate.

---

121 Lillian Feder, quoted in Rollo May, *The Cry for Myth* (New York: Bantam Doubleday, 1991), p. 28.

122 C. G. Jung, *Two Essays in Analytical Psychology*, vol. 7 of *The Collected Works of C. G. Jung*, 2nd ed., trans. R. F. C Hull (New York: Pantheon Books, 1966), ¶ 115.

- Ask what hating this situation, condition, person, or organization serves in and for you.
- Is there pleasure in this hate that keeps it popular in your life, like a film you never tire of watching?
- Is it corrosive, painful, arresting, suffocating or otherwise restrains you from living your life more fully?
- Is the object of hate yourself in the form of self-loathing?
- Is it something one, including yourself, does rather than who or what one is that attracts your hate?
- Imagine for a moment what would change immediately or fairly quickly if one day you reconciled with the one you hate.

Writing Meditation: The Power of Hate, Part II

> Possessed by the emotions of envy and hatred, one does not want improvement for oneself, does not want practical solutions; one is satisfied if the situation of others worsens.[123]

The other side of our own objects of hatred is the experience of being hated, pushed out, minimized, trivialized as someone without worth because of the destructive force of hatred by another. Again, that presence of Other may be oneself in a different format. On a national level, shortly after the numbing effects of September 11, 2001, when the Twin Towers were incinerated in New York City, one of the first responses was disbelief: How could we be the recipient of so much hate? What did we do to warrant such a backlash on us as a people, as a nation? What is the cause of so much hate? But very quickly these penetrating questions were replaced by revenge, which cancelled out any authentic national self-reflection. An opportunity was sidelined and displaced by vengeance, another form of hate, as national policy.

They are legitimate questions each of us may pose when we discover we are the recipient of another's intense derision. Perhaps it too begins in disbelief, or in a shock of non-recognition. At other times we may know full well what has brought on the psychic and emotional energy of so much hatred for us. It is a deep wound, I believe, to be hated and for

---

123 Wolfgang Giegerich, *Soul Violence: Collected English Papers,* vol. 3 (New Orleans, La.: Spring Journal Books, 2008), p. 421.

slander to be spread about who and what we are. Its truth or falsity is, at this moment, irrelevant. It can slice so deep as to attack the fortress of our own identity and begin to dismantle its walls, pull down the turrets of our own self-respect and destroy the drawbridge of our self-esteem. Being hated pushes us into a region where we may be most vulnerable not just to the force of hate but to its effects on the rest of our lives as we live more tentatively, a bit fearful of performing actions that could incite further splenetic attacks. We shrink into a form that is less than we are capable of sustaining, even a mere shadow of what we are capable of being.

- Describe a situation wherein you fully realized that you had become the object of hatred for another or a group.
- What, if you stay with the feelings of that experience, did that knowing do to your own image of yourself and the values that give that image sustenance and staying power? Did you begin to feel alienated from your identity, even begin to question who you were?
- What did you do in response to such negative emotions toward you?
- How long have you been carrying the feelings of being hated as well as the image of self that may have been seeded then?
- Did those feelings stem from you toward you?
- Did they originate from outside of you and confirm or deny your own self image and level of worth and value?
- If a personal myth is, among other attributes, a way of structuring reality along certain lines of strength as well as along certain fault lines, then did the myth you have been living suffer some disintegration?
- When you reflect on it, what did being hated offer you about the nature of who and what you are?
- Have you in any way reconciled within yourself this hatred leveled against you to heal a split self?
- Were there any truths, realities, or credible aspects of yourself that surfaced and became much more fully conscious as a result of the negative regard aimed at you?
- Are you able to write to the Hatred, not to the person or circumstances that initiated the hate, but to the Hate as its own entity? The question arises from my belief that Hatred is a universal principle and a primal force at rest, asleep or roiled and active in each of us under certain moments of assault.

Writing Meditation: The Myth of Forgiveness

> The function of ritual, as I understand it, is to give form to human life, not in the way of a mere surface arrangement, but in depth.[124]

> To become a more forgiving person, to decrease the hold of powerful and ingrained psychological factors, requires a confrontation with oneself.[125]

Some important quality and dimension of ourselves is liberated through the act of forgiveness. As hatred and resentments can incarcerate and even incinerate the best and most vital energies within us, so can forgiveness be a way to curb a wound, especially when forgiving is an act of generosity that accepts the fallen nature of ourselves and others. In *Total Forgiveness*, R. T. Kendall suggests that not forgiving is one strategic way we use in holding power over the other person or situation that offended us, while forgiving restores a calmness in our minds and hearts.[126] A deep liberation ensues from the act of forgiving.

- Choose an event in your life where you have mustered the courage to forgive, for it is an act that requires great sacrifice, a yielding of the wound to something more liberating.
- Describe what the circumstances were that brought you to forgive another, or brought you to forgive the other in yourself.
- Describe as well the effects of such forgiveness, whether the other accepted, acknowledged or even heard your gesture of amnesty.
- Was it important to you that the other acknowledged your gesture?
- A second inroad into this mysterious human capacity to forgive an Other is to describe a current situation in your life where you have not yet forgiven but perhaps wish to.
- What would be the terms of such a forgiveness?
- What situation would have to arise or one which you would create, in order for this act of forgiveness to occur?
- If you are not yet ready to forgive, describe what elements seem to obstruct your path, like a fallen tree, or a boulder from a nearby emotional mountain, that keeps you from moving forward.
- Imagine if you will what your life would be like on the other side of this act of forgiveness, if not a complete and open reconciliation.

---

124 Joseph Campbell, *Myths to Live By* (New York: Penguin Group, 1972), p. 44.

125 Karen, *The Forgiving Self*, p. 38.

126 R. T. Kendall, *Total Forgiveness* (Lake Mary, Fla.: Charisma House, 2002), p. 47.

- Is there a desire or a wish in you to forgive, but for many reasons, perhaps, you wish to carry the stone or rock of non-forgiveness around your neck or in your shoe a bit longer?
- What energies might be released in you to inform your life with greater vitality if forgiveness were enacted as a gesture of generosity to another and to yourself?
- What part of yourself is unlived so long as this burden of being hated/wounded continues to live off your blood?
- As a ritual meditation, write out, whether anyone ever sees it or not, a prayer, a petition, a prose proclamation of forgiveness, addressed perhaps to yourself and/or to another.
- After you have done so, wait a few days and then recollect this prayer or petition or proclamation and ask if your life has shifted at all as a result of this writing ritual.

Writing Meditation: Remembering the Discarded/Dismembered Self

I'll see it when I believe it.[127]

To feel the sadness, to mourn, is, therefore, not only to reclaim love, but to reclaim a piece of ourselves and our aliveness.[128]

At certain junctures in our lives, we dissect to protect the full range of who we might become. Myths can aid us in conjoining our disparate parts through a narrative that knits us into a coherence; they can also be dismembering, as so many mythologies, classics in literature, operas and paintings reveal: dismembering is a mode of not wanting to re-member.

As we struggle to adopt, to adjust, and to yield to life's demands and currents, expectations and assumptions, limits and liabilities, illnesses and deficiencies, we can sever those parts of ourselves that need to be enfleshed in the world, in favor of perhaps a more secure and less intimidating life. To the extent we perform this self-surgery, we are to that degree already dead, or on the last stages of a respirator. Lopping off parts of ourselves in order to "fit in" may be one of the grossest violations of ourselves that anyone could force on us, including our own self-mutilating.

---

127 Rollo May, quoted in Whitmont, *The Alchemy of Healing*, p. 42.
128 Karen, *The Forgiving Self*, p. 55.

I remember being told a story years ago by someone who offered workshops worldwide, most notably but not exclusively to and for women. A large segment of these weekend or week-long retreats was deeply involved in reclamation and retrieval: to re-collect and re-member the unlived parts of oneself. The person who conducted them related an image that had seared itself into her: the image was of a woman in her 70s engaged in a body awareness exercise. Shortly after the body movement exercise began, she was writhing on the floor in agony, in a fetal position, weeping for the unlived parts of her life she had successfully ignored and shunned for decades, perhaps in the service of another's story. Her own plot was buried in the debris of service. Now, in this embodied remembrance, that part of her myth reared up and wanted to be recognized as unlived, and was not happy about it, as the woman was in the latter years of her life. On the floor, she contorted in fetal agony, seeking rebirth right then, full of the suffering of urgency.

Such revelations arrest us in their power; they can debilitate us when the realization rushes in like a violent spring storm. Some belief, some assumption, some remark we decided to believe in and canonize, can and has stopped many from fulfilling what they know to be their destiny. But such destiny is a cooperative, needing active individuals to participate in its unfurling.

I invite you to visit this very poignant terrain and to ask some fundamental questions of the discarded self that you are. When remembered, the discarded self carries as much reality as that self you have lived out. One's personal myth contains gaps, open places, what is discarded, dismembered, left out, left over, put into left field, and left there. Personal myths include ragged maps of roads or highways not taken, unmarked cinder paths that beckoned but were ignored for the faster asphalt of surety free of ruts and uneven travel as well as unpredictable road blocks.

- Describe what in your life right now you realize has not been lived and may never be. You be the judge of that last part of the above statement.
- What desire, dream, project, travel, skill, art that you know to be part of you, has been taken out of your backpack?
- Framed another way, what outcast parts of your own psyche, carried within your personal myth, can you re-collect and acknowledge?
- What are the conditions, beliefs, or the life circumstances that have brought you to pull from the rucksack?
- What are the terms of the "psychic police force" that have pulled you over and demanded you leave this part of yourself along the highway?

- What might have to occur for you to reinstate that part of yourself as not only vital and viable, but necessary to reclaim? Is there room for it in your present field?
- If you were to imagine your life with this part of yourself not only powerfully present but integrated into who you are now, what would be different in your life?
- What is the greatest fear or apprehension you carry if you were to activate this part of yourself?
- Currently, is this unlived or unintegrated part of yourself a wound, an affliction that you carry?
- Are you just as glad that you did not live that part of yourself out?

Writing Meditation: Secreting the Secret Self

Myth expresses the functional relationship to the environment and to the psyche itself.[129]

As you can see, how you tell the stories about your life reflects your self-image and also predicts, to some extent, how much or how little you expect in the future.[130]

The elements of our personal myth include what is not said, not spoken, not shared, but may have been allowed to hide privately in the deep recesses of our lives. One of these elements is our secrets. Secrets can hold the taboos we have constructed or have been placed on us. Secrets shape us from the inside out. Some individuals and even nations hold secrets for decades. They are powerful energy fields because they hold a truth that is not shared but remains in a closeted part of our souls. I think we both fear and love our secrets. They hold something essential back from being present to the world, a form of secret knowledge that itself contains power. Our secret self, however, secretes itself into our lives in ways we may not be aware of. Within a secret, we live in a constant tension between holding the secret in hiding and wanting, very often, to tell it to at least one person.

How powerful it is when someone in intimate conversation instructs us: "Please tell no one what I am about to tell you. If it ever got out that I . . ." We listen, ears wide open, to what we are about to hear of this person's closely-guarded narrative. Some numinous or

---

129 D. Stephenson Bond, *Living Myth: Personal Meaning as a Way of Life* (Boston: Shambhala Publications, 1993), p. 195.

130 Carol Pearson, *The Hero Within: Six Archetypes We Live By* (New York: HarperCollins, 1998), p. 19.

sacred quality attends secrets, and when one is shared with us, for perhaps the person can no longer contain it because the vessel it was in no longer tolerates the pressure of the story, secreted away, to give itself a voice. In hearing the secret, we enter an initiation, perhaps into some privation, some perversion, some pathology of the person. Or the secret can be of a positive thought, idea or action that the person wishes to remain unsaid. We have just been offered a ticket and now we step deep into the corridor and then into the theater, of that individual's personal myth.

Hearing someone's secret self exposed can be an exhilarating and hugely responsible experience. It may even prompt or evoke in us a desire to share one of our own secrets; that is how potent hearing a secret can be. I think we sense in our nature that some healing may accrue from storying the secret to another. Tremendous psychic energy gathers around our secrets and that same energy can be curative, healing, like a salve or unguent applied to a bodily wound. Secrets organize ourselves in new and unforeseen ways; secrets shape our mythos. Telling or writing down our secrets, or one in particular that haunts us periodically or continually, continues to torque who and what we are, both to ourselves and others.

In this writing meditation, go as far as you wish with it. No one will ever see what you write. But if you have never given your secret a voice, it can enslave you, keep you from wearing anything else but an orange jump suit as a prisoner of your own image. Of course, not all secrets are negative and debilitating. We are going to explore both sides of what secrets can possibly carry within us. One writer has suggested, along this pathway, that "we weave our memories into narratives from which we construct our identities."[131] We can hear within the folds of such an insight the tangible presence of our personal myth. Again, we spiral back into the past but never with exact replication, because it has shifted with our new histories that are being re-newed and added to each day:

- Describe a secret that you have told no one. Let it be a secret that, if known, would bring shame, guilt, remorse, or negative feelings from you and for you by others. This secret need not be of something you did but could include something you thought, wished for, imagined, held and may still hold as an obsession.
- Give it as full a narration as you can recollect. Consider and accept the fact that what you write may be part recollection of exact facts and part a fictionalizing to fill in the gaps. Both are almost always present in remembering as an act of imagination. Let both in.

---

131 Leonard Scheingold, quoted in DeSalvo, *Writing as a Way of Healing,* p. 149.

- When you have finished writing it, ask yourself: if others knew this about me, what would their opinion of me be compared to what it is now: positive, negative, impressed, and disappointed, for instance? The number of impressions may be wide and divergent.

- Ask as well: has this secret deflected me from my true path or directed me towards it? Has my secret been a sign post to follow rather than a force that redirects me in my life's journey? Could it possibly be both?

- Here is the important part of the meditation: describe as closely as you can the feelings that arose in you in the act of writing your secret. The secret has its own life, its own wants and desires; writing the secret out will stir up some of these feelings in you. Give the feelings of the experience now, not the secret itself, a voice.

- A second secret: describe something you did, wished for, desired, held or hold sacred, strove for and may continue to. Perhaps it is something you do not want known you did for someone, content instead and even pleased and comforted by the fact that no one knows this about you. For what we keep secret adds a texture to the fabric of who we are.

- When you are finished describing it, recall the feelings that arose in you or were evoked by the writing itself which offered this secret its own public language for the first time.

- The final ritual: take these two pieces of writing and destroy them in a ritual. You might burn the pages, tear them into tiny pieces, drop them in the trash, bury them somewhere—I have witnessed all of these possibilities—so that no one will ever see them.

- This ritual is one of burial, not of the memory but of the expression of that memory. Ask yourself at the same time: do I wish now to let the power of that secret go? Can I, in the writing of it and now the destruction of that expression, allow that secret to float out of my life as a center of power? May either of these secrets, exposed to the air of writing, now have shrunk in importance? Give this last some thought; however, it is important to ritualize the end of this meditation.

Writing Meditation: Wounding into the Work

The soul can exist without its therapists but not without its afflictions.[132]

Wounds, hurts, afflictions we inflict or have had inflicted on us are not random or without some connection, even a method hiding within their surfaces. Our wounds can frame us as well as shame us. Both are crucial to the continued construction of our personal myth in the same way that the workers who paint the Golden Gate Bridge begin their task again as soon as they have finished. In this method of constant renewal lurks a myth of the soul.

---

132 Hillman, *Re-Visioning Psychology*, p. 71.

In fact, where we are marked, scarred, tattooed with hurts, dismembered by cruelty, resentments and infections is already a narrative of ourselves that is mythically-inflected through suffering. I suggest as well that our destiny is in part marked and measured by our woundedness. Our wounds place us in the world in a particularly unique manner; the wound is where something is buried, a burial site, or where something hidden splits open, breaches to reveal a memory, a site of pain, of suffering and death. But it can include a joyful sense of new freedom as well, based on a deeper understanding of those energic flows in us and others that can both bloody and bless us, often at the same moment.

James Hillman reminds us that our markings and wounds are ways into soul, into a way of imagining ourselves in the world that is not unrelated to myth.[133] He asks us rather than to diminish or treat the wounds we carry so to domesticate them, that instead we engage in "pathologizing the myth onward,"[134] which is to follow the soul's course, not our model of it, to pay close attention to "what the imagination is doing in its madness."[135] An open receptivity is required to allow the wound its own voice, tenor and attitude. Wounds, in fact, create or impregnate attitudes.

Given his insights into the essential act of bringing the wounds that possess us forward, gather your courage to work the following meditation:

- Remember and describe a wound or trauma that deflected you from the life you thought you were to live; instead, may it have put you on an alternate path that has become your life, or an important aspect of it?
- Has it shaped your life's interests, preoccupations, even obsessions to accomplish something in the face of such injury?
- Or with the complicity of such a wound or wounds? Here I am suggesting that our wounds can be accomplices in our life's work, offering us energy rather than sapping it from us.
- Write about the original affliction and its aftermath as it has shaped or given a form to your life that would not have occurred without it.
- Remember here that we are using writing as a riting process, wherein some act of recovery and even restitution is encouraged in the process: remembering, riting it, writing it; relaying it or relating it to others.

---

133 Hillman, *Re-Visioning Psychology*, p. 74.

134 Hillman, *Re-Visioning Psychology*, p. 74.

135 Hillman, *Re-Visioning Psychology*, p. 74.

Writing Meditation: Acknowledging a World Wound

> A culture is unsalvageable if stabilizing forces themselves become ruined and irrelevant. This is what I fear for our own culture.[136]

One need not look very far to see many instances of where the world is wounded, inflicted, conflicted, and infected: pollution in the natural order, the political terrain, the ground of peace and justice, equality, a sense of fairness, conflicts between peoples over ideas, ideologies, prejudices, natural resources, violence by companies, regimes, governments on its own citizens. No longer is it enough to concentrate exclusively on our own vulnerable sore spots and injustices; the world herself is in need of care, if not cure. In this meditation we want to identify a world wound, which could be as close as your own family or neighborhood, your own city and its unique culture.

- Describe where you see a world wound. What damage does it cause? Is it in your home and family, your neighborhood, your city or town? Is it more national in scope or even global in its toxic reach?
- What action, attitude or thought, however small, can you contribute to its acknowledgement, to making a larger population aware of it?
- What do you imagine could be worked on for its healing?
- Do you imagine a way or ways in which you could, individually, slow the wounding and festering, modify the widening gap that increases the size of the wound and its complications?
- Might you contribute to its lessening effects by:
- Being less negative towards others in thought and action?
- Entertaining less violent thoughts?
- Revealing more positive regard for yourself and others?
- Being less addicted and engaged in anger?
- Placing the needs of others in front of yours?
- Using less of resources?
- Being less restless, anxious, busy, active?
- Continuing to educate yourself towards fuller and deeper levels of consciousness?
- Hating or disliking or abusing yourself and others less?
- Punishing yourself and others less, or at all?

---

136 Jane Jacobs, *Dark Age Ahead* (New York: Random House, 2004), p. 24.

- Developing a daily ritual in which you pray for, send good thoughts and positive energy to world leaders so they might be more open to new alternatives regarding national or global problems, shortfalls, infections, co-operations?
- Writing an editorial or a letter to an on-line post or to a local newspaper so that your opinion or insights can be heard by many?
- Being open to different ways that you think about solutions or even the nature of problems that should be grasped more psychologically and mythically, less so politically?
- The goal here is to shift, in however slight a way, the energy field that sustains and manages this infection so it remains in place for any number of reasons to benefit others.

6

RITING THROUGH THE EMBODIED SELF

> Myth is a song. It is the song of the imagination inspired by the energies of the body.[137]

> Odysseus' journeys and subsequent telling of those voyages is an imaginal attempt to retrieve and reunite *biology and biography*—to get the story right—and to return home.[138]

While related to the last chapter on woundedness, this chapter is different because it explores much more specifically our incarnational selves, which is one of the most intimate expressions of our personal myth. Like myth, our bodies are in constant destruction, disintegration and reconstruction, even reanimation. Like myth, our body is in continuous renegotiation with our desires, memories and the world—all within shifting limitations and an often oscillating world view. Our life journey is as somatic as it is psychological, emotional and spiritual; therefore the personal myth living within us and our inhabiting it, is an enfleshed mythos, connected deeply and in a sustained way with our attitude and stance in the world, as Joseph Campbell has observed. Towards the beginning of *The Flight of the Wild Gander* he notes: "Mythology is the womb of mankind's initiation to life and death."[139] Each of us then carries myth within the cells of our bodies and in our narratives throughout a lifetime. The body's own story is as integral to exploring personal myth as is any other dimension of our becoming. Studies with organ transplant patients have even confirmed that our various organs carry our narratives in their cellular structure and that certain kinds of stories appeal to different organs.

---

137 Stanley Keleman, *Myth & the Body: A Colloquy with Joseph Campbell* (Berkeley: Center Press, 1999), p. xiii.

138 Dennis Patrick Slattery, "Nature and Narratives: Feeding the Fictions of the Body in Homer's *Odyssey*," in Slattery, *The Wounded Body: Remembering the Markings of Flesh* (Albany: State University of New York Press, 2000), p. 23.

139 Joseph Campbell, "Bios and Mythos," in Campbell, *The Flight of the Wild Gander: Explorations in the Mythological Dimension: Select Essays, 1944-1968* (Novato: New World Library, 2002), p. 34.

Campbell further deepens our grasp of the body's mystery and complexity by observing that "When you say 'my body,' you are talking about a collage of environments, an organized somatic world, that all says 'me.'"[140] Moreover, as we have pointed out repeatedly, a libidinal energy attends the body as well as the mythic template of our lives. This energic field between self and world is an enfleshed presence in process of becoming and disintegrating as it reenacts the ancient cycle of birth, growth, death and renewal.

Such a somatic milieu includes all that we have inherited in and through our bodies: perhaps osteoarthritis from your mother or father, a propensity for athletic achievements, a flare for music and the dexterity of your body to play instruments, speed in running that reminds you of your grandfather as an athlete in college, being ambidextrous like your uncle John, a tendency to put on weight even with a lean diet and lots of exercise, a problem that your father and sister contended with their entire lives witness the connection between lineage and predisposed physical tendencies.

Yet there is another embodiment we must explore in this chapter: the body as imaginal, or capable of containing and entertaining rich worlds of the imagination in and through our flesh. Our bodies are a way into such a realm, depicted quite beautifully by many writers and poets. One of them is in a fine little book by Robert Bosnack: *Embodiment*. In it, and influenced by the work of the Islamic scholar, Henry Corbin, he reveals the subtle and intelligent body that images themselves contain and sustain. From a list of qualities pointing to such a reality, I want to mention a third feature of our embodiment he develops: "Thirdly, there is the fact that we are embodied by imagination, that imagination grows itself a physical body."[141]

The gestures we engage, consciously or unconsciously, often contain and remember an entire history of a family member or several relations. A family history can live in part, and be reincarnated in any of us who carry the signs and inclinations of ancestors. There are times, for example, when I make a gesture, innocent enough, like the rapid movement of quickly placing my thumb and first finger on each side of my nose and sliding them down until they touch once more; such an action instantly recalls the same gesticulation my father performed so often that it became part of his biography for me. When I gesture in that way

---

140 Keleman, *Myth and the Body*, p. 30.

141 Robert Bosnak, *Embodiment: Creative Imagination in Medicine, Art and Travel* (New York: Routledge, 2007), p. 10.

I ritually conjure him into my presence in a motion that is both imaginal, memorial and enfleshed. Then, without warning, entire scenes, like dramatic vignettes, will suddenly unroll before me, some pleasurable and others filled with pain. The gesture invites a narrative, and the story that emerges finds a solid roost right against my own tale; I see something through the two stories, both embodied, imaginally recollected and sometimes inflamed.

In this chapter we will remember, gesture, move and dance; we will embody our past and our present through the flesh that we are as we recall Bosnak's insight that the imagination contours a body around it in an outward expression of its own image and intentions. I suggest we do not have bodies but rather *are* embodied, and not just in the physical sense but in an imaginal deployment as well. James Hillman reminds us that the psyche does not want to be taken only physically, but it also responds in pathology when not taken "somatically enough."[142]

Yes, there is of course a physical body that defines us; it is first the medical body of quantification with height, weight, ailments, aches, afflictions, heritage, prowesses and promises. There is also the imaginal body that is closer to expressing our personal myth, the body we invite in daily to comprise part of our daily story in its dress, fabrication, sculpting, exercise—in short, the body we imagine ourselves to be. It is the body of desire, of disappointment, of limits and of forgiveness. Let's turn to that body and give it a more intense presence in language.

Writing Meditation: My Somatic Consciousness

The body is both a process and a destiny. It has its own way of thinking, feeling, perceiving and organizing experience—an innate way of forming its responses. Our personal myth is in part about the body's journey, continually recreating itself in unique ways to form an individual personal structure called the self.

- Use writing a description of your body to become more conscious of your somatic self.
- Describe your body as it is felt and seen, not the quantitative dimensions of it. What does it say back to you in the mirror?
- What is the narrative that the body holds for you? What story seems to be most embodied, most sustained in your current life? Describe the plot of this living flesh.

---

142 James Hillman, *Re-Visioning Psychology* (1975; repr., New York: HarperPerennial, 1992), p. 82.

- What changes do you notice in your body that affect what limits as well as the prowess you possess?
- What limitations in your embodiment have also the possibility of opening you to new freedoms?
- What is the experience of being an aging body that appeals to you and/or that repels you?
- What qualities of the aging body do you find most challenging to adjust to, to accept, not to orphan or exile from your life?

Writers' Responses

I knew it was growing, a little mole with defined edges that over the course of a year darkened, raggedly expanded, and began to look like the dismembered body of a squashed fly on my lower, left leg. I knew it was dangerous—life threatening—still I ignored it. How many times had I run down the lava steps to the ocean and dove in, narrowly missing outcroppings of jagged rocks into which sets of waves crashed, and swum blindly, begging, bargaining, pleading, "take me!" Time and again the sea tossed me back to the earthly contract. Defeated, with heavy heart, and heavier footfall, I returned to the family household, to the familial madness, into which I had agreed, at some long-forgotten level, to play my part.

When the mole started to grow, the part who whimpered, "it's too hard, I never imagined it would take so long, be so cruel," found a blessed way out. I wouldn't have to slit my wrists and bleed out in a warm bath, my mother's often-voiced preferred method, "comfortable" and "clean." I didn't have to overdose on drugs and be labeled a "good seed gone bad" as might have been spoken of in regards to my grandmother. Only let the mole grow. Family and friends would circle my bedside, hold my hand and whisper "what a shame, so much life ahead, so much potential." A martyr's death. That was it. I could die a martyr's death and be done with the failed attempts in the uncooperative sea.

So I waited, went ahead with half-living and let the mole grow.

When did it happen? When did I decide to take up my destiny? Was it the beauty of the music that surrounded me as I attended conservatory? Did my ear whisper to my heart, "if you die, you will never hear Beethoven's Ninth or Chopin's 'Rain Drop Prelude' again?" Or was it biology, after two decades of rejecting dolls my body began to crave holding a baby of my own. Was that part of the contract? It certainly wasn't looking into my mother's dark, hard eyes. But it may have been in holding my grandmother's soft, wrinkled, hand when it could no longer bring the bottle to her lips. . . .

In the end I didn't lose the leg. I gained a whopping big scar, ugly with its down-to-the-shin-bone incision upon which a skin graph rested precariously after being scraped from my left hip. Through ragged holes the freshness of the wound seeped as the edges of the hip and leg skin began to merge, gingerly held on by one hundred and thirty-two stitches. My father gasped when he saw it. Truth be told, I gasped too. (And the music soothed me). My father insisted paying for the plastic surgery. But in that moment, the voice that became my own rose and softly, firmly said "No." (Tiare Newport)

"Not my heart!" I heard myself say after leaving the cardiologist's office, having had yet another EKG and then an electrocardiogram. "My heart is strong, good, not arrhythmic, not ill. I have a good heart, am light-hearted, full of good cheer of the heart." But the scopes and listening devices said otherwise, something about a sinus node falling asleep instead of conducting all chambers of the heart to beat in synch. Now, with "a-fib" the heart had two beats, two rhythms and so on to blood thinners I went to avoid clotting and perhaps a stroke.

I felt betrayed by my heart; I had exercised regularly, been faithful to my weight watching, careful of what I ate, ceased smoking, drank less; but the heart responded with a chaotic beat, an irregular rhythm—silent, yes, but a slight jab of pain periodically, or a moment of breathless abandon when I was not even exercising.

I felt split from myself with this heart-felt betrayal. I did not know what was coming, but I had dreams of pacemakers and surgeries to repair the heart. My story began to change from one who was athletic, sprightly in his 60s, to that of an invalid; I saw myself walking the streets carrying a cylinder of oxygen tubed to my nostrils and knew that aging had overtaken me. The plot of my story now included possible clots in my heart. A sense of unworthiness began to overtake me. I felt out of rhythm with the rest of my life. (Writing Participant)

Writing Meditation: Embodied Stories

We cannot separate the stories we are drawn to once or many times, without considering their attraction as well to our somatic heritage and destiny. Reflect then for a few moments on the kinds of stories you most enjoy and those which have the least energy for you. I pose this question because of a belief that the stories we are attracted to and those we find repugnant or distasteful are all somatically inflected because they mirror something in our own embodied dramatic structure.

I can see too that these stories could ground us in our bodies further or they might also release us from our own embodied lives. Some stories, for example, hit us with such visceral power that we carry them around as shaping principles or patterns because of their persuasive energy. Stories have the power to make us ill or heal us from long-sustained cuts.

- Think of a story or two that you like to return to, be it in a work of fiction or non-fiction, a play, or a film.
- Describe what qualities or characteristics of the story most appeal to you, even parts that you wish to incarnate in your own life.
- As you read or experience a story that has great appeal, what visceral changes occur to you?
- Where in your body do you feel the conflict or friction that intensifies as the story develops?
- Are you in any way ashamed or uncomfortable with the kinds of stories that attract you the most?
- Do you sense in any way that the stories that attract you are too narrow, too much the same, lacking variety or newness?

Writing Meditation: The Narratives in Mementoes

There are things we carry or keep secreted in our rooms because they carry such powerful emotions from an incident in our lives: a locket, a medal, a stone, a dried flower, a medallion, a clot of earth, a tooth, a feather, a ring, a photograph, a piece of cloth carrying a far-away scent, a letter from someone now deceased or lost in the haze of history. These objects can carry and convey a powerful fragment of our own development, an arrested moment in our lives or a moment of sudden revelation and growth; when we return to them, the entire narrative of their being and the context in which they arrived in our lives, is lived once more, poignantly, as the memory ripens into a more intense reality because of the new context it now fits into.

- Give voice and expression to one of these mementoes that are so important for you to preserve in some fashion.
- What is its story? Describe its context and its content.
- Is it important, for instance, because someone precious to you touched it once, or wore it or wrote it? The physical proximity adds power to the object, making it analogous to a totem.

- Let your memory move back and rest on something that still carries great emotional presence for you.
- If it were suddenly taken from you, would you feel a loss, enough to grieve over?
- What is it about the object that continues to nourish you?
- Try, instead of writing from your point of view, to let it speak from its point of view. What does it wish to say?

Writers' Responses

I am the necklace that Amy Pinkerton, then Hall, gave Hallie on her graduation from her master's degree program at The Mandel School of Applied Social Sciences. I am a little, understated piece of jewelry. Hallie mistook me for sterling silver, but I am platinum, with a little sliver of diamond tucked into a platinum charm circle. I am the gift of a best friend, of a roommate, of a "girlish time," although a professional time. A mark of accomplishment; a celebrated milestone. My purchaser, that would be Amy, is extremely devoted to recognizing special events of all kinds—births, anniversaries, holidays . . . but the choice of such a timeless piece of jewelry as I am—not fad or fashion, but stoic and lovely—seems additionally prudent and forward-thinking somehow. Sturdiness and Preciousness. I am the necklace that fad or fashion can be added to. My job is to grace a neck almost without second glance, and yet the person is more special with it, and looks different without it. I am subtle sparkle. The fact that my little diamond is nestled into a doughy circle of metal protects me from delicacy. Platinum. As elegant, understated, tough, and transformational as the friendship between the two. And jewelry gods willing, the durability to last as long. (Participant, Cleveland, Ohio)

The Peridot Ring

Remember that day in Agra? Tough luck being on that group tour and visiting the Taj Mahal in the blazing noon sun. You couldn't look at the white marble without sunglasses, poking them down or up just long enough to snap a photo of the world's most famous ode to love.

We hadn't met yet.

Friends told you that jewels were big in India. But you were typically jaded. Even the embedded semi-precious stones in the Taj disappointed you: matte inlays that didn't glitter.

116

Then the bus stopped at a jewelry store. You asked for peridot, your birthstone, figuring the clerk wouldn't have any and you wouldn't have to spend money in a tourist trap.

But he responded, "One moment, please," and brought out two pieces.

One was a square-cut medallion in a pink gold setting. The other was me: a rectangular-cut stone also set in pink gold, tailored, not flowery.

I was too big for your ring finger, but the clerk assured you I could be adjusted back home.

The cheapskate in you stood aside. What the heck, you said, "I'll take both."

Yes!

First, I had to do my duty. A single woman walking the streets of Ahmedabad, you slipped me on your left ring finger and feigned the story of a fantasy journalist husband who couldn't make the trip. I protected you, as you protected me, adding thread to keep me from falling off your hand.

Eventually I moved to your larger middle finger. You figured you'd wear me at least during the two-week solo journey in India. It's been 19 years.

If people ask how I got that chip, you say, "I knocked the ring in a hot tub with a National Geographic photographer."

The full story is that you joined a group of Sunday magazine conferees, including the speaker/photographer, for relaxation in a public whirlpool at Disneyworld. Wild woman? Hah!

Once, you thought you'd lost me somewhere in the apartment. You knew it was over with Scott. A 15-year age difference doomed that from the start. You thought in (sad) (anger) fear, "I've lost Scott and now I've lost my ring." But I was hiding near the carpet edge. Scott wasn't completely lost either. Your lives are separate. But the respect and appreciation never went anywhere.

I've been with you all along, the constant reminder that you have traveled, unattached, to India and Burma and Cambodia and Kathmandu and Zanzibar and Oman and Timbuktu. I've kept you grounded in a world of adventure as you've plied the nine-to-five world in Ohio.

I just hope I don't hold you back from your most audacious adventure—the exploration of your heart. (Peggy Turbett, Cleveland, Ohio)

Writing Meditation: The Story I Have Yet to Embody

> What is a myth? A story that grows out of the history of bodily process to orient life and give values.[143]

To translate bodily energy into language is to engage in what I call a somatic semantics. Language and embodiment are mirrors of one another. In the space or gap between the words and the reflection abides our personal myth. I would say that our skin is like a parchment on which is inscribed the terms of our unique plot.

Stanley Keleman, in conversation with Joseph Campbell, observed that "our body structure determines a mythic way of thinking and gives us an identity."[144] Our bodies and the energy field they create and absorb from others, is the matrix space for personal mythologizing. Our biography is in constant conversation, in complement or in conflict, with our biology. Patterns in our life story can be discerned in our body patterns, diet, gestures, favorite forms of exercise, and fashion. The stories we tell ourselves repeatedly and those we tell others are not divorced from the deepest levels of our somatic consciousness; to be conscious is to be aware of our physiology as imagined. The soul has a form and its formative shape is in large measure somatic. Our destiny as well is somatically inflected so that the body we are and the destiny by which we pattern ourselves form a unity that we call our identity.

- When I look back from where I am now, what part of my life am I proudest of achieving?
- List two or three.
- When I reflect on where I am currently on my life's path, what is most satisfying?
- What is most diminished?
- What part of my life am I still to embody?
- What is the story that remains incomplete that I still have the desire to accomplish in and through my embodiment?
- Is the body I am now sufficient for such a challenge?
- Is my image of my own somatic being a deterrent to my accomplishing or living into the part of my life still unfulfilled?

---

143 Keleman, *Myth and the Body*, p. 5.

144 Keleman, *Myth and the Body*, p. xiii.

Writing Meditation: The Body Diseased or Wounded

A writer I read years ago made an observation that has stayed with me. Dudley Young wrote in *Origins of the Sacred* that the word *blessed* and the word *bloodied* came from the same etymological root. Using etymology to reveal a psychological truth, he revealed that where we are bloodied by the world is often the same affliction that blesses us. Our wounds are then a cause for wonder; they can carry within them a blessing, a gift of the sacred that reveals to us what we have missed. Only the blow that bloodies us may reveal this truth as a blessing.[145]

The lesions we have grooved into us contain insights needed for our destiny to be fulfilled a bit more.

- Describe a wounding you have lived with that, over time, revealed something you needed to recognize, know, implicate in your life.
- What is the story of the wound? What did the wound have to say to you?
- Have you reconciled your life with the wounding?
- How did you come to a place of mutual toleration and acceptance?
- If you have not come to such a place, describe where you are today with this wound. Let it be a physical ailment, or an affliction brought on a physical ailment.
- Are you able to sustain a conversation with the wound over time?
- Have you ceased speaking to it and it to you?
- Is there today a wonder in you regarding the wound, what it serves and what way you are in its service?
- Do you remain to this day confused, upset and uncertain about the wound's existence in your life?
- Has the wound altered your perception of yourself or pushed you to take stock of what your life's purpose is?

Writing Meditation: Poetics of Affliction

My own experiences of woundedness have on more than one occasion found expression in a poem—my way of trying to grasp the contours of such an affliction. The body's suffering brings on or evokes a site of language, a poetic knowing that language can use to calm the trauma of emotion that gathers around body woundedness or a suppurating emotional sore.

---

145 Dudley Young, *Origins of the Sacred: The Ecstasies of Love and War* (New York: Harper, 1992), p. 46.

The body "is an image of both depth and surface, of deep mysterious interiors and often codified exteriors; what affects it in either region becomes the ground for constructing those meanings that haunt the body visible and invisible."[146]

A few years ago, as I was bombarded by a series of tests to determine whether or not I had prostate cancer, I became terrified of the disease as well as the surgical methods for eliminating it if such were so. Once, as I sat in the urologist's waiting room, frightened of the biopsy on the prostate I was to undergo, I began to write a poem of my feelings in the moment on the back cover of a magazine in order to lower the barometric pressure of my interior darkening weather patterns:

Silent Places of the Body Under Siege

In the Cancer rooms of the clinic
is a forest of words that terrify.
Like beasts they move between us
sitting on the quiet chairs
their lairs the slippery dark
places of our bodies.

Quiet green lighting is broken by the beasts
describing angiograms, edemas—fluid
in there that is not good—
thrombosis and metastasize.

What is it to part the screen of the word
Cancer
and see, as above the lintel of the Inferno:
"Abandon all hope ye who enter here"?
Invisible birds with sharp yellow beaks
fly through the halls unmolested
past the outbursts of laughter of far

---

146 Dennis Patrick Slattery, "Introduction," in Slattery, *The Wounded Body: Remembering the Markings of Flesh* (Albany: State University of New York Press, 2000), p. 10.

too cheery receptionists.

We sit in the antechambers of Hell
or by the lowest, widest spiral of Mount Purgatory
with others peering at us
seeing into one another's ailments.
The man next to me breathes
with gurgled sounds from his hollow chest.
He looks over his glasses and stares at
my Levis as if they might have a heart condition.

I wear deodorant today to beat back the stress
and cannot keep knives out of my mind.

A patient enters holding a bag of liquid
with a line snaking into her arm under
the long sleeves of her blouse.
A snake bite of venom keeps her fluid in motion
and the rest of us sit thumbing magazines
looking for even a shred of our own stories
hidden in the pages full of healthy images
of young people whose teeth
are far too white and whose laughter
carries no contagion.[147]

The poem was a release valve that allowed me to reassess my own mortality. It gave my fear a voice and my potentially cancerous body a place to nest. It also offered a plot to my affliction, a story to hold it with—both hands.

- As best as you understand poetry, write a poem to your wound.
- Or, let the wound write a poem to you. Listen for it.

---

147 Dennis Patrick Slattery, *Casting the Shadows: Selected Poems* (Kearney, Neb.: Morris Publishing, 2001), pp. 25-26.

- Or write a poem to the situation in which you were afflicted, physically hurt, diseased, even dismembered.
- Let the wounded part of you gain its voice, something we often neglect in our understandable obsession to cure the wound, to erase and efface it or to silence it. Now, through a poem, face it.
- After you have finished, ask yourself: what, if anything, is different for having given the wound or the situation around it a poetic utterance, even a plot line to hold itself within?

Writing Meditation: Fiction and Physiology

What has never anywhere come to pass, that alone never grows old.[148]

Our personal myth lives in one of its most vital presences in our flesh. Our own incarnated selves inhabit the soul that guides us and offers at every step of our journey direction and purpose. The realm of poetry offers what has not been or may never be; nonetheless, it harbors poetic truth that is deeper and more lasting than the truths of our everyday lives. It carries as well an intuitive sense of knowing, one that is spontaneous, immediate and pushes to the white hot nugget of truth of our afflictions. While we are historical beings folded continually into the fabric of time, we are also poetic beings who can dwell imaginally in the improbable world of fiction, that "as if" standard of our experiences mentioned above. Where the two collide marks also where they collude and in that collusion our personal myth takes shape and gathers form as we become more conscious of its contours.

In a profound study of the philosopher Aristotle's small but insightful book, *The Poetics*, S. H. Butcher writes that "the truth of poetry is essentially different from the truth of fact. Things that are outside and beyond the range of our experience, that never have happened and never will happen, may be more true—poetically speaking,—more profoundly true than those daily occurrences which we can with confidence predict."[149] I believe this very quality of never having happened creates a corridor into the study of our personal myth, for myth is in part a fabrication that highlights what might otherwise remain below the floorboards of

---

148 Friedrich Schiller, quoted in S. H. Butcher, *Aristotle's Theory of Poetry and Fine Art*, 3rd ed. (New York: Hill and Wang, 1902), p. 171.

149 Butcher, *Aristotle's Theory of Poetry and Fine Art*, p. 170.

consciousness. Its emergence is through our visceral selves, our own embodiment. In that spirit, let's finish a story about the body transformed, reordered, reshaped; in your creation, trust what it is that appeals to you about where the story should go from the quoted ending. Whether you know this story by the Czech writer, Franz Kafka, or not, trust what your own visceral reality wants to make of it to extend the plot. Don't censor your response; simply be present to what surfaces on its own. Here is the beginning of the story:

> When Gregor Samsa awoke one morning from troubled dreams he found himself transformed in his bed into a monstrous insect. He lay on his back, which was as hard as an armour plate, and saw, as he raised his head a little, his vaulted brown belly divided by stiff, arch-shaped ribs, and the bed covers which could hardly cling to its height and were about to slide off completely. His many legs, pitifully thin compared with the rest of his bulk, waved about helplessly before his eyes.
>
> "What has happened to me?" he thought. It was no dream. His room, an ordinary though somewhat small room for one person, lay peacefully between the four familiar walls.[150]

- In your own way, feel into the body of this man that has been transformed into an instinct. Imagine the improbable as if it were true.
- Do not become too rational about the trajectory of the story you wish it to take. If you know the story, do not try to recreate it; take it in a direction that your own embodied creative impulses suggest to you.
- The story is mythical from the very beginning; what of your own personal myth might want to connect with it?
- Resist the impulse to resolve the story; pay more attention to the process of creating it as an action.
- Write from your own embodiment, your own felt sense of yourself as an enfleshed being confronting such a moment in the life of another. Trust where you are taken.
- Part of our purpose here is to engage the story with such affective sensibility that our own consciousness is widened and deepened by the creative act of writing.
- Write as much as you need to in order to complete the narrative.

---

150 Franz Kafka, "The Metamorphosis," in Kafka, *The Metamorphosis and Other Stories* (New York: Oxford University Press, 2009), p. 29.

Writing Meditation: The Fiction in the Affliction

> The archetypal questions we might therefore pose at this juncture are: What god or gods reside in the wound? What does the wound want? What is the disease asking? What is the story that it poses or proposes? What plot wishes to be born through the wound?[151]

Some deep connective tissue exists between fiction and afflictions. By fiction here I mean a storied account, be it of an actual historical event or, like the narrative in the last meditation, one that did not happen, will in all probability never happen, but that is not sufficient to take from it either a poetic or a mythopoetic truth that enlarges our orbit of understanding.

In this meditation, we will look at a description from a surgeon, Richard Selzer, who in his forties began a successful writing career. He chose as his subject matter what he knew most about: the operating theater as well as the patients he saw and treated in his rounds at the hospital he was connected to in New Haven, Connecticut.

I want to use one of his stories about the body wounded and allow us to imagine it from the place or habitation of our own woundedness. Again, I will ask you to finish the story based on the origin of its plot. It is a vignette by Selzer based on a moment with a patient he encounters on his rounds. What happens at the beginning is not pleasant, nor need it be. What is important is the body wounded and in crisis that may startle something awake in our own wounded being and unveil another quality of our personal myth, the patterned way we exist, make decisions, and perform in the world.

Moreover, it is a story about the body's boundaries, which another writer, Antonio Damasio has written so well on in the following way: "One key to understanding living organisms, from those that are made up of one cell to those that are made up of billions of cells, is the definition of their boundary, the separation between what is *in* and what is *out*."[152] Along the sliver that separates the *in* from the *out* is one dominant locale where our personal myth forms and is most active negotiating these two realms that can be in conflict

---

151 Slattery, *The Wounded Body*, p. 15.

152 Antonio Damasio, *The Feeling of What Happens: Body and Emotion in the Making of Consciousness* (San Diego: Harcourt Brace, 1999), p. 135.

or in accord with one another, even mirroring one another. So, imagine the following scene that Selzer depicts:

> "Don't come in! Stay out!"
>
> Just so does the woman answer my knocking. But I am already inside the room. On hospital rounds, a knock is only a gesture.
>
> "Are you all right?" I ask her through the bathroom door.
>
> There is no answer.
>
> "I'll be back in a few minutes. Please get back in bed. I want to examine you." I turn to leave. Then I see advancing from beneath the closed door the blot of dark shine. I step closer. I crouch, peering. I slide open the door which separates us. In a hospital the doors cannot be locked.
>
> The woman is naked. She sits on the toilet, bent forward, her pale white feet floating on the jammy floor. Nearby, a razor blade dropped from one painted hand. The other hand cannot be seen; it is sunk to the wrist within the incision in her abdomen. Bits of black silk, still knotted, bestrew the floor about her feet. They are like the corpses of slain insects. The elbow which points out from her body moves in answer to those hidden fingers which are working . . . working.[153]

The scene is a difficult one to enter. Yet, it is powerful in its simple forceful prose. The images make it vivid, vital and profound in the way the body may be entered and instructs us as to the power of writing to create a wound that may moan in our imagination for many days after reading it.

- Where might this vignette go from here?
- Where are your own bodily sensations involved in this scene and where might you take it and where might it want to take you?
- Where is the opening greatest for you as you read it and then reread it?
- What might be the point as well as the plot from here?
- Consider taking the point of view of the woman or the surgeon and write from that point of view.
- Feel free to shift perspective so we as readers see the story unfold from a different angle.
- Take the point of view of the incision, the opened wound, and let it have its voice in the scene.
- What might be calling from inside you to complete in the story?

---

153 Richard Selzer, "Raccoon," in Selzer, *Confessions of a Knife* (New York: Simon and Schuster, 1979), p. 32.

- Trust what arises and work your writing from that place.
- Note closely where the story ends for you.

Writing Meditation: A Leg Up on One's Myth

> Where narratives are formulated, they may be shared as myths. Myths typically focus on the major and challenging elements of human life.[154]

Reading of afflictions can contain a healing poultice for me as reader in part because the imagination is at heart analogical and embodied. As we read we can often feel viscerally the narrative in the "as if" mode I suggested earlier. I believe this is possible because the embodied psyche in each of us is relational and connective in its fundamental impulse. We have the gift of being able to "imagine into" the life and the suffering and joys of others, which is the powerful mystery of stories themselves and the energy they can carry into us and we into them. The power of stories can then cultivate a greater presence to the suffering of others through a deeper sense of compassion in us. To feel this response connects us on a deep level through recognizing the presence of suffering, both our own and that of the stories that define afflictions.

As we entertain two last writing meditations for this chapter, keep in consciousness how this is so as you feel in an incarnated way what is taking place in you as you read. My sense is that quality stories, poetry, and art generally, complete something in our fractured selves, salve us, through what Edward Whitmont refers to as "the law of similars" wherein "like cures like."[155] When reading, we contact something in us that has a correspondence in the words read and the experience carried by the language. Then reading and imagining become homeopathic in its energy flow from inner to outer. Reading becomes a mythopoetic activity wherein healing begins to integrate what I sense is wounded in me through the wound in the work I enter imaginally. Wounds work wonders in drawing out from others the affliction they bear. Let's take a poem from this arena:

154 Peter Willis, Timothy Leonard, Anne Morrison, and Steven Hodge, eds., *Spirituality, Mythopoesis & Learning* (Mt. Gravatt, Queensland: Post Pressed, 2009), p. 3.

155 Edward C. Whitmont, *The Alchemy of Healing: Psyche and Soma* (Berkeley, Calif.: North Atlantic Books, 1993), p. 5.

Leg Fright

No sooner do I sit down in the crowded
quiet medical lab cubit
than my right leg twitches, spasms and I
want to start writing something about
body chaos,
blood that howls between fences
and the electric charge burps through
the right thigh—proud to express that
something is not right.
Pulling blood from my right arm
will slow the leg down,
a leg that wants to be out
in the parking lot splashing in
rain puddles[156]

Poetry, fiction, art, music, if it is any good, contains no *messages*. But they do evoke insights and deeper levels of awareness or consciousness. Some field of sentience is activated in us such that we see differently by means of the experience that the words, images, and sounds capture. So it is I sense with this poem.

- On a very literal level, what happens in the poem?
- On a more imaginal or narrative level, what takes place in this patient through his leg?
- What does the poem make you aware of?
- Without violating the poem, but rather to move it closer to home, where in your own life have you felt the yearning to be outside splashing in rain puddles?
- What in your own body signaled another calling or indicated to you another way of living?
- What were the terms of your own walking and splashing that you had taken from you that you wished to reclaim?

---

156 Slattery, *Casting the Shadows*, p. 30.

Writing Meditation: Evoking an Ancestor

All knowing comes by likeness.[157]

The great neo-Platonist philosopher, Plotinus (204-270) came on one of the most sublime psychological truths regarding learning that was subsequently taken up by writers in many fields of study. Likeness, to my thinking, is at the heart of the myth-making impulse and even the mything energy that we claim when we are attracted to something that demands we pursue its inferences.

Implicated as well is the narrative part of the soul that seeks connections with other narratives, other images, that confirm its own identity and existence. We are each affirmed in both body and soul by narratives that present analogies to our own stories, whether or not we are conscious of them. Working in this way with the contours and contents of our own personal myth, we engage not analytical but imaginal reflection[158] that both broadens and deepens our own wakefulness as mythic beings, even mythic matter, for myths are our mother (mater). Myths mother us into a fuller sense of our identity. Myths matter to us because they make present and encourage the mothering in us that nourishes and provides the love needed for growth.

One important area we will end this chapter with is the mothering that ancestry can provide: their memory is mothering. The early Greek world knew this when they aligned Memory with a goddess, Mnemosyne. She it was who in the myth, mated with Olympian Zeus for 9 nights; each morning Mnemosyne gave birth to one of the 9 Muses. So the myth of Memory herself guides us in our remembrance of an important ancestor that we want to recover by remembering this person in a bodily way.

We each carry with us some images of persons, places and mementos of our histories, In each of these Mnemosyne is present to encourage us to keep these shards of our past alive in the present through the connective energy of remembrance. We are attached in our origins through the Dead. Remembering an ancestor, which does not have to be, but may

---

157 Plotinus, *The Enneads*, trans. Stephen MacKenna (Burdett, N.Y.: Larson Publications, 1992), 8.1., p. 76.

158 Willis, Leonard, Morrison, and Hodge, *Spirituality, Mythopoesis & Learning*, p. 3.

include, a blood relation, sheds crucial light on our personal myth. We might ask: what is it about that person, young or old, relation or friend, even someone who entered our lives to influence it profoundly, then exited, leaving the trace of their presence stamped into the wax of who we have become? This person can be a mythical, fictional or historical figure as well. I have for years been mentored by Odysseus and Athene, for example, as well as by Dante Alighieri through his *Divine Comedy* and Father Zosima in Fyodor Dostoevsky's *The Brothers Karamazov.* It may be helpful to go far back into your own biography to see more clearly the trace they had on you, but it is not essential. The following are some prompts to encourage your meditation. My sense is that when we remember who it is that rises up in us, we are remembering at the same time a valuable treasure in ourselves that recollecting coaxes us to retrieve and honor with a fully-embodied consciousness.

- Is there someone from the past who is always with you, speaking to you and you to him/her?
- In what way do you honor that person today, and perhaps on a regular basis?
- If you have now decided on a person or a pet that has mentored you in some profound way, but whom you have never addressed, perhaps you could begin a dialogue now.
- Create a dialogue with that ancestor and record it.
- Was anything left undone with the piece of your biography that might now furnish you an opportunity to complete it, even if it is one-sided?
- If that ancestor were alive today, what might the two of you do together?
- What would be two essential observations, ideas, or feelings you might want to share with this ancestor?

Writer's Response

I have no images of ancestors, but I did have a strong connection to the two paintings on the wall in the back room [at the Dallas Institute of Humanities and Culture], one of a man, the other of a woman. I went there for inspiration and found a very strong connection, even a bond, with each of them.

My mythic ancestors are in the next room, on the wall, side-by-side, male and female. They look so much alike. I think they are royalty. Asian. Chinese. Ancients. They speak to me, silently. She smiles, ever so modestly. It's in her eyes. Her gentle expression says she loves me. I feel honored to be loved by such a grand lady. Her love is warm, tender, embracing, nurturing, nourishing, glowing softly, and containing me in her presence.

He does not smile. His love is made of sterner stuff. I feel his strength. He is hard, but in a comfortable way, or rather to say in a way that is not fearsome. He has met his fears and he is no longer afraid. And yet, he is always vigilant, always ready to act, even as he sits quietly, not prepared to act; that is, ready to act but without anticipating action. His solidity is monumental, as a mountain is monumental. Placidly awesome.

I feel both of them, separately and together, inside of me, available to me, as if their energy could complete me. I feel immensely grateful. I look at him and bow my head. I look at her and bow my head. Amazing Grace. (Annemarie St. John)

Writing Meditation: Gesturing an Ancestor through Bodily Movement

The key concept of morphic resonance is that similar things influence similar things across both space and time. The amount of influence depends on the degree of similarity . . . all of us are more like ourselves in the past than like anyone else.[159]

Movement is the great law of life. Everything moves. The heavens move, the earth turns, the great tides mount the beaches of the world.[160]

To be in motion is our natural state; rest is essential between periods of movement and both are necessary for a balanced and whole-some life.

Far from thinking that our bodies are separate from emotion, psyche, mind and spirit, it would be truer to think of them as one entity, as Trudi Schoop, a dance therapist does. She gave a talk to an audience of dance therapists in which she observed: "So I no longer concern myself with any division of the human. From my whole person, I address myself to another whole person; to all of you whole persons, in fact."[161] We will deepen our

---

159 Rupert Sheldrake, "Mind Memory and Archetype: Morphic Resonance and Collective Unconscious," *Psychological Perspectives* 18, no. 1 (1987): 9. Also available at http:// www.sheldrake.org/Articles&Papers/papers/morphic/morphic1_paper.html.

160 Mary Starks Whitehouse, "The Tao of the Body," in *Aesthetic Movement*, ed. Patrizia Pallaro (London: Jessica Kingsley Publishers, 1999), p. 41.

161 Trudi Schoop, "Motion and Emotion," *American Journal of Dance Therapy* 22, no. 2 (2000): 91.

understanding of personal myth if we follow her idea that we exist within an underlying unity despite feeling at times like a collage of separate parts. Exploring personal myth has as one of its intentions to feel that unity in an incarnated holistic way.

One insight that can grow directly from the above is that we exist in our own time and in the time of our ancestors. I have, for instance, watched one of my two sons make a gesture that mirrors one I make regularly or that my father used to make. Now their physical contact with their grandfather was very minimal over the years; nonetheless, in that short space, or perhaps in their genetic memory base, they in-corporated this gesture. Gestures can be mythic, memorial, and deeply meaningful for one when he/she becomes conscious of its origin as part of a previous person's-hood, his/her way of being in the world under certain circumstances.

All of these observations have as their intention to lead us to discovering through bodily gesture the presence of an ancestor. At play here as well is that ancient motion of the spiral: for in embodying someone from the past, we enter the timeless sweep of the spiralic psyche as it renegotiates its relationship with the history of another.

Some elements of who that ancestor is may be discovered in the complexity of bodily gestures that bring that person forcefully into presence. For in some tangible way, that gesture carries or embodies a segment of that person's personal myth. We live out our myth in part in the way we gesture ourselves—as ritual acts—into the world and then pay attention to the way the world gestures back to us. Movement is the basic blueprint we follow in dialogue with the world and those we meet within it.

- Think of someone who you would like to make present through your bodily movement.
- Was there a certain way that person performed a task, for example, in the way that person held a fork, sat in a chair, walked across a room, drove a car, walked, stood in conversation with others?

For example, when I enacted a gesture of my father's in a workshop conducted by Marion Woodman at Eranos in Switzerland some years ago, he was suddenly and palpably in the room. My gesture enacted a question he would ask often: "What time is the bus?" because for decades he rode the bus from Lakeshore Blvd. in Euclid, Ohio to downtown Cleveland where he worked in a modest job for the Cleveland Electric Illuminating Company. And, as he asked the question, he walked with a rapid pace. Being tall and thin, he had a long gait and I remember never being able to keep up with him, so swiftly could he cover a mile walking. He reminded me a bit of the Mad Hatter, the rabbit with the large pocket watch in *Alice in Wonderland*.

In the workshop, then, I moved around the room asking anyone whose eye would catch mine: "What time is the bus?" After a few minutes repeating his question and his gait, I viscerally felt a fuller sense of not just enacting my father, but actually becoming him through a mimetic somatics, an imitation in my own body of his former gestures. I tuck this illustration in right here to ground the way you might think about embodying the other in bodily movement that collapses temporality between the past and the present.

Part I

- What characteristic or two stand out for you that might most effectively bring that person to life in and through your own embodied motion?
- Enact that person as best you can. Once you begin, imagine the person, not what you are doing to enliven and even enflesh him or her.
- Do not analyze what you are doing. If you authentically allow the memory of the ancestor to take you over for a few minutes, you will feel more deeply something of that person's essence, the soul of their presence, their own personal myth gaining life through your embodied imaginal re-gesturing.
- Try to remain in that embodied motion in space and time for about 8-10 minutes. It will take at least that long for you to feel that person migrate into you, infiltrating your own feeling life.
- When you feel that you want to stop, do it gradually, as if you had been in a deep meditation or dream state and wish now gently to return to the waking world. If your experience is like mine, you will realize that through the body you have entered a dramatic dream space and that another has been living in and through you in the landscape of eternal presence. In fact, you have been existing and moving in two personal myths simultaneously.

Part II

- After a few minutes, turn to your journal and consider these few questions:
- What was it about this person that brought you to choose him/her to embody?
- What was your own experience like, now that you have stepped out of the role—for it was a dramatic role you were giving shape and style to—as best as you can recollect it.
- What memories, scenes, or vignettes arose in you as a consequence of embodying the other as ancestor?
- What of your own embodiment took shape and form that perhaps became conscious to you for the first time?

My hope is that this chapter allowed you to achieve a greater consciousness of the body as lived rather than a body you have. Within the borders and boundaries of our personal myth, we are embodied as part of our essence rather than the body being something "I" possess. Shifting our angle this way will reveal the power of personal myth as a gestural energy field to be felt in our flesh and not simply as an idea or element we inhabit.

7

RITING THE SELF AS/AND OTHER

The Other Within embodies anti-structure . . . hence, the obstacles to his or her inclusion in the structures of society and psyche abound.[162]

We build our relationships based on projections. The person who I perceive mainly through my projections is an imago or alternatively a carrier of imagoes or symbols.[163]

One of the most powerful and provocative themes in literature is that of the Other as Double. The narratives that develop the self as an Other continue to inform our sense of who we are as not only singular and whole but multiple and varied. In our own house are many manifestations of our total being. I can think of several literary works that carry this theme deep into our imaginations: *The Epic of Gilgamesh* reveals the more primitive natural man, Enkidu as Gilgamesh's civilized double; Patroclus in Homer's *Iliad* dresses as Achilles and enters the battle against the Trojans, only to be slain by Hector who, for a moment, believes he has just slain the Greek hero; Dante Alighieri is both the pilgrim in his *Divine Comedy* as well as the creator of that journey in poetic memory; the poet Dante is and is not the pilgrim he writes about; William Shakespeare's last play, *The Tempest* moves to a reconciliation between Prospero, the wizard of the island and Caliban, his dark primitive double, who the exiled King of Milan finally acknowledges and integrates as his own; Fyodor Dostoevesky's marvelous short story, "The Double," relates the way we split and live in two separate realities at once; Nikolai Gogol renders in his short story, "The Nose," how a part of us can split off and become an autonomous personality in the world; Oscar Wilde's *The Picture of Dorian Gray* reveals how his moral life can gather in a painting of the debauched young Dorian while he remains, at least to all appearances, virginally young, not unlike Narcissus himself; Joseph Conrad's *The Secret Sharer* tracks a young ship captain who

---

162 Daniel Deardorf, *The Other Within: The Genius of Deformity in Myth, Culture and Psyche*, intro. by Robert Bly (Ashland: White Cloud Press, 2004), p. 31.

163 C. G. Jung, *Dream Analysis: Notes of the Seminar Given in 1928-1930*, ed. William McGuire, Bollingen Series XCIX (Princeton, N.J.: Princeton University Press, 1984), p. 50.

confronts the double nature of himself and through it gains a sense of his own authority; Nathaniel Hawthorne's "The Birthmark" contrasts the more primitive Aylmer to the young brilliant doctor to reveal the former's wisdom about the cost of scientific experiments to create perfection. James Joyce's *Ulysses* doubles in 20th century Dublin the ancient Greek epic poet's world of myth, legend, history and poetry to illustrate the mythopoetic power of refashioning an old epic in modern dress; Flannery O'Connor's short story, "Everything that Rises Must Converge" reveals the racial prejudice of a white woman who confronts a black woman on a bus wearing the same hat she has on. It exposes to the white prejudicial imagination that she also shares in what she believes is beneath her own racial status.

The list could be extended; the point is that this doubling of self into Otherness is one of the deepest psychic patterns existing in us; it reveals in part through doubling the shadow of ourselves, what we would rather bury than believe is part of our own legitimate legacy. Yet the double can reveal gold in us that we have denied in ourselves, so this rich mythic figure in all of our psyches is not exclusively negative and destructive. It can also serve as our guide, or as pyschopomp, that leads us both more fully into the world and deeply into our own recesses where untapped resources await.

But perhaps in the Roman poet Ovid's collection of mythic tales in his *Metamorphoses* do we discern the most potent myth of Otherness, in fact its mythic origin, along with its intrinsic paradox: the Other is I. I embody the Other as much as the Other incarnates me; becoming aware of such a truth allows us to recognize so much of what our Shadow self carries in the darkness of unconsciousness until we bring it into our awareness, and for our purposes, through the ritual of writing.

Recall for a moment in "The Myth of Narcissus and Echo" when Narcissus, having spurned the advances of Echo, whose misfortune was to fall in love with him at first sight, arrives alone at the clear virginal pond in the forest. This myth offers an opportunity to contemplate the nature of the Other that we all carry as part of our personal myth. In reading the plot of Narcissus, we are translated into a different way of seeing that unfolds the place of self-identity through Otherness. When time allows, give yourself over to this classic collection of stories that highlight transformation. Give particular time to the "Narcissus and Echo" story, which appears in a section of Book 3 of Ovid's classic text. I recommend the fine translator, Allen Mandelbaum's edition of this text.[164]

---

164 Ovid, *The Metamorphoses,* trans. Allen Mandelbaum (San Diego: Harcourt, Brace, 1993), pp. 90-96.

I have been developing the idea in this book of writing reflections that myths, like poems and dreams, are forms that serve as invitations to meditation, stirred as they are by the power of the stories themselves in their imaginal movement and in their images. Mythopoesis is, as I have written elsewhere, a different form of imagining, one that includes the metaphysics as well as the physics of the physical. They present to us a way into seeing that ordinary perception bypasses or simply deletes. Thus, even to look into the still waters of myth as psychological reflection is already to be connected to the Narcissus/Echo narrative.[165]

While there is not enough space to entertain all the details of the plot, our concern here as we prepare for writing meditations on Otherness, is the moment when Narcissus approaches the virginal pond nestled beautifully within the shadowed forest. He is alone, isolated and thirsty as he approaches the water's lip. We recall that water is the only one of the four elements which allows reflection, a mirroring of what is before it or above it. But it requires a stillness, both in the person and on the water's surface. On this rich image, C. G. Jung observes that "Our unconscious . . . hides living water, spirit that has become nature, and that is why it is disturbed."[166] Another writer, Robert Johnson, whose theme is the shadow, a prominent image in this chapter, observes that water from the deep artesian well can be a source of "the deepest spiritual nourishment of humanity" if one has the courage to seek out the living water of life.[167] Self reflection, if not carried to extreme, can be a source of nourishment and rich sustenance within the daily diet of our lives.

I believe that deep knowledge as nourishment can emerge from the eternal pond into which Narcissus gazes to satisfy a thirst, to quench it in the virginal solitude of dense doubling. Let us gaze on the water ourselves for a moment. Ovid describes it as

> Silverlike,
>
> gleaming, bright. Its borders had no slime.
>
> No shepherds, no she-goats, no other herds

---

165 Dennis Patrick Slattery, "Narcissus, Echo and Irony's Resonance," in Slattery, *Harvesting Darkness: Essays on Literature, Myth, Film and Culture* (New York: iUniverse, 2006), pp. 266-287.

166 C. G. Jung, *Archetypes and the Collective Unconscious*, vol. 9, part I of *The Collected Works of C. G. Jung*, ed. and trans. R. F. C. Hull and Gerhard Adler, 2nd ed. (Princeton, N.J.: Princeton University Press, 1971), ¶ 52.

167 Robert A. Johnson, *Owning Your Own Shadow: Understanding the Dark Side of the Psyche* (San Francisco: HarperSanFrancisco, 1991), p. ix.

of cattle heading for the hills disturbed

that pool.[168]

The pond is an untouchable place, like Narcissus himself; his nature is already mirrored in nature's locale because they are a unity. Place is without blemish; it is virginal, untainted, unpolluted, as I think we have a desire to be ourselves, where no stain or pollution infects our lives; we may expend huge tanks of psychic energy daily to maintain such a persona. It is an analogue of a desire for perfection, for purity, untainted by the world's messy body.

Drawn by the beauty of the natural setting, Narcissus approaches and lies or kneels down by the lip of the pond to satisfy his thirst. In satisfying it, he encourages another appetite to rise up in him. Such is the dynamic process of a consuming imagination. Now he sees and gazes in wonder at the unknown image that rises up to meet his own face as he stoops lower, towards the water. Ovid relates how he stares not once but twice, so the image of himself is echoed visually through him, and he gazes unblinking "at the twin stars that are his eyes."[169] C. G. Jung offers a helpful insight into the nature of water that bears on Narcissus' disposition at this moment: "Whoever looks into the water sees his own image, but behind it living creatures soon loom up; fishes, presumably, harmless dwellers of the deep—harmless, if only the lake were not haunted."[170] But, we might ask, what is the quality of this double seeing, where anyone of us in the Narcissus moment engages a double seeing, a duplicate imagining of the self that cannot be separated from the natural world? I wonder if this is another form of our Otherness that we do not recognize today on a cultural and ecological plane of awareness? In the myth, Narcissus' doubleness is made possible as a mode of perception by the natural order's clear and unpolluted presence. What is prompted in the moment is nothing less than a sense of wonder: "he now is struck with wonder by / what's wonderful in him."[171] Mythically, a dawning awareness of his double signals the time of his initial trouble:

Unwittingly,

he wants himself; he praises, but his praise

---

168 Ovid, *Metamorphoses*, p. 93.

169 Ovid, *Metamorphoses*, p. 94.

170 Jung, *Archetypes and the Collective Unconscious*, ¶ 52.

171 Ovid, *Metamorphoses*, p. 95.

is for himself; he is the seeker and

the sought, the longed-for and the one who longs;

he is the arsonist—and is the scorched.[172]

In his doubling, but now divorced from Echo, he is ensnared by Eros, in desire, yet absent an exit strategy out of the labyrinth of self-fixation, which has grown like a chrysalis around him, but which began with the healthier action of self-reflection. Otherness, or if I may use the participle, "Othering," is a form of mothering that smothers, or can, if one does not allow a bit of irony to intercede between one and the image that fixates. Self-knowing is end-stopped, the myth suggests to me, because of self-fixation which paralyzes. In self-fixation, the Othering qualities that arc beyond me are deleted; I become a victim of my own Otherness and therefore only a shadow of what I am possible of being. My impulse is to protect myself from the Othering quality within me, so I may live a life fixated on a single image within my small pond. As soon as I recognize my second, my double, as myself, I am then opened to the possibility of new knowledge. My doubled Other provokes that in me by making me not one but two. The world assumes a more intimate image because I am now aware of its reflective nature, if not its double face.

All desires and appetites have vortexed for Narcissus into one. All of the action funnels into a final revelation, not of self-knowing but of self-fixation, which succeeds in keeping one hidden from one's self. Fixed on his one image, all other forms of Otherness no longer become possible to imagine: "I'm he! . . . / my image cannot trick me anymore. / I burn with love for my own self."[173]

The myth invites so much more reflection, but we must leave Narcissus here, absorbing the revelation that has loomed out of the water. He will soon wither in self-fixation by the virginal pond's rim. When, later, those who wish to bury the young man search for his body to hoist it onto a funeral pyre, they find in its stead "a flower, / its yellow center circled by white petals,"[174] a thing of beauty, not to be possessed, its life short and lovely for anyone to behold in the natural world. We can, if we gaze with wonder on the natural object of beauty, see something of our own flowering nature within its white petals.

---

172 Ovid, *Metamorphoses*, p. 95.

173 Ovid, *Metamorphoses*, pp. 95-96.

174 Ovid, *Metamorphoses*, p. 97.

As we each imagine the myth in our own way, we discover something of the grotesque and the gold in the images of the myth; we find Otherness that is us at the same instant, and it nourishes us even if/or because it reveals something of our own poverty of vision and inclusion. I have given this story ample space in the present chapter because I hope to use it to illustrate how our own personal myth can open to an ancient story and be transformed in the way we see ourselves through the clear virginal waters of poetry. Patterns in the myth resonate with our own echoic selves that is part of Otherness and Self. The power of the mythopoetic becomes most vibrant in the act of imagining, which is the purpose for giving Narcissus and Echo its warranted presence here.

Writing Meditation: Mirroring the Myth

Even while I have left so much out of the myth, offer a response to the story as I have related it:

- What part of it did you connect with?
- Where did the story strike you, resonate with you, or remind you of something in your own life?
- If myths carry a good portion of their strength in the act of remembering, what in your own past carries any segment, image or quality of Narcissus and/or Echo?
- What analogy in your life is Echoic ,that continues to repeat to you something you may have a tendency to forget or bury as undesirable or upsetting?
- When have you found yourself gazing into a reflection of yourself that threatened to swallow you if you continued to gaze at it?
- Or if it did swallow you and pull you down and out of your life, describe that condition or situation.
- Did the myth not touch you on any level or create any analogy in you? Describe how it did not.

Writing Meditation: Shadowing the Other in Prejudice

This thing of darkness I / acknowledge mine.[175]

In a fine little book by Robert Johnson, he develops the importance of paying conscious attention to the shadows in ourselves to minimize the projections of its often destructive content on to others.[176] Too much looking into the light casts a long shadow behind us, as C. G. Jung has observed so well.[177] Johnson relates the intriguing story of the origin of the term "bogey man." It derives, he writes, from old India wherein each village chose a man to be the "bogey." We might substitute the word "scapegoat," which derived from the Hebrew tradition. At the end of the year he was ritually slaughtered in order to carry the evil deeds of the community with him, thus purging them of the transgressive nature of their behavior.[178] In appreciation of his impending "service," to the community, he was treated royally while he lived by having all his desires satisfied by the tribe.

This "bogey man" carries the collective shadows of a people. Without this annual ritual purging, the evils and offenses of a people might be too much to bear. We can readily think of examples in our own day where this same mythic enactment is ritualized in law, custom, attitudes, institutional prejudices and conventional wisdom. It is a way to keep the "Other" in its deformities, abnormalities and pathologies out there, to keep us insulated from what we might have to face "in here." Absent integrating these deformities, our personal myth remains intact but static. Yet it carries also the distortions brought on by shadow material unfaced and unexplored. My own sense is that what we project out at "bogey" is immensely crucial to identify as part of our personal myth.

The word "prejudice" comes from the Latin, meaning to "pre-judge," or to label without knowing. It is a powerful psychological method of keeping the Other at a distance, to maintain a sense of purity about our selves, away from the shadow that roils beneath the

---

175 William Shakespeare, *The Tempest*, ed. Robert Langbaum (New York: Signet Classic, 1987), act 5, scene 1, lines 275-276.

176 Johnson, *Owning Your Own Shadow*, p. 31.

177 Jung, *Dream Analysis*, p. 123.

178 Johnson, *Owning Your Own Shadow*, p. 33.

floorboards. Prejudices carry their own mythic energy and signify an archetypal behavior that is part of human nature.

- Describe a strong prejudice in you that has been actively present in your life for some time.
- Describe a prejudice in you that has evolved recently.
- In your description can you identify its origins? Parents, friends, media, your own development, for instance?
- How does this prejudice serve you in your daily life in specific situations?
- What does it protect you from or allow you to be aggressive about or to retreat from?
- What has happened when this prejudice has been assaulted at the citadel where it holds court?
- What beliefs or self-images does the prejudice protect and serve with unfaltering allegiance?
- As a wall, what does the prejudice separate out?
- What does this prejudice allow you to impeach with impunity?
- If you were to entertain letting it go by allowing it in as part of your personal mythology, imagine what might be the consequences.
- Does your prejudice increase your stature in your own and others' eyes?
- Does it diminish who you are but you are willing to trade it off to continue to cling to this prejudice?
- If for a moment you were to acknowledge that this prejudice constituted something crucially important in yourself, what response would you make to this possibility?

Writing Meditation: Conversing with the Shadowed Other

It is impossible to avoid being a carrier, vessel, or container of shadow material or shadow figures of the psyche. If we deny or ignore that part of ourselves, we will be haunted and hunted by energies that can threaten to tear one down by dismantling one's sense of self. Robert Johnson makes clear how the shadow "can rob us of energy."[179] It can also steal from us our own life if we are placed in a position to live out the lives of others—parents, siblings, teachers, friends—instead of our own destiny.

Johnson claims as well that "the self is a complex energy system"[180] that needs to conserve, construct, and maintain itself from assaults on its power supply. When the shadow makes its presence felt, we can, if we detach from it for a moment, feel the energy in us

179 Johnson, *Owning Your Own Shadow*, p. 38.
180 Johnson, *Owning Your Own Shadow*, p. 38.

wane, shift, or dissolve, leaving us feeling dispirited, depressed and without that *élan vital* that makes life feel as if it had benevolent meaning and energic surety of purpose.

One way to make a connection with the shadow is through conversation as a rhetorical ritual wherein we allow the voice of the other to speak without censorship and without protest.

- Allow yourself a ritual space and time for this conversation, not when you are distressed but when you can calmly and openly allow an exchange to surface.
- Write down what arises without worrying or monitoring your responses; the more you censor or delete or control the responses, the more the ego is in charge to make sure the shadow remains domesticated, if not intimidated.
- Listen closely to the voice of the shadow: a parent, a teacher who criticized, a friend or work colleague who never found you good enough, even your own voice as harsh critic.
- Name the voice of the shadow: terrible mother, scolding uncle, critical teacher, demeaning acquaintance, negative critic, unhappy child. . . .
- When you begin a conversation in writing, you will be cast in a dual role: yourself in dialogue with the shadow persona and the persona leveling resentments, negative attitudes, critical swipes, or demeaning assertions at you. The courage to take it, not to respond in kind, is a sign of great strength and restraint in yourself.
- You may find in the process that you need more than one conversation to arrive at some insight, but I suspect the revelations will come fairly soon after you begin.
- At the end of your conversation—and it does not have to end with some resolution or finality—allow it to taper off with a desire to continue at another time where you left off or to begin in a new place.
- When you feel you have gone as far as you can with the shadow in this meeting, end it as if you were parting with a friend or finishing up a phone conversation. Finalize the ritual with a salute and friendly parting. Perhaps even consider continuing the discussion at a later time.

Writers' Responses

The following is a dialogue created by a participant who found it surprising how quickly the shadow wanted to be given a space to speak:

Shadow: I am your fantasy of guilt, shame, low esteem and I will continue to remind you of these shortcomings when you least expect me.

Participant: Yesterday you rode with me in the car and tried to ruin the leisurely ride I took along a favorite scenic highway that I love to visit when I can. The afternoon was a sunny Sunday. I kept trying to come back to the beauty of the present but you would not give me the peace I so strongly sought.

SH: I wanted to spoil it and as many other experience you have that give you pleasure. I will continue to seep into every moment of your life to unsettle you and steal your peace of mind. You will not know the meaning of the word "serenity."

P: My wish is to purge you from my life, but in truth I know that is impossible. I want to acknowledge here, and to you directly, that you are the presence of joylessness in my life; you destroy joy and my feeling of gratitude for being alive.

SH: That is my task. I need to feel superior to all others because that feeling sustains my fantasy of myself. Oh, yes, I have a sense of myself as you have one of yourself. Then, because I am small and meager, I can feel larger, more forceful and more in control. You will bow to those intentions I carry with me when I invade your quiet moments.

P: I think I will cease playing by your rules; I am a loving, generous person. That is what I need to do to flourish. Your destructive presence in trying always to set the agenda of how people should be is a form of tyranny. I do not choose to be tyrannized.

SH: Try to dislodge me from your imagination and from the memories that debilitate your sense of yourself. I wield great power and will not give it up without a fierce battle. I have been with you for a long time.

P: I will unsettle you and your fantasy; the energy flows both ways.

SH: you will have to gather a much greater force than you possess now if you hope to unseat me. I am the persistent voice of NGE: Never Good Enough. I will compare you to me or to others and you'll always lack, always come up short as inadequate no matter how many successes you enjoy in the world . . . .

A second writer working to converse with the shadow without animosity or conflict, wrote the following:

MR: I promised when we ended our last conversation that we would talk again.

SH: You returned as you said you would. Good. I did not voice all I wished to last time, so I now have another opportunity.

MR: When you haunt me as figures in my life that seem bent on destroying my sense of who I am, I am not happy.

SH: Happy is what I don't wish for you—until you honor me, make me a pat of your decisions, consult me when you are undecided about something important to you.

MR: OK. I can do that and will begin to accommodate your wish to be consulted so long as you do not tyrannize by making all the decisions.

SH: That's fair. I want to be a formidable presence in your life, not left in the basement along with old clothes or a bicycle you never ride anymore. When I am down there, my resentment grows and then I will explode on to your consciousness to bowl you over.

MR: What might be a good way to give you space in my waking and even in my dream life, for I feel you take advantage of my sleep to haunt me. Those are the nights I sleep so fitfully and wake up exhausted.

SH: Do not try to be someone or something else in order to avoid me. Be you with me intact. Be you in your imperfect state. Be you but not in any explosive way. Continue to be you in a creative way.

MR: Who are you, really?

SH: Parts of your past split and hurt, wounded and splintered. I am the wound that keeps on oozing and will make a mess with my excretions.

I am the young part of you that could never please your father, that was attacked by him verbally when he said things to you in your youth like: "You are worthless; you will never amount to anything, you piece of crap." I am your father's projection of his own self-loathing from his timidity and then from his alcoholism. I am the part of your father who denied himself life but came alive in the spirit, the spirits of drink and excessive rage. You carry that grieving wrathful piece of him in me.

MR: Will the mourning ever lessen?

SH: Keep talking to me and it will.

MR: Are you my addictions as behaviors, repeated in order or as attempts at healing? But fail, because I don't yet recognize you as my addictions?

SH: You are catching on. I have had enough for today. I liked the exchange with you and look forward to another, but soon. Don't bury me in the basement or in a closet or in a cupboard in the garage and think all is well. It is better, but far from well.

MR: I agree; let's talk within the next week or ten days.

SH: (Silent, but with a nod of the head).

Writing Meditation: Self as Other Prejudiced

> Jung used to say that we can be grateful for our enemies, for their darkness allows us to escape our own.[181]

The other side of carrying this "inner enemy" out into the world in order to insulate ourselves from its devastating energy as well as the courage needed to integrate these monsters of our lives, is to be the brunt or victim of prejudice. We can, as I have many times, learn something essential and core about ourselves by what happens when we are singled out and prejudged for our religious beliefs, our political stance, our taste in books, food, clothing, or our education, for example. I have taught at an institution where a young woman student other than Anglo-American was ostracized by her family and beaten by her husband because she dared to pursue an undergraduate degree. From within the family and her marriage, she was cast as one violating the norm and was thus made a "bogey" for her efforts. Her desire to learn by studying a field that would earn her a job and give her life great satisfaction was sabotaged by a collective mythos that punished her admirable drive to succeed.

The very way her family responded to her ambition we too can self-inflict by making ourselves the object of derision and turn the shadow material on ourselves in order to protect and insulate the egoic self from change or growth. This aspect of our personal mythology can be the deadliest element of ourselves; its self-affliction is its ironic and painful consequence. But let us take these two meditations one at a time:

- Describe a time in your life when you were the object of others' projections on you, that at the time you were convinced that you were the problem.
- Offer a narrative of what brought the intense condition on that made you the "bogey" for others.
- What ways did this affliction appear to hurt you?
- What did you do in return in responding to the pain?
- Who were the executioners of this prejudice?
- Was this prejudicial situation or condition ever resolved? If it was, in what way was it solved or diminished?
- Do you still live within this prejudice leveled at you?

---

181 Johnson, *Owning Your Own Shadow*, p. 37.

- Having this experience as a part of your life formerly or presently, what has carrying this scapegoat reality done to your own life, your image of yourself and your behavior?
- Has being a victim or object of ridicule or stereotype changed in any way the manner in which you look at others who suffer oppression and other forms of abuse?
- Has being singled out, scapegoated, made an example of, eventuated in any political or social action that has helped you to integrate this experience as a valued part of your own personal mythology?

Writing Meditation: Self as Other Held Hostage in Prejudice

> It would be exceedingly difficult to get the gold out of the shadow. People are as frightened of their capacity for nobility as of their darkest sides.[182]

Sometimes we perform a prejudice on the shadow material of our lives by assigning it to a small room in the castle tower as a negative agent best kept out of sight. But, as Robert Johnson so perceptively encourages us to consider, in the shadow is where the gold is often to be found, our own gold, the gold of a life that has not sought it nor may even have accepted its presence. I like to think of the shadow in this way, having lived in the scorching heat of Texas summers for 25 years: where there is shadow there is shade, and where there is shade exists a respite from the heat of the sun; too much illumination is as unhealthy as too much shadow. To rest in the shadowy glen of a grove of live oaks along a moist river bank is to feel the gold in nature.

Johnson suggests that there exists so much "hero worship" in our culture because most people are fearful of the heroic gold lying within. We are then seasoned for fearing the best in ourselves as much as we are in confronting the worst impulses of our nature. Heroic qualities, nobility of soul, and a generosity of spirit are for many to be avoided as much as distressing and destructive forms of thought and action. The power of myth resides here in part, for myths, as Rollo May has written, is what "hold us together." They provide us with psychic structures as well that give us coherence, shape and meaning.[183] I would add that a personal myth does not particularly like or invite change, or in being made to change,

---

182 Johnson, *Owning Your Own Shadow*, p. 45.
183 Rollo May, *The Cry for Myth* (New York: Bantam Doubleday, 1991), pp. 44-46.

generally speaking; but it is essential for consciousness itself to expand and deepen. Growing out of aspects of our personal myth keeping us ensnared in old habits of thoughts, imaginings and outworn harnesses, is another way to avoid the soul's inherent nobility. But to recognize such nobility carries with it an imperative to act on it, which frightens many back into their shell of the ordinary. A move from a familiar unity to the foreign terrain of polarity and diversity opens the way for a third, new reality to enter. When that occurs, in the tension new knowledge has a chance to gain a foothold.

- A prejudice against our own great-souledness can assist us in avoiding an unlived part of our life that we sense is essential for our self-definition as a whole person. What is that part in you that you recognize as being left in the closet or the cedar chest of yourself, unlived, waiting for the right season that never materializes?
- Part of our shadow is what we might do, or sense we could do, to incarnate our generous, noble, unique, novel, one-of-a-kind self. Describe this shadow of dark gold in you.
- Imagine for a moment what the terms could be to let this part of who you are surface in a splendor that would change the course of your life or enrich the course it is currently on.
- What force, presence or belief in you continues to successfully block or sabotage or arrest and incarcerate this aspect or dimension of yourself?
- Is there a way of modifying or customizing this shadow of gold to allow you some access to it in your life in a real, embodied way?
- Will you be content or discontented to allow this aspect of your noble nature to remain unlived?
- Is there a ritual that you might create and perform in order to allow this unlived part of yourself to be real-ized?
- What other form might this noble nature of you that is still in potential, incubating in the caverns of your soul, become a real part of your existence?

Writing Meditation: From Contradiction to Paradox as Other

As soon as a person projects a bit of his shadow onto another human being he is incited to this kind of rancorous speech.[184]

---

184 Marie-Louise von Franz, *Projection and Re-Collection in Jungian Psychology: Reflections of the Soul* (Chicago: Open Court Press, 1995), p. 21.

Another way to understand the power and the purpose of our projections is to think of them as ways of making self as other, thereby deluding ourselves into believing we have solved an inner contradiction. We have in fact just camouflaged it and forestalled an authentic resolution. We can quite easily cut the Gordian knot by simply outlawing the contradiction by outsourcing it on to others; however, the original energy that fed the contradiction remains inside us, doing its destructive work.

I like what Robert Johnson has done with the archetypal pattern of inner contradictions: he believes that transforming it into a paradox keeps the tension intact but the grating and grinding noise that contradictions can create to a low drone. Often these inner contradictions we are heir and susceptible to have their genesis in fear. He cites the wisdom of C. G. Jung, who remarked: "Find out what a person fears most and that is where he will develop next."[185] If we accept Jung's observation, then there appears to be a fatedness attached to what we fear because it points to where we are headed. So to turn or transform our *contradictions* into *paradoxes* can effectively bring it to consciousness and assimilate it. Such a resolve, though, takes immense courage, for to enter it, one must relinquish control.

Johnson returns to an ancient symbol, the mandorla, as a psychic geometry for transforming contradiction into paradox. Perhaps, he suggests, we might even redefine the heroic as "the ability to stand paradox."[186] This ancient symbol consists of two circles overlapping; where they overlap creates an almond-shaped area that contains the material from both circles and, in my view, looks like an eye turned on its side, like the eye of a cat! It is certainly a new way of seeing from an angle other than a horizontal one. I can remember seeing this image in many of the churches in Italy, especially in the elaborate golden mosaics in cathedrals in Rome, for example, in the church of Saints Cosmos and Damian that stands on top of a small hill overlooking the Forum Romana. In it is contained the elaborately regal figures of Christ and his mother, the Virgin Mary, the earthly and heavenly images that unite in the mandorla design. An entire cosmos gathers in the sacred figures inside the mandorla.

I further enjoy Johnson's linking the mandorla image to poetry: "the mandorla is the place of poetry."[187] Poetry is the expression in language of paradox, where two antithetical poles meet in a new synthesis or unity, yet each retains its distinctness. Johnson believes further

---

185 Johnson, *Owning Your Own Shadow*, p. 92.

186 Johnson, *Owning Your Own Shadow*, p. 92.

187 Johnson, *Owning Your Own Shadow*, p. 103.

that where the images overlap is "a mystical statement of unity."[188] Stories themselves carry this mandorlic image; stories struggle through conflict and contradiction not to reach a resolution, necessarily, but to entertain paradox as the central action of the journey.

I want to add to Johnson's astute and psychologically, if not mythically rich, observations, by asking us to think about what we *altar* and what we are willing to *alter* in our lives. To altar something is to put it up in a tabernacle for safe keeping and for continuous worship. It is sacrosanct and is neither to be questioned nor challenged. We tiptoe around it in silent obeisance. I think this act is fine, but it can be the genesis of contradictions when life circumstances that impact changes in our personal myth begin to suggest that something altared must now be altered. Here arises an opportunity to shape-shift contradiction into paradox by making the closed protective circle of what we have altered now be allowed to altar itself in the mandorla. We move and develop from one psychic geometry to another and deepen our understanding in the process.

A life contradiction implies an Otherness that we will not allow to be reconciled; it is the Othering of ourselves that the closed circle cannot tolerate. It breeds contradiction and this contradiction can in turn birth prejudice, hatred, and resentments, thereby further demeaning or trivializing what does not fit our narrow and comfortable patterns of awareness. The mandorlic imagination, by contrast, opens something up and out into another space where the two sides of an idea exist in the almond space of a more tolerant and graceful geometry. Instead of insisting that our imagination "pick sides," we open to the tension that is present within the two dimensions and we wait, openly, for a third—the *tertium quid*—to appear that can often contain the wisdom that each side carries. Let's see if this might be true for us:

- What contradiction do you suffer from now?
- What are its terms? It can be an idea, an image, a belief, a value, a conventional wisdom held for decades, a career, an idea of parenting . . . .the possibilities are endless.
- Can you step back for a moment and recall when the force of a contradiction entered what may have been a comfortable belief or position before this new energy entered to disrupt?
- Where is the greater energy in this contradiction?
- Or is it spread through the two sides equally?

---

188 Johnson, *Owning Your Own Shadow*, p. 103.

- Now, draw a mandorla in your journal. Let it take up the entire page. Make it big enough to write in it. The mandorla should look like a large version of this shape: (). This is the space where two circles of contradiction create a unity within their own diversity.
- Write out in each side of the circle the terms that contradict, one in each circle.
- You may want to step away from it for awhile if you feel the tension and sense no compromising position where the two sides might co-exist within the mandorla in a paradoxical partnership, without resolution but at ease with one another.
- Think of the space of the mandorla as that of a reconciliation but not a resolution. We are not interested in fixing something at this point, only with finding a space for the two sides of the contradiction to create some form of partnership. That may be as good as it gets.
- Write out what comes to you inside the mandorla. You are after allowing some credibility to become a part of the new wholeness within the differences. Simply be as honest and authentic as possible.
- If nothing comes to you, so steadfastly have both sides been altared in your mind, then set it aside for now to allow the psyche to entertain what is perhaps a new way of seeing.
- When some alteration becomes a possibility, write it out.
- Your task is to move away from any hierarchy of making one better than the other and giving them equal status.
- Trust that the psyche will work this material into a new format that could relieve you of tremendous pressure to fix something; rather, it offers space for something to grow from the positive energies that feed the contradiction.

Writing Meditation: Running Towards the Roaring Other

Psychologically, wherever there is danger there is potential and opportunity.[189]

At various moments we each realize glimpses of Others who we may come to recognize are us that most of the time we don't comprehend as part of the cast of characters that comprise the ensemble of ourselves. Being offered these moments can be revelatory and open us to dimensions that surprise and stretch who we believe we are. The following poem by Antonio Machado recognizes just such a side-bar glimpse:

---

189 D. Stephenson Bond, *Living Myth: Personal Meaning as a Way of Life* (Boston: Shambhala Publications, 1993), p. 65.

I

Don't trace out your profile—
forget your side view—
all that is outer stuff.

II

Look for your other half
who walks always next to you
and tends to be who you aren't.[190]

Not being us is a deflection, if not an illusion. One of these Others that we may want to ignore or avoid and pretend is not walking beside us is Fear. What we fear is Other; here I am speaking of the way Fear itself is Other, regardless of what that Fear fears. On this very point, mythologist D. Stephenson Bond asserts that "whether or not the eruption of powerful internal experiences turns out to be a breakdown or a breakthrough depends upon the ability of the person to give it form and meaning, upon the ability to mythologize."[191] This ability he refers to is a combination, I sense, of courage and creativity in the face of the Other. Within the experience he names, we can be deconstructed and/or reconstructed by means of its powerful presence. C. G. Jung too saw immense value in becoming acquainted with the other: "This process of coming to terms with the Other in us is well worth while, because in this way we get to know aspects of our nature which we would not allow anybody else to show us and which we ourselves would never have admitted."[192] We become our own best acknowledgement of that portion of our personality that while seeming foreign, is in fact a most intimate part of our construction.

Another writer who I find very helpful on this point is the mythologist Michael Meade. The Other can take the form of what frightens and scatters us, or comes up behind us as an unknown presence and strips us of our identity. It can, however, as Bond's quote that begins

---

190 Excerpt from Antonio Machado, *Moral Proverbs and Folk Songs*, in Robert Bly, James Hillman, and Michael Meade, eds. *The Rag and Bone Shop of the Heart: A Poetry Anthology* (New York: Harper Collins, 1992), p. 366.

191 Bond, *Living Myth*, pp. 65-66.

192 C. G. Jung, *Mysterium Coniunctionis*, vol. 14 of *The Collected Works of C. G. Jung*, ed. and trans. R. F. C. Hull and Gerhard Adler (Princeton, N.J.: Princeton University Press, 1970), ¶ 706.

this chapter affirms, be a place of insight and courage, not emotional paralysis. In his book, *The World Behind the World*, Meade voices an old African story that bears directly on a large outline of our personal myth.

Meade relates a story of the abundant life on the African savannah. The major occupation of all who live there—animals, plants, tribes—is life and death. The herds at various times of the year are extremely plentiful. Lions especially love to hunt these herds in the tall grass by using a specific strategy: "they send the oldest and weakest member of the pride away from the hunting pack. Having lost most of its teeth, its roar is far greater than the others and much more threatening than its ability to bite. The old one goes off and settles in the grass on the other side of the herd where the hungry lions wait."[193]

Soon the herd moves in between the old lion and the fierce hunters. When the herd is startled by the terrifying roar of the old lion, many immediately begin to run from the source of the fear and directly into the gaping mouths of the young lions who kill what they need. "'Run towards the roar,' the old people used to tell the young ones. When faced with great danger, run towards the roaring, for there you will find safety and a way through."[194] One can hear the wisdom in the story, even the myth in the method; one paradoxically heads to what seems the greatest source of danger and escapes with one's life, but only if one has the courage to execute this risky move, one that challenges all energies of self-preservation with no credible warranty attached. To go against the natural instinct, to defy the logic that appears to govern the situation, is heroic in that it reveals an imagination that trumps instinctive responses that would normally get one killed.

- Think of what frightens you in life right now, something or someone that carries an intense fear for you.
- It could be a diagnosis, a person, an idea, an insight, a revelation, a situation, an uncertainty. Choose what is roaring at you right now.
- What might be a way of running at it? A ritual? A war cry? A physical act?
- Turn and face the roar.
- What will it take out of you to run at it, without reserve or caution?
- Write this out for yourself. Even writing about it is a form of running at it in a riting ritual.
- Only you can decide whether the roaring you head towards is fangless or saber-toothed.

---

193 Michael Meade, *The World Behind the World: Living at the Ends of Time* (Seattle: Greenfire Press, 2008), p. 3.

194 Meade, *The World Behind the World*, p. 4.

- What is the consequence of running at the roar?
- Regardless of the outcome, are you better off for having run at it?
- The roar is the Other in you that saps your energy. Have you gained some of that energy, even courage, back from having taken a run at the roar?
- Are there other Others roaring at you that you might want to consider giving a run for its roaring money?
- List one or two Others, regardless of whether you want to go towards them now.

Writer's Response

The roar for me is being alone. Alone would be without family. Alone would be without hugs. Alone would be without friends. Alone would be in sickness. Alone would be in death. Alone would be psychically and emotionally in a darkness. A fear I have is the feeling of being surrounded by water, on an island and alone. I can run at this aloneness. I can run at friendlessness, lovelessness, sickness alone, and death alone. I can run in it with as much courage as I had when I declared at the age of 19 to my shrink, "I want to be an interesting old lady and to be an interesting old lady I know I will need to have problems." So here is another problem.

Other problems of my life I ran towards: a father's betrayal with my money and losing my college money. I got to school. I earned three degrees on my own. A brutal husband who abused me and who for a time broke my spirit. I left him. I faced those problems and survived them. I've flourished in spite of them. And so I may be alone now. What if this aloneness is a shadow on the wall and may not exist?

When I had a car accident two weeks ago I was in the hospital and told my friend that I felt it was okay, if I had died, I was ready. She said, to me, "I'm not ready to lose you." That day I felt such love. My students love me and I love them. My family's love for me I can feel. So why do I feel alone? This is a feeling that I felt before and now it seems to be stronger than at any other time of my life. Is this another problem to face to become an interesting old lady? Is this just one more road, the last road, the road that was always there? Is this instead a whimper from my soul in the water not abandoned but nurtured and I can't see it? I am not alone. I am denying my soul's existence every time I say I am alone. It is a toothless roar that means that nothing is and never was there. It is a shadow without form and teeth. I'm not alone. It is one more leap towards the light that I can make. It is my leap of faith that I'm not alone. It's a leap that there is no roar and the lion has no teeth. It is an act of grace in itself believing that this is so. (Joan Canby)

Writing Meditation: Sword and Shield for the Other

> For it is one of the typical qualities of a myth to fabulate, to assert the unusual, the extraordinary, and even the impossible.[195]

> I prefer to think of 'Self' less as an entity and more as a kind of awareness in process.[196]

Our last meditation on Otherness begins with two quotes, one pulling us toward a further understanding of myth and the other toward self as a narrative identity in motion, like the plot of a story. In our life story are dragons, beasts, gargoyles of monstrous shapes and devious and torqued proportions that we, as warriors in our own right, move *to* and retreat *from*.

Two instruments that we carry with us most of the time, often hardly visible but no less tangible when called upon, are a sword and a shield. We use the sword to attack the Other when we feel invaded or put upon and need to aggressively protect what is valid and valuable that comprises our personal myth. The shield, however, is what we slip behind when away from home and use to ward off or deflect what we have judged to be threatening. So sword and shield are two instruments we may have learned not to leave home without.

Let us end this chapter by imagining a couple of things about sword and shield. First of all they are not blank, throw-aways but integral parts of our equipment for dealing with life's wayward moments. Imagine your sword and shield; instead of writing about them, draw or sketch them:

- Draw your sword using crayons, pastels or pen and pencil. Having color in them might vitalize them in a more intense way.
- Give yourself plenty of space to sketch the sword and make it large enough to be able to inscribe on its blade or handle what the sword's name is and what its motto is.
- Choose one or both of these inscriptions, but what you inscribe on it is an expression as outward gesture of your personal myth. What is it that your myth needs to say?
- Make it as embellished as you wish, keeping in mind the great archetypal image of Excalibur, King Arthur's famous sword in the Medieval epic of the Round Table.

195 C. G. Jung, "The Origin of Myth," in *Jung on Mythology*, edited by Robert A. Segal (Princeton, N.J.: Princeton University Press, 1998), p. 73.

196 Paul John Eakin, *How Our Lives Become Stories: Making Selves* (Ithaca, N.Y.: Cornell University Press, 1999), p. 40.

- When you have finished crafting and embellishing your sword, turn to your shield.
- What is its shape? How big must it be to protect you? What coverage do you require in order to feel safe when attacked by deflecting the negative energy from you?
- Draw on the shield words, images, scenes, as with Achilles' great shield crafted by Hephaestus for the Greek warrior at Troy and described in Homer's Iliad.
- What words might the shield have emblazoned on it as a protective talisman?
- What images do you want to face the world with when it becomes hostile or pushes against your space in it?
- When you have finished, record how you wish to use the sword. In what life situation, real or imagined, even remembered, might it be necessary to unsheathe it?
- The shield might have many uses currently as something that you can hold up between you and the world as a buffer or as something that deflects, to buy you time to find an appropriate strategy.
- Describe the situation that you feel a need to be protected from in order to deflect it from yourself.
- Would there be any situations that normally call for either sword or shield or both that you might be willing to set down both instruments in favor of another way of confronting these situations?
- Describe them.

Writing Meditation: A Ritual of Unlearning

And the string of his bow will have forgotten to whir![197]

My thoughts are not myself. My thoughts are exactly like things of the world, alive and dead. Thoughts grow in me like a forest, populated by many different animals.[198]

Generally, our trajectory in life is towards further learning, understanding, and grasping the new to encourage our own development. One might say that unlearning something is yet another form of knowing, but it has a different feel to it. The soul needs to let certain ideas, attitudes, points of view, or perspectives go by the roadside in life; it is like an uncoiling of

---

197 Friedrich Nietzsche, *Thus Spoke Zarathustra*, trans. Clancy Martin (New York: Barnes and Noble Classics, 2005), p. 13.

198 C. G. Jung, *The Red Book: Liber Novus*, ed. Sonu Shamdasani, trans. Mark Kyburz, John Peck, and Sonu Shamdasani (New York: W. W. Norton, 2009), p. 250.

something that no longer serves the good in you. Only you can finally discern when it is the right time for relinquishing a learned response by unlearning it and letting the knotted rope fall from one's waist. But to do so is to allow the self (1) to be consciously open to the Other; (2) so that new knowledge can grow from it (3). C. G. Jung writes that in the numerology of the ancient Greeks, the number three is "the first that is uneven and perfect, because in it we first find beginning, middle and end."[199] His observation shows us that without a risk, without a meeting of the Other that is us, we will not reach the revelatory new Unity of the third. We remain stuck in the 1-2 punch of our own ignorance.

Here we will work to describe one quality, characteristic, idea, or image of self or other that it is time to unlearn. For example, one might think of unlearning:

- Being angry too quickly or at all.
- Dependency on others for how s/he feels.
- Speed, acceleration, replaced by an openness to the slowness of life's events.
- Morbid thoughts, destructive ideas about self or others, or feelings of remorse or guilt that are decades old with long expired shelf life dates.
- Something not serving you as it did but is still collecting rent from you on a daily or annual basis.

We could ask: what is it that unlearning might afford or offer you? You might consider as well what moved you to choose what you brought up to unlearn.

Writers' Responses

1. I want to unlearn the desire for perfection. It steps in the way of expanding and progressing my knowledge and abilities. I feel a stronger energy accomplishing something I didn't expect to than the negative energy I feel failing something I thought I could conquer easily. (Brandon Chasse)

---

199 C. G. Jung, *Psychology and Religion: West and East*, vol. 11 of *The Collected Works of C. G. Jung*, ed. and trans. Gerhard Adler and R. F. C. Hull (Princeton, N.J.: Princeton University Press, 1977), ¶ 179.

2. I shall unlearn unworthiness and powerlessness. I am not Eve, the downfall of mankind. I am Eve, she who braved to taste the fruit of knowledge. I am not cut from my family cloth, but a strong pattern that is woven through the fabric of all of existence. I let go of my belief in limitation. I renounce any belief in my lack of value. I am beloved and powerful beyond measure simply because I am here. I want to unlearn anything that contradicts this truth. (Robin Miller)

3. I want to unlearn DEPENDENCE, on knowing my fixed destination or fixed course; as if I were assigned to air-traffic controllers and THEY delegated where journeys begin and end. These controllers determined the flight patterns of others without any human contact. I want to UNLEARN being subject to the subordination set up by other forces I cannot see or measure, nor be restricted by textbook prohibitions. (Beth Ellen Jack)

4. I want to unlearn that I have to steal myself away, to hoard my light for fear of depletion or darkness. I want to unlearn I'm a tray of hors d'oeuvres devoured at a party. I want to unlearn "not enough" loss limit, or lack. I want to unlearn scarcity and poverty, that empty is an end and not a beginning. I want to unlearn that life is merely survival, rushing to and fro with urgent desperation—to be late, always on time, but never fully arriving. (Brian Dietrich)

5. I want to unlearn the habit of dam building. I have always feared going fast, following the river freely or far. A dam built on older dams, and as those fail I am like a frenetic beaver, fearful of the flow and of the fraternity needed for destruction. (Sarah Sethofer)

8

RITING THE SPIRITUAL SELF

> Where earlier psychology tried to see through religion for its psychopathological content, we are now trying to see through psychopathology for its religious content.[200]

> No science will ever replace myth, and a myth cannot be made out of any science. For it is not that "God" is a myth, but that myth is a revelation of a divine life in man.[201]

We will use this chapter heading to explore a number of ways in which the mystical impulse or desire in each of us finds multitudinous manifestations. The language of today is that people are moving from being religious to embracing spiritual dimensions or qualities of their being that can be lived daily. I take this split or diversion in the road to suggest that rather than organized religion as one's basis for prayer, worship, meditation, and rituals, more people are discovering that having services in one another's homes in groups of 4 or 14 instead of belonging to a local parish or a multi-thousand mega-church, is more conducive to spiritual reflection and interior deepening. Others have joined religions from other parts of the world. Still others are happy with their particular day of worship in large numbers in a formal congregation.

A recent three-part series, *Religion in America,* on *Frontline,* revealed the history of religion as basic to our founding as a nation and that, in spite of the often-heralded "separation of church and state," such a split has not deterred a marriage between religion and politics in America. It also related the immense diversity in the city of Los Angeles, which hosts multiple mosques, temples, shrines and other buildings of worship that together allow diversity in religious expression by the hundreds, if not thousands of mutations today.

Still others prefer the tranquility of yoga classes, communing in nature through walks, hikes, or camping, while others have developed meditation techniques as well as reviving the

---

200 James Hillman, *Re-Visioning Psychology* (1975; repr., New York: HarperPerennial, 1992), p. 106.

201 C. G. Jung, *Memories, Dreams, Reflections*, trans. Richard and Clara Winston, ed. Aniela Jaffé (New York: Pantheon Books, 1963), p. 340.

ancient practice of *Lectio Divina* where one meditates on a single word in a passage from scripture, a poem, a sermon or other religious texts in order to imagine into it more deeply. The increasing popularity of "Twelve Step" Programs to give those addicted to substances or behaviors, or those individuals who live or have lived with addicted individuals a community of support with a strong spiritual baseline. For many, joining such groups has led to a profound spiritual awakening. Clearly, we have as a culture entered a period of intense pluralism in the way we imagine and communicate with the transcendent or the immanent nature of the divine, the Sacred Other, both feminine and masculine presences, or those mysterious presences of life that echo a deeper, more universal, or more inspiring manifestation that offers people measures of solace, solitude and serenity. All of the above are threaded deeply into our personal myth and are thus worth exploring in writing meditations.

Joseph Campbell beautifully expresses this deep connection between myth and a sense of spiritual participation when he notes that "A mythologically-grounded culture presents you with symbols that immediately evoke your participation: they are all vital, living connections and so they link you both to the underlying mystery and to the culture itself.[202] The popular mythologist is important in this chapter for another reason. So influenced was he by Indian thought, especially that of Ananda Coomaraswamy, that he built his mythic edifice in part from the latter's contemplations, among which is this observation by Coomaraswamy: "the various cultures of mankind are no more than the dialects of one and the same spiritual language."[203]

Another persuasive writer on this enigmatic topic of spirituality is Evelyn Underhill, whose work, *Mysticism* written in 1922, is a magnificent account of the mystic and his/her relation to the poet. She also wrote a shorter version of this large text, *Practical Mysticism*, in which she observes: "to give up one's own comfortably upholstered universe" is the task of the artist, the poet and the mystic. She goes on to affirm that "like animals, the mystic and poet strive for a directness of apprehension which we have lost. The terrier gets and

---

202 Joseph Campbell, *Pathways to Bliss: Mythology and Personal Transformation* (Novato, Calif.: New World Library, 2004), p. 4.

203 Joseph Campbell, *The Flight of the Wild Gander: Explorations in the Mythological Dimension: Selected Essays, 1944-1968* (Novato: New World Library, 2002), p. 34.

responds to the real smell, not a notion or a name."[204] I want us in part to entertain the camaraderie between the mystic impulse and poetic logic, for together they offer many insights into the spiritual dimension of our being. Let me offer this literary example of a writer dear to Joseph Campbell, me and perhaps you.

In one of several works on the poet James Joyce, Campbell writes of a moment in *A Portrait of the Artist as a Young Man* experienced by young university student in Dublin, Stephen Dedalus. One day Stephen is walking along a beach in his customary introspective solitude, when he notices ahead of him a woman knee-deep in the waters of the strand, her skirt hiked up to reveal her bare legs. He also notices in the same instant that "Her bosom was as a bird's soft and slight, slight and soft as the breast of some dark plumaged dove. . . . Heavenly God! Cried Stephen's soul, in an outburst of profane joy."[205] He is pulled immediately out of his solitary musings to gaze at such a wondrous sight. Joyce coins a term for this instant of revelation in the young man's life, which easily extends into any of our experiences that captures a similar moment of awakening: "esthetic arrest."[206] Campbell goes on to describe its significance in the passage from Joyce's novel: "It is an eternal moment. . . . What he sees is not simply a lovely girl, but a ray of light of eternity. It opens his third eye (his inward eye); the world drops back a dimension; his life is now committed to this seizure."[207]

The life of vital spirit seems to be a calling, a vocation, a bringing or coaxing out of oneself to something grander, more mysterious, more satisfying in the quest. Spiritual journeys, pilgrimages and voyages are all indeed quests for what may never be attained. But this is hardly reason not to push off from the shore to spiritual recovery and renewal and to pursue the pilgrimage with all the depth and amplification that one can muster.

---

204 Evelyn Underhill, *Practical Mysticism: A Little Book for Normal People and Abba: Meditations on the Lord's Prayer* (New York: Random House, 2003), p. 27. For a more involved discussion, see her extended exploration, *Mysticism: A Study in the Nature and Development of Man's Spiritual Consciousness*, 12th ed. (1922; repr., London: Methuen and Co., 1930).

205 James Joyce, *Dubliners, A Portrait of the Artist as a Young Man, Chamber Music* (New York: Random House, 1992), p. 321.

206 Joseph Campbell, *Mythic Worlds, Modern Words: On the Art of James Joyce*, ed. Edmund L. Epstein (Novato, Calif.: New World Library, 2003), p. 42.

207 Campbell, *Mythic Worlds, Modern Words*, p. 40.

The poet Rainer Maria Rilke offers us one of the most economical poems that renders a calling to a spiritual life, to open the heart to the mystery of one's own being:

Sometimes a Man Stands Up During Supper

Sometimes a man stands up during supper
and walks outdoors, and keeps on walking,
because of a church that stands somewhere in the East.
And his children say blessings on him as if he were dead.
And another man, who remains inside his own house,
dies there, inside the dishes and in the glasses,
so that his children have to go far out into the world
toward that same church, which he forgot.[208]

An important dimension in the life of spirit, the mystical impulse, gathers around being called, or called forth, or called to. It can be a blessing and often insists on one being dislocated from the normative and familiar, perhaps even being bloodied a bit in the process. Some initiation is inevitable. James Hillman observes that "a pathologized awareness is fundamental to the sense of individuality."[209] Such a pathological state or condition is often the genesis of a spiritual quest for the wholeness waiting to be discovered deep in the Self.

Writing Meditation: Your Church in the East

No one's center is like someone else's. Find your own center, not the center of your neighbor; not the center of your father or mother or family or ancestor but that center which is yours and yours alone.[210]

---

208 Rainer Maria Rilke, "Sometimes a Man Stands Up During Supper," in *A Rag and Bone Shop of the Heart*, ed. Robert Bly, James Hillman, and Michael Meade (New York: HarperCollins, 1992), p. 60.

209 Hillman, *Re-Visioning Psychology*, p. 112.

210 Malidoma Patrice Somé, *Of Water and the Spirit: Ritual, Magic, and Initiation in the Life of an African Shaman* (New York: Penguin Books, 1994), p. 199. I am indebted to Dr. Sandra Easter of Pacifica Graduate Institute for revealing this source to me.

- Return to Rilke's poem above. Read it aloud to yourself once or twice.
- As we have done in a previous chapter where poems were used as evocative methods to stir the imagination, let the poem work on you. Be receptive to what it wants you to notice both in its setting and in its action.
- It is, as you see, a poem contrasting two ways that one may respond to the call of spirit. Something in the world wants us, goads us and offers us an opportunity to move into the unfamiliar terrain where the rules of engagement are not quite as clear as those we have learned or manufactured to plod through the more repetitive landscape of our lives.
- You might want to speculate, who you most feel your life has copied: the first or the second man, or one of the children of either one.
- You can assume the persona of either one of the children or one of the men, or both.
- What, finally, might you identify as your church in the East, traditionally the direction of a new day, new life, and rebirth?
- Describe your church in the East and offer a narrative of when you were called and under what circumstances.
- Have there been several churches that have called you, that were so engaging that you stepped from the table of your daily life and journeyed outdoors to pursue it?
- What have been the consequences of such a road taken rather than refused?
- On the other hand, have you heard the calling and refused it, said "no, not right now, I'm busy" to the church in the East?
- Regrets? The right move then? Your current mantra?

This calling is so important to meditate on; it is the voice of talent, the vocative call of Life, of Divinity, of the deeper Self, that is uncertain how often it might knock on your door and call you: "Call me Ready" or "Call me back later."

Writers' Responses

Sometimes A Man Stands Up During Supper and . . .

It's "as if" I were reaching to open the door at Seven-Eleven on Royal Lane when the tall, black man opened it for me. I was overcome with the realization that "this was not right." My mother, a lovely Christian woman, daughter of a sharecropper family, taught me never to meet the eyes of a black man. But she was wrong and today, as a young mother living in north Dallas, I looked him squarely in the eyes and said "thank you." He smiled.

That's the first time I can remember consciously rejecting something one of my parents taught me. Years before I sat in the pew listening to my father preach, thinking "that's the dumbest thing I've ever heard" but I was much too smart to say that, then or later. More than once in my life a thought has flashed before my eyes; I wondered what would happen if I just stood up and uttered those words, "that's the dumbest thing I've ever heard."

Some years ago I remember having a conversation with a minister whose speech patterns told me he would understand. My children were grown and now I sought Mike out for some counsel after he said to me in a discussion of some importance, "Marilyn, that just won't pass the smell test." That challenge so resonated with me that I shared my history of avoiding confrontation and he helped me chart a path through a legacy, one for which I was very grateful but could no longer acknowledge as *real* to me. His last words that day were, "you know Marilyn, you will make this walk alone." With these words embedded in my being, I took the first step and I've been walking ever since.

It's been true. Most of my early steps were solitary, but along the way my children, one at a time, have joined me. An occasional interaction with friends of 50 years surprises me, which brings me to the realization today that I'm not *leading* anyone. I never have that desire to speak out "that's the dumbest thing I've ever heard" but rather, for me, it just doesn't pass the smell test. So while it's true that I'm making this journey alone for the most part, I have so many grand epiphany experiences with those whom I encounter along the way, I no longer feel an obligation to correct or confront them. How does one argue with *smell?* (Participant, Dallas, Texas)

A Meditation on

"Sometimes a Man Stands Up During Supper"

My father stood up during supper

And walked outdoors seeking his Grail,

Walking west until he reached the Far East.

He didn't return for thirty years,

Confused to find the table empty but for faded dishes

Dusted with the faint echo of a dinner long cold.

I stayed behind, one of the dishes and the glasses

Discarded and forgotten at the table.

I sang my blessings in a thin solo

As my siblings looked on in shattered silence.

I wanted to go too.

Fourteen years later,

Hearing and heeding the cry of a gasping soul

Like my father before me, I stood up during supper and walked away,

Leaving behind the dishes and glasses of a marriage.

Three score year and six into my journey

I've heeded that cry several times,

Once walking east from LA to DC,

And again, acquiescing to Eileithyia's[211] edict, to become a midwife,

Now I've stood up and walked away from supper again.

As I listen intently for the mandate in this cry,

I hear a faint chorus.

Could that be the echo of twenty-five hundred children singing blessings?

(Elizabeth Fairchild)

3 Years of Rites

Meditation on Rilke's poem

"Sometimes a Man Stands Up During Supper"

That walking out

that keeping on a straight line to the East

is a very masculine journey.

That heroism thrills the children, elevates their sight,

encourages them on; and if he cannot stand up spiritually, becomes inert, and dies,

---

211 Eileithyia is the Greek goddess of childbirth.

they mourn without knowing why, carry discouragement.

But the feminine walking out is mostly spiraling out,

curving round to clean the dishes and making many, many suppers, nourishing the walkers as she widens the circles of her path, a labyrinth to the East.

And her children are glad, blessed, when she doesn't sit still in the center, becoming a spider to them.

The danger for our masculine side is wandering off

when walking out

and for our feminine side to walk in a closed circle. (pcraig, Dallas, Texas)

Writing Meditation: Altaring the Spirit, Altering a Life

I had the feeling that I was caught in the middle of a vast intelligence, something that knew I was there and wanted to do something to me. I was still holding on to the bundle of light as well as to my own sense of being fully conscious and physically present in this strange world.[212]

What the African writer Malidoma Somé captures in his experience of a ritual that takes him to another realm are the words "vast intelligence." Rituals like the one he has entered through his tribe increase awareness and stimulate a connective tissue between self and other, especially with the living and the ancestral dead. Rituals have the power to make the past dramatically and psychically present through their enactments. They harbor within themselves an aesthetic which can, in ritual "bind together an object and a value in affect" such that something of a spiritual and aesthetic sense congeal in ritual.[213] The ritual behaves as a mystical spiral that links the now with an eternal present that might be termed spiritual in design and permanent in its consequences.

Creating an altar is one way to enact a presence that has power and propulsion in that it can propel an individual or a community into another dimension of awareness and

---

212 Somé, *Of Water and the Spirit*, p. 244.

213 Robert Plant Armstrong, *The Powers of Presence: Consciousness, Myth, and Affecting Presence* (Philadelphia: University of Pennsylvania Press, 1981), p. 20.

sensibility. A ritual like creating an altar in your study, bedroom, or living room is an aesethetic/spiritual activity that gathers power in its performance.[214] In such a ritual performance, what was profane can be altered into the sacred. Creating an altar is nothing short of a ritual founding. Mircea Eliade believes that "every sacred space implies a hierophany, an irruption of the sacred that results in detaching a territory from the surrounding cosmic milieu and making it qualitatively different."[215] To create sacred space as a ritual site in your own home is, as Eliade further believes, to become aware that "sacred space reveals an absolute reality and makes orientation possible."[216] Such a ritual draws out the presence of something that matters to you, makes it more conscious and thereby adds a mythic dimension to your life by means of it. Not only its memory but its mattered presence are brought into a formal relation with your daily life, markedly enriching it.

In my own experience of constructing an altar 8-9 years ago, and then adding to it over time, attending it, cleaning it of incense ash, dusting the figures, maintaining its spiritual field in my study where I can see it when I sit here typing, provides me great solace and a solid compass bearing. My felt experience is that this space, which is the top flat surface of a low bookshelf, provides an energy field from which emanates not only the spiraling smoke from incense sticks, but a powerful vigorous constellation from the figures, dirt and stone gathered from many countries of the world as well as gifts from several important people in my life. While I have listed some of the contents earlier, I want to return to them in a moment.

The structure and contents of my altar have their own coherence that I did not work out beforehand; it is just there, present and powerful with its own melody not created consciously by me. One writer suggests in his discussion of quantum fields, that "coherence establishes communication; the better the coherence, the finer the telephone network and the more refined wave patterns have a phone."[217] In the flow of communication that is a consequence of this ritual altar that alters, it makes present both coherence and joy. Happiness, suggests another writer, "comes out of an inner harmony, not on controls we

---

214 Armstrong, *The Powers of Presence*, p. 11.

215 Mircea Eliade, *The Sacred and the Profane: The Nature of Religion,* trans. Willard Trask (San Diego: Harvest Books, 1987), p. 26.

216 Eliade, *The Sacred and The Profane*, p. 30.

217 Lynne McTaggart, *The Field: The Quest for the Secret Force of the Universe* (New York: HarperCollins, 2002), p. 43.

exert over great forces of the universe."[218] Going with rather than pushing against comprise a part of the ritual action of altar creation that can be as simple or complex as your own soul dictates.

In her own work with other women, depth psychologist Sandra Easter writes that "Holding the chaos and complexity of the dynamic relationship, it [the altar] serves as a ritual container where the relationship between us can be opened and closed."[219] One can hear the energy present in her astute observation: to hold the chaos and complexity of energies in an equilibrium witnesses how the energy field of the altar is poignant and provocative. I suggest that such a construction creates within one's intimate lived space a spiritual-symbolic field of force that exposes one to the vast energy fields of the created world. So let us try our hand at constructing an altar as part of unfolding our personal myth.

Just to give you an idea, if this perspective is new for you. I mentioned earlier in this book that my own altar is comprised of little statues from religious and mythic traditions in many parts of the world; dirt from sacred sites in Ireland and various parts of Texas that have special meaning for me; rocks with labyrinths, faces, and designs on them; prehistoric fossils millions of years old; two stones I pocketed from a visit to the Third Reich's constructed Terezin Ghetto 40 kilometers north of Prague in the Czech Republic; gifts from various folks who mean a great deal to me; incense burners and sticks of incense I burn when I write; feathers picked up on my travels from fields, roadsides, our 5 acre forest behind our home; shells from beaches up and down the California coast, the south Texas coastline and two sites in the Caribbean. Things like that. The only criterion is that they mean and hold special value for you and in some mysterious way both comment on your history as well as complete who you are.

- You can design an altar or draw it or write it out—whichever works for you.
- What mementoes are important that you have tucked into drawers, that you carry with you or are meaningful objects from special moments in your life?
- What is it about these specific items you want to hang on to, to treasure, by ritualizing their presence on your altar?

---

218 Mihaly Csikszentmihalyi, *Flow: The Psychology of Optimal Experience* (New York: HarperPerennial, 1999), p. 7.

219 Sandra Easter, "Beyond Biography: Mending the Ancestral Web" (Ph.D. dissertation., Pacifica Graduate Institute, 2011).

- How does being able to gaze at them individually and, just as importantly, within a field of meaningful objects, enhance their relevance?
- Think of each of these items as a memory vessel or reservoirs or container of energy that embraces something critical to your personal myth that you might feel less complete without.
- Consider how each of these items might be your connection to an ancestor, which could include the Earth herself, another person, another country, a place that continues to teach and instruct you, or a pet you no longer have.
- Look at how you might place these items in relation to one another. Their juxtaposition actually inaugurates a story between them as well as a dialogue on these two moments of your history.
- How you arrange them is a mirror of an essential part of your interior landscape that your personal myth embodies.
- Notice too what you have decided to exclude from your altar; think of them as a sacrifice to the altar in their absence.
- Are you able to speculate on what you might add to the altar in the future, say a trip you are planning, or a person you are to visit after a long absence, for instance?
- Remain conscious of ways you might bring back with you something that would add further leavening and texture to your story, as a remembrance. It is something that, in its altering power, might aid your selection by making present what would fit into the contents of what your altar contains now.
- Finally, as you gaze on your altar's objects, either drawn in a notebook, written out, or actually compiled and arranged, do you see any flow to your story, any narrative to the objects that begins to link them in any patterned awareness? At times in our life we need objects to lead us to discern patterns hidden in plain view. Altars and rituals around them can evoke such relationships.

Writing Meditation: Surrender to What Cannot Be Known

> Myths form a bridge between the terrifying abyss of cosmological ignorance and our comfortable familiarity with our recurrent if tormenting human problems.[220]

The quote above by mythologist Wendy Doniger is from a fine book on myth that develops this large theme of intersection that myths gather around. My own response to her work is that the spiritual and the mythic are often more intimate than we might first consider.

---

220 Wendy Doniger, *The Implied Spider: Politics and Theology in Myth* (New York: Columbia University Press, 1998), p. 22.

Surrender can occur where two worlds intersect in a field of meaning that can be dramatic, though temporary, as well as profound, permanent and life-altering. Let's consider in a writing meditation some of these qualities within an act of surrender.

First Surrender

In some life circumstances, yielding to larger forces, presences, gods and goddesses, spiritual imperatives, or a transcendent mystery, is not giving up and in but more a behavior to accommodate life's imperatives that may take us beyond the rational and manageable. In this spirit:

- What have you surrendered to? Surrender here is meant as a giving over your entire self to a force or presence or imperative that insists on or invites relinquishment. What we surrender to is mythic on this scale.
- As a consequence of this surrender in your past, what has shifted in your life?
- If placed in the same position, and knowing what you know now, would you willingly yield to it again?
- When you surrendered, what in fact did you give up or sacrifice?
- Has the price tag been more-or-less what you expected at the time, or did you think of it at all?
- What attitude or disposition did you have to shift into and adopt before you were able to surrender?
- Thinking back on it, could the act of surrendering have been at the same time an assertion of something that had been hidden underground?
- It is possible to surrender to not knowing, or not controlling or not managing. What is it you gave yourself over to?
- Did the surrender lead to a deeper mystery, a further confusion, and/or a moment of clarity and certainty about something in your life?
- Did you lose something of yourself, either temporarily or permanently, as a result of the surrender?
- Are you in a place in your life now where that particular surrender is no longer necessary? Did surrendering to it at the time put you in a place that would be unnecessary now?

Second Surrender

- What now in your life have you surrendered to?
- Describe as best you can what its terms are or were.
- Could you shift in your life what you once in your past surrendered to and what you are now surrendering to? Are they interchangeable?

- What parts of your over-all narrative do these two surrenders speak to and about?
- By reflecting on both of them, do you discern any pattern or awareness that is part of both of them, that ties them both into a spider web of a unified narrative?

Writer's Response

Mother Mercy

The pillar of mother Mary Herself has been removed,
The church has fallen and with it, the angels.
The lutes and harps of heaven are silent,
The Child never lived here.
The silence is deafening in the cold darkness that never knew love.
Mother Earth has tipped to father sky and all falls into nothing,
A barren field of no dreams only the toil of forgotten passions swept away by an icy wind.
Oh to return to the Ocean which knew no boundaries,
And escape this desert wasteland of lovelessness. (Gabriel Hilmar)

Writing Meditation: Imagining Your Own Death

> Being aware of one's mortality and conscious of one's death takes a person beyond the ego's concept of time as an endless resource. . . . It opens the heart to value existence in a new way.[221]

Even speaking about death makes most people queasy in a culture that generally denies death by keeping its reality hidden, veiled and on the sidelines. What is most inevitable becomes most intolerant for conversation in many households. The death that we imagine, however, is with us all the time. I would say that every waking moment, when it becomes conscious of itself, carries the penumbra of our mortal limits. As such, death is a mythic

---

221 David G. R. Keller, *Oasis of Wisdom: The Worlds of the Desert Fathers and Mothers* (Collegeville, Minn.: Liturgical Press, 1993), p. 73.

announcement and a mythic activity, even as we make great efforts not to let it happen any time soon.

Not long ago, my wife suffered a severe stroke early one August morning. After I found her in the hallway losing consciousness, then calling 911 while our older son rushed out into the night to stand in the street with a flashlight to guide the EMS vehicle to our front door, I held her under the crushing reality that she might die in my arms. Death visits, intrudes, announces itself, abducts, holds us hostage and is, finally, the last visitor in our lives. To ignore it while working on meditations on personal myth would be beyond naïve because it would side-step the completion of our cycle on earth.

Prepare for death as we can, I am not sure how successful most people are in their preparatory minds when the reality knocks suddenly and pulls our front door from its hinges.

Presently my wife is recovering, both in physical movement and in speech; Death now roams the hallways and bedrooms of our home as a guest we do not want to ask to depart, yet feel uncomfortable because we are not more clearly fated to its Presence. So be it. When we read Emily Dickinson's immortal poem on mortality as undergraduates or later in life, we are made aware that it is memorable beyond so many other creative works on the subject:

712

Because I could not stop for Death—
He kindly stopped for me—
The Carriage held but just Ourselves—
And Immortality.

We slowly drove—He knew no haste
And I had put away
My labor and my leisure too,
For his Civility—

. . .

We paused before a House that seemed
a Swelling of the Ground—
the Roof was scarcely visible—
the Cornice—in the Ground—[222]

Courteous, inevitable, polite, permanent, unhurried: Death carries all these qualities. To mark our passing we have invented an epitaph to be carved on the stone or a mausoleum or on the casings of our ashes as our final words, our last script. The ritual of mourning is the last rite of passage to mark our transport from the living to the dead. For many souls, it is the most mythically alive moment of their existence.

- In imagining your own death, what is it you wish to have carved or engraved or most remembered as some quality or belief or saying that you used or was used about you by others? It is often composed of a short phrase or sentence that gathers up who one is into a single sentence or phrase. What is that single sentence or phrase you wish to mark you life?
- If appropriate, what is it you would like buried with you? What mementoes, journals, CDs, poetry, writing, gifts from others you wish to accompany you in this crossing?
- What is to be destroyed at your death? Anything you left behind until your death that you wish to be annihilated at this moment?
- What do you wish to be said at your death? If you were reading your own life description, what might it say? Write it out now.
- If cremated, where do you wish your ashes to be scattered, buried, strewn, or preserved in a vessel?
- If you could choose where to be buried, where would it be?
- Is there a question you sought responses to in life that was never adequately answered? Can you state that question now?
- Any question is a form of a quest; what was it you quested after in life? That may give you a hint as to the question you pursued.
- Do you have a vision of the terrain and conditions after this life that you can give expression to?
- What is your fantasy, belief, conviction, hope, or desire in the next life? What might give you the greatest satisfaction in creating this reality you hope for?
- Within the realm of your spiritual life, what is the most important thing you said YES to in life?

---

222 Emily Dickinson, *Poems by Emily Dickinson*, ed. Mabel Loomis Todd and H. W. Higginson (Boston: Little, Brown and Co., 1912), p. 138.

- Contrarily, within the realm of spirit, what is the most important thing you said NO to in life?
- The last two are based on my assumption that the central questions, yeas and nays we pose to ourselves and the world, carry some important value of the contours of our personal myth.

Writing Meditation: Riting the Awakened Self

> We know a thing only by uniting with it, by assimilating it, by an interpenetration of it and ourselves. It gives itself to us just insofar as we give ourselves to it.[223]

There seems little doubt that we live in a time and place where our uniqueness and distinctiveness, even our autonomy, carry strong mytho-cultural values we are asked to emulate and strive for. Perhaps we are in a period that might be called the (r)age of the individual. In such a climate of self-absorption, it may be hard to imagine giving oneself over to something like what is outlined in Evelyn Underhill's perceptive observation above. Interpenetration rather than controlling mastery is a difficult concept if viewed within the cult of the individual. But it seems an essential interchange within the spiritual dimension of our being.

We live in a tension, then, between individual growth and a contrary impulse of giving over to something beyond us with such intensity that we penetrate its being as it penetrates ours. Such a mutual overlapping could be understood as a definition of love. As we get older and grasp more, an urge may grow in us to connect on a deeper level with others, including the natural world, the cultural frame we exist within, and the spiritual realm we may sense in tandem with our mortal limits. Perhaps you feel in yourself at this stage of your life an impulse of awakening, of loving on an entirely different level that is more encompassing and satisfying. It springs from a natural desire for what one writer calls "heartfelt knowing," another way of grasping a deeper form of love, which he describes as "a quality of being" rather than a function.[224] It is interested less in self-improvement than on expressions of gratitude.

---

223 Underhill, *Practical Mysticism*, p. 11.

224 Gerald G. May, *The Awakened Heart: Opening Yourself to the Love You Need* (New York: HarperCollins, 1993), p. 10.

Love awakens some qualities dormant in us and makes us feel a bit restless, a little ill-at-ease because we intuit at certain moments of our lives that something is absent, needing presence, to allow us to be more present to ourselves, others, and perhaps a divine source or origin from which we emanate. Variations on how this might be satisfied has led to a vast pluralism in spiritual practices, where, for example, engaging in one's work is now being referred to as a spiritual practice. The psychiatrist Lionel Corbett writes in a new book that psychotherapy itself is a spiritual practice. He further observes: "Essentially, our spirituality is our personal myth, our way of understanding the nature of things."[225] A friend of mine referred to his own teaching as his *ministry*. What I am witnessing is a new lexicon that I prefer to call mythic; our practices, both professional and personal, carry a mythic substructure that gifts our lives with a deeper meaning. Such is the power and presence that collects around awakening, which can be captured effectively in the ritual of writing.

- Do you or have you sensed an urge or impulse to connect with some power, force or presence beyond yourself that you might call spiritual?
- Can you return to the origin of that impulse, or what could be construed as a calling to what transcends you?
- In what way is it asking or insisting that you respond to it?
- What are its obligations that you sense in responding to it?
- Does it carry a wisdom that you feel a need and a desire to respond to?
- Is there a trust demanded of you that you might have to yield to before giving yourself over to this presence?
- If you choose to say no to this invitation, what do you imagine will be different in your life?
- If you choose to say yes to this invitation, what do you imagine will be different as a consequence?
- Does yielding to this calling frighten you, exhilarate you, excite you or evoke other emotional responses in you?

---

225 Lionel Corbett, *The Sacred Cauldron: Psychotherapy as a Spiritual Practice* (Wilmette, Ill.: Chiron Publications, 2011), p. 20.

Writers' Responses

There is a presence of the sacred within me that is evoked by literature, kindness, learning, flowers, true fellowship. This divinity has an energetic spirit, a sharing, loving soul, and a hopeful passion for people and learning. She's vibrant, people are attracted to her, she laughs, teaches, eats to her heart's content and judges not. This divinity allows me to lift outside of ordinary consciousness and see brighter lights, have better conversations, and feel less anxiety. She's here now, and she moves gracefully through my chaos.

Her sense of humor shines brightly. She's open-minded. She knows no fear. Yes, when she's with me, I'm alive, I'm EFFECTIVE, I create art and meaningful relationships, I have more clarity; yes there is divine consciousness—It's called beauty and love.

She embodies me through writing, literature, hearing, talking, learning. I feel her lightness, she tingles.

My other side suffocates her because she's worried about what others will think, she's different, lonely, beautiful, so I entrap myself, give myself chains, build a prison around myself. That prison has no purple flowers.

My Dark side. How do I see her as my friend? Addiction, fear, self-loathing. She loves pain, so laugh at her, tell her she's fooling herself, this is no white cottage Sarah.

You've changed already. Stay that way. Be true to your divinity, let GO of the fear, alone time is your friend, it's your medium,

The wind will blow it over, Jesus just kissed me on the cheek,

put his hand on my hair,

I will let it shine. (Sarah Colburn)

In childlike exuberance, I extend my arms in great affection to nature. In the drawing that emerged from my soul yesterday, I wanted to draw Mother Nature in the beauty of the evergreen. I see it and feel it in my communion with nature, in particular trees as they sway, dance, and greet me. In their many moods and seasons, they are constant. Mirroring this environment is the ocean, beside which I once lived. Heard her subtle rhythms at night as tide lapped the shore. In wild storm, the strong waves pounded down—and other times tranquil as a pool. She reflected my myriad moods. I walked with her as I walked my dog each morning and night, spiraling through sunsets and rises, and star-strewn skies. She accompanied me. Creatures, warm and brown, eyes glistening, aware of life, alive in the present moment. My sweet dog, Abby, the sea lion heads that pop up from the ocean surface, curious and spontaneous. The wide-eyed doe and her fawns with huge ears and eyes that see and hear me, and stand like a statue, then relax and know I mean no harm. I am connected to the creatures, and to the trees, and to the ocean—and their spirit finds its way back to me. We are One. In a sense, I embrace myself in a joyous reunion, pure love, all accepting and eternal. My drawing of Mother tree turns out to look strangely similar to me. Her branches reach out to nurture me and I reach back in childlike awe——a Divine connection. (Natalie Larkin)

The numinous Other is invoked as I shed my persona

shoes, jewelry, clothes

And step down into the temenos I have consecrated over 20 years

A simple, partially enclosed hot tub

Rented by the hour, on a hillside

With a view of trees, sunset, mountains, lake, city,

The occasional voice of coyotes,

The scent of sage and pine,

And frequent moonset.

This is my sacred place, my chapel,

Holding Fire, Water, Earth, and Air

A womb of safety, comfort and rest.

The submerged body shivers and sighs

As that heat envelops and enters the cells

Then, in and through

Silence

Song

Movement

Stillness

The Goddess and The God are present.

What flows from this rite

Is an Embodied Divine Presence.

Spacious and trusting,

I know what I did not know,

did not want to know,

or have forgotten

Because I am with Those who can encompass me

And I, like Rilke's "She"

Stretch beyond what limits me to hold Them. (Marilyn J. Owen)

Writing Meditation: The Central Question

Living one's myth doesn't mean living *one* myth. It means that one lives *myth*; it *means mythical living.*[226]

Within the mystic spiral, a geometry that many cultures and civilizations of the past have venerated as a powerful universal symbol for life itself, there may develop in each of us a fundamental question that guides or goads our quest in life. I call it the Central Question. It may stem from our past, come on us in moments of meditation, reading, or reflecting on our lives, or it can suddenly abrupt into our lives through the poignant fissures of an illness, the death of a loved one, an unexpected event that throws us out of the orbit of our daily lives into a reflective moment that takes us deep into our being's fundamental purpose.

I have witnessed in conversation with a friend questions suddenly crop up between us: "What is this all for? What is it pointing to? What is its purpose?" We may engage some possible responses or leave the question resting quietly in the calm pool of silent mystery. Nonetheless, the question itself is important to ask and to navigate through at several stages in our lives. If you have not thought about it, then this meditation might be a ripe occasion for you to ponder it. I bring back the spiral here because it is such a rich image of our lives recursively folding back on themselves without ever duplicating the past. As Jill Purce writes of it, "each winding marks a containment and a completed cycle in the development of the whole; but, as each is a part of the whole, the completion is also a beginning."[227]

---

226 Hillman, *Re-Visioning Psychology*, p. 158.

227 Jill Purce, *The Mystic Spiral: The Journey of the Soul* (London: Thames and Hudson, 1980), p. 15.

Let us then enter the tabernacle of the spiral we are currently moving around and entertain a few ideas that might lead into a question that is in the forefront of your mind or one that you may be formulating for the first time:

- What is my Truth?
- What is my Wisdom?
- Is it possible for me to learn and to trust more?
- What contribution can my Truth add to the world's Truths?
- What is my unique question that keeps me questing?
- What do I continue to or wish to begin to say NO to?
- What do I continue to or wish to say YES to?
- What other Central Question might I hear within myself or craft consciously to move me along this spiral of my life's curving trajectory?

The assumption at work here is that the Central Question I pose to myself and, by extension, the world, carries within it reverberations of my personal myth. The quote that begins this meditation suggests that this same myth may be multiple within a coherent unity so that we allow what might feel like others' myths, or fragments of this one, to become a part of the overall pattern or design of my myth. My personal myth is a patterned way of perceiving, purposing myself in the world and in plots of self-reflection.

Writing Meditation: Riting the Projected God

> These images of God that we erect and pray to are of a God fashioned out of what we need and what we wish for. . . . Our pictures of God come from longings still with us.[228]

Whether we practice a faith or belief in a God or Gods within a formal religious ritual or discover the divine, the sacred, the transcendent, in the world of matter, including human matters, perhaps we have a prayer life that allows us to address the Divine Other. This

---

228 Anne and Barry Ulanov, *Primary Speech: A Psychology of Prayer* (Atlanta: John Knox Press, 1982), p. 27.

source or sources may offer us great comfort at times of afflictions, suffering, loss, confusion, or the onslaught of destructive impulses towards self or others.

Within this prayer life we each have fashioned/discovered a form or image of divinity that suits us, works for us, and is perhaps borrowed from a long tradition. Or it may be a recent discovery that we find unique in part because it offers comfort when life pushes down on us or when we feel a deep gratitude for what has been given us. So this meditation carries two parts: one is the origin and development of this prayer life that you may have worked years to craft, or it may have been gifted to you in a moment of spiritual enlightenment. The other is the form or image or idea of divinity that you address in and through this way of imagining the sacred in your life and perhaps in all life. Let's begin with the prayer life quality you engage and foster:

Part I: The Form of Prayer Life

- When and if you pray, what form does it take? I think it can include singing, dancing, body movement along the rhythms of the larger world's rhythms, silence, stillness, walking and feeling gratitude, petitioning—the mutations are endless.
- Does your praying consist of wishes, desires, wants?
- As you reflect on it, what is the content of your prayer life?
- Has your prayer life changed over the years? Describe two of its major shifts.
- Does it continue to change even today? Have you found a form of praying or several forms that satisfy your life currently?
- What "benefits" have been gained from your prayer life? It may have nothing to do with acquisitions or relinquishments, though it might.
- What limitations do you currently feel about your way of praying, your method, your manner of prayer?
- Are you seeking another format for your prayer life?

Part II: Our God or Gods Images

To whom or to what we pray comprises the central question of the second part of this meditation:

- What form, shape, image, idea, emptiness does the divinity assume that we pray to? If none of the above applies, give your own response to the deity that resides within/without or both.
- What is the emotional, intellectual, embodied, imaginal experience that is offered to you in praying?

- Does praying change anything fundamentally? Is this communion more a felt sense with the sacred, in whatever form it takes, that you seek?
- What do you seek, hope for, wish to settle into when you pray to this transcendent/immanent presence?
- Would you use the word "mystical" to describe what the experience is like in these moments of prayer?
- Do you consider your ancestors or all the ancestors in any way divinities that can guide, mentor or teach you in this life?
- What "gifts" do you receive from this divinity?
- What "gifts" do you offer this divinity?
- Have you created any special place for these moments of prayerful meditation that helps to invite the divinity or divinities in?
- When you pray to your image of the divine, do you sense on a more palpable level the presence of mystery, the numinous, or the supernatural? I know these are big terms, but adjust their frequency to make sense of your own experience you struggle to describe.
- If for some reason, this force or presence that is elicited or honored in prayer were to disappear, what difference might it have on the way you live and on the values you hold?

Writer's Response

I'll start with Divine Consciousness. It exists. How else can I write to find out what I do not know? How else can I know when I write? I put the tip of my pen against the white of the paper and the lines become the container, holding my psyche, holding my spirit, keeping my body in a place, keeping all together, all present. This is creation. Is it my creation? With certainty. Am I the vessel, as I sit by the trickles of water from the fountain, shadows across the page outlining the edges of my hand, casting the sinewy spires of the palm tree that waves in the wind, occasionally brushing my body? Perhaps.

And if I am the vessel that connects the sound and the touch and the feel and the images and the words that flow, am I a soul container? I am not the sole soul who senses and who thinks. Within these lines, yes, but not within all lines that contain. The container, my container, our container is the presence of the Divine. The divine. The Divinity. That Divine consciousness, Knowing, that comes in the presence of water, that comes in the presence of shadow in the now of the moment of today. (Teri C.)

Writing Meditation: Riting into the Numinous

> It is altogether amazing how little most people reflect on numinous objects and attempt to come to terms with them, and how laborious such an undertaking is once we have embarked upon it.[229]

> Too few people have experienced the divine image as the innermost possession of their own souls. Christ only meets them from without, never from within the soul.[230]

I want to use both quotes above from the *Collected Works of C. G. Jung* to highlight the terms of this meditation, which follows closely and may even overlap some with the preceding one. The numinous is sacred space, sacred mystery, sacred energy and powerful presences that all implicate the mythic realm of being. Myths and the numinous are both meaning-engendering and meaning-intensifying moments of heightened awareness of what is invisible but palpable, not measured in the quantitative sense but mean something essential mytho-spiritually.

Whether we had the language for the experience, we all have moments of numinous presence, of the mysterious sacred that can hit us like a lightning bolt, as it did Saul as he rode toward Damascus in pursuit of further Christian persecutions, or it can descend on us as illness, as a terrible crippling accident, or as a financial collapse in our own economic lives; it can also appear as a profound stillness, or a subtle whisper when we suddenly become aware of what has been hidden. The numinous in whatever form has the capacity to dramatically alter our lives and thrust us into greater depth and reflective knowing.

The numinous is not, strictly speaking, an outside event but an inside manifestation, an experience of sudden awareness, a revelation, a shock of recognition that affects us to the core of our mythic being. It can be delivered to us as an idea, an image, an event, a story, a dream, a revelation, or something overheard, that transforms us on the spot. We may sense

---

229 C. G. Jung, *Psychology and Religion: West and East*, vol. 11 of *The Collected Works of C. G. Jung*, ed. and trans. Gerhard Adler and R. F. C. Hull (Princeton, N.J.: Princeton University Press, 1977), ¶ 735.

230 C. G. Jung, *Psychology and Alchemy*, vol. 12 of *The Collected Works of C. G. Jung*, second edition, eds. Herbert Read, Michael Fordham, and Gerhard Adler, trans. R. F. C. Hull (Princeton, N.J.: Princeton University Press, 1974), ¶ 12.

in this instance a new pattern arise in us that enshrouds the world in new apparel with an intensity that we have never felt before. It may feel at first very impersonal and "out there," but transmit at the same time a fierce energy that invades us "in here" with a force that refigures our vision of the world and ourselves.

In addition, a numinous experience may be a moment of contact with something that we feel a need, later, to write about, to paint, to dance, so to give it a form that we can revert to in moments that call for a need to renew it. Various writings of mystics attest to this moment that often conveys with it a sense of sublime unity, a delicious sagacity of both atonement and at-oneness with some presence or energy much larger than ourselves and yet shockingly familiar, even intimate. Some habit or series of routine ways of thinking and behaving are suddenly dismantled, replaced by a new vision of yourself and life generally. This moment when something breaks through has been called by one writer a "core experience," that can be so severe as to "lead one to fall out of one's myth."[231]

In the crevasse created by this breakdown into newness, a new myth may begin to take shape to affect even the style of our imaginings and the behaviors that used to be part of our somatic lexicon. We begin to imagine the world's terms differently, with a new-found openness and largesse. Gerald May calls this spiritual awakening a "unitive experience." In it, "one feels suddenly 'swept up' by life, 'caught' in a suspended moment where time seems to stand still and awareness peaks in both of its dimensions."[232]

I have experienced such an instance of the intrusion of the numinous while traveling in other countries and visiting sacred sites, while walking through the Terezin Ghetto north of Prague, in a monastery in Kentucky, while walking in the woods or hiking in the mountains, in reading a powerful classic work of literature, or poems that stir this dimension of consciousness, at the births of my sons, at a religious ceremony in a cathedral or church, in the presence of certain music, at a ritual where I or others were being initiated, or alone sitting deep in a kiva early in the morning in a Native American tribal land in Utah or New Mexico. These moments imbed themselves into the fabric of my story and become so

---

231 D. Stephenson Bond, *Living Myth: Personal Meaning as a Way of Life* (Boston: Shambhala Publications, 1993), p. 104.

232 Gerald G. May, *Will and Spirit: A Contemplative Psychology* (San Francisco: Harper and Row, 1982), p. 53.

powerfully present in it that they change the trajectory of my narrative. Give some thought to your own numinous engagement now:

- Reflect on one or two experiences you believe carried the energy of the numinous.
- Describe one of them in as much detail as you can recall. In the details of these moments or instances resides important qualities and impulses of your personal myth.
- What happened leading up to the moment? What, for instance, were you thinking about or going through in your life at the time?
- What were the circumstances of the experience?
- What or who was present in the experience to give it such force?
- When did this event occur in your life?
- Have you given it shape or form since then in any way?
- What might you do now as you reflect on it to reveal its contoured presence?
- Have you shared this experience with anyone?
- What is the feeling-tone attached to giving this experience expression in language?
- In what way does this experience continue to live in you?
- Has it shifted at all in your memory over time? Does it continue to transform you today?

Writer's Response

I don't know if I can describe the depth of what I feel—
How tentative I have felt at every step, how tentative
every turn, every choice.
How I always seem to be asking permission to be here—
"Is this OK, God? If I have fun here?"
"Can I really take this journey,
spend this money,
enjoy this life?"
"Won't someone else be wrecked, somehow,
because I have said 'Yes' to Life?"
Oh, the fear that has shadowed my every step;
A lifelong dance with Shadow.
And finding, sometimes, the flipside, Courage—

To change the things I could

To make decisions

To ask for help

To take a step . . .

Just like the story of my birth,

I muster up my Courage

and take that leap into midair.

"Because in midair, you can't change your mind!"

My new friend says. . . .

That is surely a dance with my

husband, my lover, my daimon

Trickster.

He must love me so much,

to plot his plots

to propel me screaming and shrieking

out of one situation and into another.

My lover and my torturer, this Trickster.

And how I felt his caress the night before this trip.

After weeks and weeks of his laughter torturing my ears.

The plagues of Egypt that had descended on my house:

Bunnies in the garden, rats and wolf spiders in the bedroom,

Squirrels in the closet—

Ripe fruit dripping and dropping from the trees—

More than I could make jam with,

More than friends and neighbors could absorb,

And more at home, still waiting for me.

And ants, ants welling up like a tide through the floorboards.

That was it, it did me in.

I felt my grip slipping from my dreams—

Home, hearth, family, responsibilities clung to me on every side.

I sank down in fearful misery

at the foot of the buffalo in my dream—

"I can't do this," I thought.

"I simply cannot stand here alone facing the unknown any longer—

My strength is gone, and my knees are bending."

My breath left me in short, miserable gasps—

Failure failure oh dear god I cannot do this

I give up. . . .

And you, dear Buffalo—

nuzzling my neck—

your warm, soft breath washing over me…

And the voice of my friend on the phone, reminding me,

"Beth!" she says, "But you've been amazing—

You've taken the bull by the horns!"

And like a key in some kind of lock,

I felt my heart turn over inside me.

Gasping, crying,

I tried to speak my gratitude—

Unable to express the depth of the well of love inside me—

For in my dream,

in my despair,

in my weakness and misery and

utter capitulation to failure,

to the completely unfathomable mystery of

how to *live*,

I remembered—I never let go of the Buffalo's horn. . . .

"I didn't let go!" rings in my ears,

I didn't let go—

And now, with absolute mystery as to what comes next,

I get up and pack my bags,

wash my face,

And set forth on the next leg of my Journey. . . . (Participant)

Writing Meditation: Riting the Religious Self through Ideas and Images

> First, imagination can be described as a rule-governed form of invention or, in other terms, as a norm-governed productivity.[233]

> In the first place, should the Gods express themselves in the psyche through its ideas, then our occupation with ideas is at least partly a religious occupation.[234]

Perhaps we have misjudged psychology and religion by creating a gap or fissure between them and often pitting them against one another. I suggest that the bridge or connective tissue that allows a fuller and more satisfying conversation to ensue between these two ways of grasping what seems mysterious and outside or beneath or above the normal ways of thought, is myth in the form of enduring psychic patterns that give shape and meaning to both spiritual and psychological experiences.

The other element here that both share and that I owe a debt to James Hillman's original work in archetypal psychology and its methodology for bringing more clearly to the surface, is vision. He explores these realms of seeing into our thoughts, behaviors, ideas and images in *Revisioning Psychology* to reveal in what way the mythic patterns we live within are akin to the visions "which govern human beings as the world believed itself ruled from Olympus and by daimons, powers, and personified principles which we now call 'the unconscious.'"[235]

As I read and think about what is implicated in his thought between psyche—myth—religion, I discover that as Gods are in my religious beliefs, so I tend to make my religion a God. None of this, to my mind, subtracts from spiritual experiences or religious beliefs—in fact the opposite occurs. I see for the first time that separating these modes of inquiry from one another truncates understanding, aborts a full vision of psycho-spiritual life and retards my own sense of each of these areas when studied isolated from one another.

My desire here is to offer a meditation in which we are asked to think about how the ideas I see the world through, the visions I carry into my interior and external life, are nothing less than the shaping forces and forming fictions by which I create both the picture

---

233 Paul Ricoeur, *Figuring the Sacred: Religion, Narrative, and Imagination*, trans. David Pellauer (Minneapolis: Fortress Press, 1995), p. 144.

234 Hillman, *Re-Visioning Psychology*, p. 129.

235 Hillman, *Re-Visioning Psychology*, p. 129.

of reality and its consequent meanings. These visions "grip us," as Hillman writes of them. In a slightly different expression which captures the same sensibility . . . in Shakespeare's *Hamlet* when, towards the end of the play, the young prince speaks to his close friend Horatio in a moment of revelation: "There's a divinity that shapes our ends, / Rough-hew them how we will,"[236] Divinity is enfolded in our ideas; gods and goddesses appear as guides in our behaviors, habits, idiosyncrasies, which can also be understood as religious dimensions of our spiritual being.

A perspective, a prejudice, a firm and unshakable idea, a belief that brooks no quarter with others—all of these can be altars, even fully developed shrines, painstakingly built stone by stone over many years so that it and a fortress can not be distinguished as an edifice that keeps me sheltered and immune from other gods, other ideas, points of view, or realms of understanding. I see this most poignantly and dramatically in current political discussions, where real debate, open conversation, an ability or occasion to shift one's point of view, a tacit or explicit respect for the other's thoughts, a sense of civility that attends opposing philosophies, are considered weaknesses by candidates who suffer under the vision of unwavering, steadfast, clear-minded, non-negotiating, ego-driven, muscle-headed, God-sanctioned posturings. Unconquerable remain all parts of the shrine, brick-by-brick placed solidly with the certainty of mortar to allow no real thought that could show one's Achilles' heel, much less a foot firmly ensconced in one's mouth! In the process, a religion of dogmatic assertions rules over one's ability to see something from another angle. Leadership as despotism appears to rule the religious roost of the political shrine that voters then pay homage to with the sacrificial blessing of their ballot.

Myth, then includes the historical, psychological and religious; we are inspirited, baptized, confirmed and may receive Extreme Unction through our steadfast ideas; behind the ideas, as Hillman invests this movement in the soul, are gods and goddesses so that spirit and psyche find a common ground. A close affinity develops in time in conversation wherein reversion, re-vision and *religio*—a turning or bending back and in, share a common weal. To speak of religion and psychology as two vastly different entities that "structure our consciousness with such force and possession"[237] is to further coerce the split in us into a

---

236 William Shakespeare, *The Tragedy of Hamlet, Prince of Denmark*, ed. Sylvan Barnet (New York: Signet Classic, 1986), act 5, scene 2, lines 10-11.

237 Hillman, *Re-Visioning Psychology*, p. 129.

wider fissure, then into a vast chasm where no one can any longer hear the voice of the Other. If we can, however, for the moment, entertain Hillman's understanding of the classical Gods as attitudes or modes of seeing and understanding, then we can allow a greater elasticity in our lives to accommodate our personal myth in deeper layers of awareness.

Finally, before our next meditation, I cite his definition or description of a God: "A God is a manner of existence, an attitude toward existence, and a set of ideas. Each God would project its divine *logos,* opening the soul's eye so that it regards the world in a particularly formed way."[238] Without reducing the spiritual life we carry within in any way, I believe that his definition opens us to the mythic quality of religion and the religious qualities inherent in mythos, most specifically our personal myth, as it extends and tapers into a larger cultural myth that also envelops us. Both religion and myth are formative ways of understanding; history may then be conceived as an overt expression of that understanding in time and space. We benefit immeasurably by exploring within our own landscape the way in which our spiritual life is also in part an attitude as well as a set of ideas about creation, my purpose, the quality of meaning I inhabit, the good life, what virtue is, how I grasp the sacred in all things as well as what offers me comfort when I consider my own mortal and wounded precincts.

- Describe in order of importance, three ideas that you worship, that is, what you give highest authority to in your daily life.
- What is it within these ideas that carry so much value for you and may even, given our earlier meditation, make present on a regular basis the numinous in your life?
- What do these ideas allow you to see that you might become blind to without them?
- What is it in these ideas that help you to shape and form your way of understanding your life as having essential meaning and that gives you a perspective of yourself in a wider context of family, community and the larger world.
- Would you ever, under any circumstances, sacrifice any of these ideas on a fiery altar of disuse? I am thinking of them as divine presences that you worship in the way you might worship the most valuable things, persons or situations in your life.
- Do these ideas successfully keep other ideas from entering your sanctuary, chapel or cathedral you have constructed?
- Are these ideas housed in separate tabernacles or do they speak to one another in divine discourse?

---

238 Hillman, *Re-Visioning Psychology*, p. 130.

- Is it possible for you to discern, within the power of these presences, what they do not allow in what you sense might be of value if they did?
- Are there any other ideas contesting any of these ideas, that even threaten to topple one or the other if given half a green light from you?
- Does any one of these ideas keep chaos or breakdown at bay?
- Do you sense that without this or that idea to shore you up daily, you might descend into the chaos of doubt, uncertainty, and ambiguity?
- Do these ideas continue to satisfy your desire and ability to continue to deepen and broaden your spiritual self?
- What, if anything, do you sense limits you because of any one of these three ideas?
- If we shifted the language here to substitute the word image for idea, what images of divinity, of your spiritual life, of your own divine presence in the world would change?
- Describe your self-image as part of a divine image you carry and nurture.
- Would you write differently about a divine image compared to a divine idea?
- Would the image of the sacred or of a God be different in your description from the idea of the sacred?

Writers' Responses

Entering a sacred space and closing my eyes. . . . I remember that beyond time, space, eternity, worlds beyond worlds. . . . the formless, the ineffable—You Are—I remember You the unknowable through the image of the Sun—the portal that opens beyond the beyond . . . the incomprehensible . . . still You Are present in all that is.

I journey and enter an ancient Temple where I meet the Dalai Lama—the face and presence of kindness. . . . I bow before the great golden statue of Buddha and pray for justice and mercy to fill me. . . . I enter the lotus garden and remember the passageway to my precious heart center. . . . I approach the red rock doorway on a high mountain path where I enter and cross a threshold that will take me to my heart center. I bow to the old blind one who stands near the archway that leads into the Light . . . Light beyond Light . . . and I walk a narrow ledge until I find the spiraling staircase down into an underworld cave where I meet the primordial sacred feminine energy, the primordial matrix. . . . the fierce presence of Kali. . . . Our Lady of Chartres, Mary—and in that space of the cave, the tomb, the womb, I access my own heart center and feel and become Unconditional Love, Peace & Harmony, the Healing Presence, Compassion. I am Unconditional Love, I am Peace & Harmony, I am the Healing Presence, I am Compassion. . . . In that space I ask . . . What am I to say today?

What am I to do today? Where am I to go today? And listen with the ear of my heart.

Leaving the cave and beginning the return to my waking consciousness, having felt the I Am Presence within me and having brought to consciousness the qualities of kindness, mercy, justice, unconditional love, peace & harmony, the healing presence and compassion, I pray they will deepen and be present/available as I move through my life today.

Am I different because of this process? It seems as if over time I have a deepening recognition that I am the Divine, I am the expression of Divinity; everything is and so duality and exclusion are lessening their grip and heaven and earth have a chance of uniting more and more in my heart. So this is part of my personal myth that helps me navigate through my life! (Karen Schneider)

I'll start with Divine Consciousness. It exists. How else can I write to find what I do not know? How else can I know when I write? I put the tip of my pen against the white paper and the lines become the container, holding my psyche, holding my spirit, keeping my body in a place, keeping all together, all present. This is creation.

Is it my creation? With certainty. Am I the vessel, as I sit by the trickles of water from the fountain, shadows across the page outlining the edges of my hand, casting the sinewy spires of the palm tree that waves in the wind, occasionally brushing my body? Perhaps. And if I am the vessel that connects the sound and the touch and the feel and the images and the words that flow, am I a soul container? Am I not the sole soul who senses and who thinks? Within these lines, yes, but not within all lines that contain. The container, my container, our container is the presence of the Divine. The divine. The Divinity. That Divine consciousness, Knowing, that comes in the presence of water, that comes in the presence of shadow in the now of the moment of today. (Participant)

I was sitting in the wooden pew so familiar to my body as we did every Methodist Sunday in old Elmwood church, next to my mother with a hymnbook and paper in the childlap.

The message was preaching itself.

When I became aware that my powerful mother was crying!

My mind opened to the fact that she was crying for her sins. . . . no word, just amazement at the consciousness that she was crying for her shortcoming.

Powerful witness. Silent.

I pondered it in my heart. All my life. (pcraig)

Writing Meditation: Riting the Numinous Animals

Animals can lead us spiritually in a variety of ways. As we will see, they can teach us about death, participate in our social and moral development, enhance our physical and psychological well-being, and heighten our capacity to love and to experience joy.[239]

Our last meditation is certainly not the least: the power of animals in our lives. I believe few of us have not had some lasting or profound intimate contact with animals. The power of animals' presences in world mythologies, in fables, fictions, religious rituals and belief systems, in our personal lives and in the food we eat, is enormous and ubiquitous. They seem to carry more than a natural presence; they align themselves with a religious, spiritual and symbolic authority as well.

For many people, their pets are valued at least, if not more, than other people, or equally with the human animals they know. In addition, animals are both worshipped and maligned, as in the phrase, "he behaved like an animal," "she is catty, watch out," or "no one is talking about the elephant in the room," or "they pigged out on a large pizza last night." Animals infiltrate our dreams, our language, our own behavior in metaphors, symbols and in our formed images of the natural order. We slaughter them, garage them in cages, zoos, kennels, sell them like objects, disrespect them in our mistreatment in raising them for food in the most abominable conditions, slaughter them in cruel ways, worship them in rituals, name them as persons, even have salons to lavish attention, treats, hair styles, groomings on them; then many owners parade them in dog shows, cattle contests, sheep contests, dog races, cockfights, frog races, horse races, rodeos—the list of ways we use and abuse animals as we monkey with their behaviors, their limits, their genetic makeup, their use in experiments for

---

239 Mary Lou Randour, *Animal Grace: Entering a Spiritual Relationship with Our Fellow Creatures* (Novato, California: New World Library, 2000), p. 7. See also Rae Ann Kumelos's web site about *Voice of the Animal,* a radio program of stories about animal wisdom, at www.voiceoftheanimal.com.

lipsticks, aerosol products, mutations, genetic alterations, cross-breedings, in-breedings, sacrifices to appease deities—is infinite.

Our treatment of animals prescribes a huge arc of extremes, from fierce abuse in raising them quickly and unnaturally for food consumption, to adoring and pampering them so that the quality of their lives far surpasses a large segment of the world's human population. Something in animals' natures mirror our own vital animal being, our instinctive lives, our sense of the world through the five bodily senses, the way we sniff around, adopt an eagle eye in negotiations, become catty toward those we are not fond of, horse around when boundaries break down, dog other people to change their mind, their vote, their money or stay as constantly busy as a beaver. When a beloved pet of long standing dies, owners may mourn for months or years over their loss.

Animals play enormous and often exaggerated roles in our lives, and our spiritual being is part of this presence. Simply peruse any Symbol Dictionary and one finds very quickly the number of animal entries that may relay their presence in antiquity, on cave wall drawings before history, as objects to harvest and venerate for their skin, fur, teeth, for their internal organs as ways of reading the future, or for their totemic presence to protect a people. In a relatively current *The Book of Symbols: Reflections on Archetypal Images*, a substantial section of the 800 page book is devoted to The Animal World.[240] In a second very thorough dictionary of symbols the General Editor writes in his Foreword: "A basic symbol is the image of an object or living thing made to stand for a concept or quality. For example, Egyptian artists made the lion a forceful symbol of power and majesty—a personification of the divine sun."[241] Animals reconnect us back to the symbolic order of being. They offer to our imaginations a living organic presence of a value or idea that sustains us and affirms our identity.

Nations as well often adopt a particular animal as a symbol to constellate their identity and their core values, what we might designate as what comprises their primary collective myth. We in the United States have adopted the eagle, which appears on our currency; the Russian bear is known around the world, as the salmon marks the Alaskan frontier of plenty. Earlier they appeared on coins, shields, buildings, temples, and cathedrals and were often

---

240 Ami Ronnberg and Kathleen Martin, *The Book of Symbols: Reflections on Archetypal Images* (Cologne, Germany: Taschen Publishers, 2010).

241 Jack Tresidder, *The Complete Dictionary of Symbols* (San Francisco: Chronicle Books, 2005), p. 6.

symbolic images of divinities as presences during exchanges of currency and goods. Three of the evangelists of the gospels are symbolized by animals.

Within the Christian mythos, one of four volumes that survived a fire is *The Bestiary of Christ,* a 467 page abridged version of a thousand page compendium of all the animals that were connected to the figure of Jesus Christ, many from the Middle Ages, which the author observes in his Introduction, citing an earlier writer: "'For the Middle Ages,' wrote Gevaert, 'the whole universe was a symbol.'"[242] As symbols, animals mirror us as well as embody the capacity to lead us into invisible realms of our being and touch deeply and permanently our personal myths.

Traditions around the world dating back to primal times have believed that animals embody a wisdom, a way of understanding and "sensing" the world that allows them to be our mentors, guides and sources of original knowledge. They are used or are present in healing rituals, in foretelling the future, in gauging climate, in reflecting the emotional or psychological, even physical state of their keepers, as well as being the embodied figure of a god or goddess. Joseph Campbell offers this insight about the animal and our own embodiment: "Biologically, in what theologians call our animal nature, we are as deeply grounded as the animals themselves: moved and motivated from within by energies."[243]

These energies are hundreds of millions of years old, he goes on to observe, such that our animal natures and the animals we love and live with, either in our homes, or, as with my family, in the Hill Country of Texas, add texture and richness to our lives. We live, for instance, with wild herds of goats, sheep and rams, recently with a pack of coyotes roaming our area, with deer that graze on our front lawn, the fox we see carrying a squirrel in its mouth, the tarantula that crawls across the gravel next to my study window, the cats that hang out on our back deck, the mice that occasionally slip into our bedroom, the scorpions that make it unwise for us to walk barefoot in to the early morning kitchen, the roadrunners that fluster their feathers in the dust beside our garage, the hummingbirds that float from flower to flower by the front window, the wasps that build nests on the back wall of the garage, the deer that we avoid every time we drive in or out of our street, the myriad species

---

242 Louis Charbonneau-Lassay, *The Bestiary of Christ,* trans. and abridged by D. M. Dooling (New York: Parabola, 1992), p. viii.

243 Joseph Campbell, *The Way of the Animal Powers,* vol. 1 of *The Historical Atlas of World Mythology* (San Francisco: Harper and Row, 1983), p. 46.

of butterflies that flutter by all the windows of our home, the snakes that move beneath old logs on our thickly-forested 5.5 acres, the birds that roost in our birdhouses and build nests in our garage, the wild pigs we hear across the street at dusk, the cats that visit each day and sun themselves on our back deck, and our two house cats we have had for a decade—all these lives surround us and inform our daily habits and joys as well as commune with our human-animal natures.

Some years ago, during a four month retreat at various monasteries, I began to notice how much animals were part of the landscape. I remember one dog in particular, Rusty, a mascot of The Carmelite House of Prayer in Napa Valley, California. I was that fall the only retreatant staying at the monastery. Rusty would be right outside my dormitory door to greet me each morning to guide me to morning service; he waited for me each day and escorted me back to my room. He was old and wise; I saw it in his eyes and in his majestically-wrinkled forehead. During the day, if I sat for more than ten minutes on a bench beside the fish pond, which I had learned to love as my private meditation spot, he suddenly and silently materialized next to me and put his large black head on my lap. I found that he actually enhanced my solitude rather than interrupted it.

We were easy and comfortable with one another; we let many of our thoughts go unsaid as we sat together watching the large goldfish surface or the bullfrogs peer out of the water with their faces and black, blinking eyes just breaking the surface. He was so schooled in the Rules of St. Benedict with his calm compassionate eyes and his daily service to me. I knew he would be a great loss to me when I departed. He enriched the quality of the sacred; without him my retreat with the Carmelite priests and brothers would not have been half as rich. Such is the power of animal presence.[244]

- Describe where and when in your life have animals played a major role in who you are.
- What have animals, or a particular pet, had on you in actually fashioning your beliefs, your world view, your connection to the natural order and your attitude to human beings.
- Has an animal or animals more generally, been a healing presence in your life, or otherwise aided you in overcoming some dramatic affliction?
- In what way has an animal opened you or pointed you to the mystery of life, or to a numinous experience wherein you sensed some form of divinity present in and through the animal?

---

244 Dennis Patrick Slattery, *Grace in the Desert: Awakening to the Gifts of Monastic Life* (San Francisco: Jossey-Bass, 2004), p. 30.

- What would be diminished or impoverished in your life if you lost an animal or the presence of the animal world.
- What in your own animal nature has been revealed to you as a result of your engagement with the animal world in any form?
- Has or does being connected to animals help to ground you in a consistent way within your own animal body?
- If animals or an animal embodies some sacred, even spiritual qualities for you, describe what this is, for it is directly connected to and relevant for, your personal myth.

Writer's Response

At one time, years ago, there were rats in the attic of my house. I could hear them scurrying about at night making scratching noises as they moved among the rafters, in the attic space, where I could not easily go. I became increasingly annoyed over the following days, or nights actually, and resolved to put an end to those miserable critters, invaders in my home and of my sleep. I climbed the ladder and set some traps and waited. It wasn't long, as I recall, before I heard a snap and I knew I had caught one. But then I heard a bumping sound, moving in starts and stops across the ceiling. The rat was not dead. It was alive, but caught in the trap, dragging it along behind him. It was not a clean kill. Not antiseptic, removed. I would have to go up there and get it, which I did.

I brought it down with me, trap and all, and took it into the garage, where I got a hatchet. Then into the garden, the place of execution. It was exactly an execution. I held it down against the ground and raised the hatchet. At that moment it stopped struggling and looked me in the eye. It was not afraid, or so it seemed to me. For a moment we had a connection, predator to prey. I paused and said something to the rat, to this animal, this living thing, something like "It's not personal." And then I brought the hatchet down. And in that instant I knew I was wrong. It was very personal. (Annemarie St. John)

9

REVIEWING AND RITING THE PATTERNED SELF

In an organic being, first the form as a whole strikes us, then its parts and their shape and combination.[245]

In our kinds of fictions the plots are our theories. They are the ways in which we put the intentions of human nature together so that we can understand the why between the sequence of events in a story.[246]

We are patterned principled persons who follow, within our infinite variations, certain forms that relate each to each and organic part to organic part that, when added together, form a wholeness or a unity that suggests, to some minds, a supreme intelligence behind and within the structures of living things. The poet, philosopher, botanist, playwright, and traveler Johann Wolfgang von Goethe, writing in the 18th century, was a visionary who saw in the natural order some fundamental first principles of organic matter that appear to share close affinities with the natural world and with the formative principles that comprise our personal myth.

Goethe's excitement grew dramatically when, in exploring the world of plants within the city of Padua, Italy, in 1786, after he and a friend crossed the Alps on foot for a pilgrimage study of the wide variety of flora and fauna Italy afforded them, he came on an idea still respected in Botany today: as he studied the fan palm leaf, he wrote later, "it gradually became clearer and clearer to me that the concept could also be valid in a higher sense: a challenge which hovered in my mind at that time in the sensuous form of a supersensuous plant archetype."[247] From this observation/discovery he concluded that the leaf was the ground or originary shape and structure of all organic life: "Everything is leaf and through

---

245 Johann Wolfgang von Goethe, *Goethe's Botanical Writings*, trans. Bertha Mueller (Woodbridge, Conn.: Ox Bow Press, 1989), p. 86.

246 James Hillman, *Healing Fiction* (Barrytown, N.Y.: Station Hill Press, 1983), p. 7.

247 Charles J. Engard, "Introduction," in *Goethe's Botanical Writings*, trans. Bertha Mueller (Woodbridge, Conn.: Ox Bow Press, 1989), p. 6.

this simplicity the greatest diversity becomes possible"[248] in the fundamental action of leaf: metamorphosis. Such a theoretical imagination as Goethe's was driven in part by a fundamental belief: all nature participates in a unity by participating in a shared form. His insight creates a further understanding of the phrase, "to turn over a new leaf," as a way to capture in colloquial parlance the act of metamorphosis.

The archetypal leaf is a manifestation of an idea of nature that has many shoots streaming off of it. Its relationship to our topic and for our writing meditations lead us to this final chapter on pattern, style, manner of being and modes of expression that typify and witness the myth we are in, and, like a leaf, remains always organic and consistently engaging a metamorphic, kinetic, and shape-shifting form. Think, then, of your life as a leaf continually unfolding through the deep structure of the spiral as its fundamental action; within the unfolding of the spiral are the nutrient structures of our personal myth that, if we can become botanists of our own souls planted in the soil of our history, both personal and collective, then we might be able to discern some of the ligaments of these patterns. Goethe's insight that he gives a natural shape to in the archetypal leaf image confirms, for me, what James Taylor develops in his insightful work on poetic knowledge. What he observes in a middle chapter captures something of Goethe's way of seeing:

> What I would summarize here is that from the most imperceptive connections of the 'spiritual preconscious' that rests within the reflexes of the first knowledge of being in the senses, to the more cultivated habit of poetic sensibility and vision, we are, throughout, poetic beings even as we live and move among the most ordinary and everyday experiences.[249]

To further this organic quality of our mythically-rooted lives, and to connect some of the branches to one another, I note another book on the curving structure to our lives so poetically intuited by Goethe and given added expression by Taylor above. In *The Curves of Life*, Theodore Andrea Cook cites the great geometer and painter Leonardo Da Vinci, to which he adds his own theory: "'the works of Nature are finite.' They move along those orderly, those vast processes of time and space which can be realized by that human

---

248 Engard, "Introduction," p. 7.

249 James Taylor, *Poetic Knowledge: The Recovery of Education* (Albany: State University of New York Press, 1998), pp. 70-71.

intelligence which is a part of them, if only it will work hard enough to collect the details."[250] One of the fundamental details of works of nature mirrored in artifices constructed by human beings is the spiral, the central focus of Cook's book. His "Cook Book" is filled with recipes on how to find correspondences in the natural order that reveal the spiralic structures in the cultural realm: "It is, in fact, almost possible to catalogue the forms of the spiral utilized by man, in rifles, in staircases, in tunnels, in corkscrews, or a hundred other ways, and to parallel nearly every one in natural formations."[251]

I am thinking, following this insight, that myth, both personal and collective, could be considered an organic sworl of psyche unique to each person or population, yet also containing impressions of what Goethe referred to above as the "archetypal plant." It is the organic nucleus out from which swirls and unfurls all of our permutations, while always remembering and adhering to that first originary principle. I sense here a complex and sustained analogy with one's personal myth, a set of guiding forms in a field of relationships, of which each of us is a composite. Beneath it, perhaps, is the substantial ground of energy fields that provide libidinal heft to this archetypal principle—as if each of us grows out and around in spiralic motion a foundational field that is our myth, created out of the soiled souls of our history, likes, prejudices, desires, beliefs, knowledge, memories and body.

In his Introduction to the revised edition of his ground-breaking book, *Field, Form and Fate*, Michael Conforti, an original interdisciplinary thinker and harvester, brings home the idea expressed above through the corridor of soul. He too turns to a biologist/botanist, Adolf Portmann, who observes in nature "the ornamentation in animals, such as colors of feathers, which have little, if any, survival value. Portmann suggests that the imperative to express one's intrinsic nature . . . is perhaps even more important than the need for self-preservation."[252] He continues to draw several solid parallels between physics, nature, and psyche in the works of several writers that have influenced his own thought: physicist David Bohm understands the implicate order as the matrix out of which everything arises. From musical and artistic inspiration, to innate ordering principles, to the generation of form,

---

250 Theodore Andrea Cook, *The Curves of Life* (1914; repr., New York: Dover, 1979), p. 21.

251 Cook, *The Curves of Life*, p. 16.

252 Michael Conforti, *Field, Form, and Fate: Patterns in Mind, Nature and Psyche* (New Orleans: Spring Journal Books, 2003), pp. xxiv-xxv.

Bohm comprehends each as "an expression of an implicate, archetypal field, finding a corresponding means of expression in the outer world."[253]

Now, in a retrospective move back into the fields of our writing, we seek to recognize any of the styles, patterns, analogies in our prose that mirror our personal myth, or that return us to basic archetypal realities that govern our lives, the divinities that define us, the perspectives we hold and hold us that bestow our lives with purpose and meaning. They might be understood as vessels that contain us. Both content and its mode of expression reflect styles of awareness, of being present, of fathoming what we make out of our experiences that place us right where our interior life rubs against the walls of the external realities that we reference daily to revision and renew ourselves. Such is the poetic response we are seeking here, one that arises out of an intuitive rather than reasoned or rational understanding that often flat-lines in explanations.

The various philosophies of life we harbor and often glorify can be used to contain ourselves, to protect us from foreign tokens that do not square with what we believe we are. They act as shields of deflection so we do not have to defect from hardened positions. James Hillman's insight here is illuminating: "Also, ideas shore up and contain our complexes. They provide shields that protect us from their onslaught."[254] Our personal myths as well can be of such substance that allows other ideas in, other complexes, to mold and hold us. They can also be armor plates that keep us safe in battle as we wave our swords to ward off intruders. My sense is that variations of this method, as well as many others, are embedded in the way and the what of our responses in these meditations. If indeed myths are, among other things, energy fields that power and guide perception, imagination, memory and fantasy in a cohesive patterned way, embodied both in ourselves and in the flesh of the world, then to reread what we have written is an act of memory/imagination to see into the patterns of the prose and to let it guide us to where the templates of the soul reside in the multiple forged fictions of our selves. Story teller Nancy Mellon has even suggested, through her research, that each organ of the body gravitates toward particular stories: "We marveled with others at how all the organic realms generate and respond to particular stories, and how nature and the greater universe support the storytelling process when it is in the service of truth and

---

253 Conforti, *Field, Form, and Fate*, pp. xxv-xxvi.
254 James Hillman, *Re-Visioning Psychology* (1975; repr., New York: HarperPerennial, 1992), p. 132.

well-being."[255] Let us meditate on these fictions and patterns that include body, nature, spirit and psyche, in a few last riting meditations.

Riting Meditation: Remembering the Patterns

> Writing helps us map our interior world. Part of laying track is letting ourselves imagine what directions we might like to lay it in. This tool helps you get a sense of your emotional geography.[256]

- As you reflect back on what you have written, perhaps the response to this meditation is not contained so much in what you literally wrote or drew, but on what was evoked in you as a result of particular or several meditation responses.
- Do any patterns that have been dominant in your life show signs of wear or wearing out? Are any of them ready to be relinquished to make room for others that are anxious and ready to enter your life?
- As you think of how to respond to these questions, yes, use what you have written but do not limit yourself to them. You may, for instance, in reading this, sense something that is no longer worthy of your living it, so first write it out. Your next act will be a willingness to let it go.
- Speak to it as a person, for in the belief or the habit of thought or way of behaving, something was in service to you.
- Give it a voice and a reality so that you can develop a conversation with it.

Riting Meditation: Sensing the Field

The repeated patterns in our lives, including repetitious thought patterns, reveal the energy channels of what Joseph Campbell designated the "mythogenetic zone, the primary area of origin of the myths"[257] we inhabit as a constant life landscape:

---

255 Nancy Mellon, *Body Eloquence: The Power of Myth and Story to Awaken the Body's Energies* (Santa Rosa, Calif.: Energy Psychology Press, 2008), p. xviii.

256 Julia Cameron, *The Right to Write: An Invitation and Initiation into the Writing Life* (New York: Jeremy P. Tarcher/Putnam, 1998), p. 21.

257 Joseph Campbell, *The Mythic Dimension: Selected Essays, 1959-1987* (Novato; Calif.: New World Library, 2007), p. 74.

- Where in your writing do you detect the presence of repeated images?
- What is the nature of these images, which can be ideas, emotions, even presences in your imagination, that continue to spring up to assist you or to haunt you?
- In what questions did they show up?
- Is there a pattern in the kind of riting meditation that brought them forward?
- Do these patterns in any way form a narrative that you can see the plot contours of? Describe it.

Writers' Responses

I am starting to see the myth of my life and to realize that although it is not completely dead it is dying as I take 2 steps forward and one back—because as frustrating as this can be, Dante's poem shows that the progress does go a long way.

I was tempted to edit, but resisted. (Susanne Scholz)

I like rough language, coarse beauty. (I like sentences structured like that last—ending in a short, often repetitive phrase.) I don't do subtle very often—or very well. (There's that dangling modifier again.) I love beginning in medias res, in the thick of it, whatever it is. Often with some mystery. "What the hell is going on?" "What does this mean?" I'm comfortable in the mystery, and, hey, you gotta build in some suspense, or else you, dear reader (or in this case dear listener) won't keep paying me the attention that I crave.

What else? I like a late fulcrum. You know that term? A concept from analyzing the structure of poetry, a fulcrum is that point where the whole poem suddenly changes direction. I like 'em late. Which is to say that I don't give a damn about a denouement.

And one last hit: I like my writing to open out, not unlike Greek goddamned tragedy, into broad, if not cosmic, concerns. Wow, man, do you see colors? (Jack)

Riting Meditation: Language Patterns

- In your prose and poetry, do you detect a sentence structure that you seem to favor?
- What about word choice? What kinds of words, in the form of literal or metaphorical expression, do you gravitate towards?

- What of paragraphs? What do they look like? Short or long or a combination of them?
- Do you sense your writing has an elasticity about it? A rigidity? Is there something in the patterned style of your prose that you notice and would like to change?
- What are you most proud of in your writing?
- Does your writing move in the structure of a spiral, a circle, a straight line, a bent line? What is your prose's geometry, its way of seeing something round about, directly, on an angle, in repeated expression? Others?
- Do you tend to begin all your sentences fundamentally the same way?
- Do you notice that you use examples or illustrations, either from your life, from others, or what you have read, for instance?
- Does the professional work that you do influence the style or format of your prose? Does you work determine your writing?

Riting Meditation: Seeking Surprises

- Looking back over your writing, do you detect what is absent, left out, or not considered until now?
- Do you wish to revise or add to any of the entries because now, with a little distance, you can discern what you did not include? Include it now.
- Do your writings place you primarily or most often in the present, the past, or the future? Is it a balanced mix? Where do you situate yourself most often in responding to the meditations?
- Did your writings make more clear, or surprise you with a belief, an attitude, a way of behaving that went unnoticed until now?
- If not directly addressing the question above, consider what was finally most surprising in the meditations, either one, several or all.
- What grew out of the (W)rites of Passage that you engaged and that perhaps brought or carried you, like a small vessel over the waters, to a new land, to an unfamiliar landscape?
- Is there an organizing principle that you were not aware of or only dimly discerned, that grew out of the writing?
- Did you see in the responses some desire, some want, some direction you wish to pursue now that was not there before you began this "pengrimage"? I use this neologism to try to connect our pilgrimage with our penning our way fore and aft.
- Was anything significant re-ordered or re-organized for you through the mysterious journey of penning yourself to the wall of your own limits? By this I mean:
- Did you detect limitations in yourself by means of the writing that you are now more ready or disposed to accept or to break free from? This might reveal itself in an organizing image or belief or behavior that holds you too tight to the past and restrains you from breaking new ground from this day forward.

Writer's Response

The concept of writing as ritual really struck me. Instead of sitting down and expecting to just jump into writing, I will create a ritual space before starting to write. I hope this will allow a greater connection with the field and make writing less of an egoic struggle.(Joe Lohmar)

Riting Meditation: Seeking the Gold Forward

I have left out of this book dozens of riting meditations that could have extended the travel for months. In light of this recognition, I invite you to respond to the last meditation:

- Out of what you have done, is there a topic, an idea, an experience, a memory—something evoked in the process, that you were not invited to write about but feel the need to because you sense its importance for you currently or as part of your past?
- Write it out. Give it as much space and reflection that it insists on. My sense is that this orphaned idea, image, experience, thought, or insight, could be one of the most important inscribings that you have done within the entire pengrimage.
- If there is more than one, give them a formed and coherent expression now. Let it lead you where it wishes to take you to make something conscious that may have been waiting all this time to be given language and publicly-expressed.

Let us end here, in the mystery of what is yet to be written. Further, let us give ourselves enormous credit for embarking on a journey that, in fact, not many even begin, frequently for want of something that does not want to be touched, disturbed, uncovered, incited or evoked. Part of the power of myth is that it wishes not to be disturbed, deflected or disrupted, for it feels that security is the way of a good life. My conviction is that you know better. Otherwise—you would have never begun!

BIBLIOGRAPHY

Alighieri, Dante. *The Divine Comedy*. Translated by Allen Mandelbaum. Introduction by Eugenio Montale. New York: Alfred A. Knopf, 1995.

———. *Inferno: First Book of The Divine Comedy*. Translated by Allen Mandelbaum. New York: Random House, 1981.

Armstrong, Robert Plant. *The Powers of Presence: Consciousness, Myth, and Affecting Presence*. Philadelphia: University of Pennsylvania Press, 1981.

Asher, Charles. *Soundings: Seventy-Five Reflections on Love and Romance, Personal Development and the Search for Meaning*. Santa Barbara, Calif.: Desert Springs Publications, 1988.

Bly, Robert, James Hillman, and Michael Meade, eds. *The Rag and Bone Shop of the Heart: A Poetry Anthology*. New York: HarperCollins, 1992.

Bohm, David. "Quantum Theory as an Indication of a New Order in Physics. Part B: Implicate and Explicate Order in Physical Law." In Bohm, *Wholeness and the Implicate Order*. New York: Routledge, 1998.

Bond, D. Stephenson. *Living Myth: Personal Meaning as a Way of Life*. Boston: Shambhala Publications, 1993.

Bosnak, Robert. *Embodiment: Creative Imagination in Medicine, Art and Travel*. New York: Routledge, 2007.

Butcher, S. H. *Aristotle's Theory of Poetry and Fine Art*. 3rd ed. New York: Hill and Wang, 1902.

Cameron, Julia. *The Right to Write: An Invitation and Initiation into the Writing Life*. New York: Jeremy P. Tarcher/Putnam, 1998.

Campbell, Joseph. "Bios and Mythos." In Campbell, *The Flight of the Wild Gander: Explorations in the Mythological Dimension: Selected Essays, 1944-1968*. Novato: New World Library, 2002.

———. *The Flight of the Wild Gander: Explorations in the Mythological Dimension: Selected Essays, 1944-1968*. Novato: New World Library, 2002.

———. *The Hero with a Thousand Faces*. Bollingen Series XVII. Princeton, N.J.: Princeton University Press, 1973.

———. *The Inner Reaches of Outer Space: Metaphor as Myth and as Religion*. Novato, Calif.: New World Library, 2002.

———. *The Mythic Dimension: Selected Essays, 1959-1987*. Novato; Calif.: New World Library, 2007.

————. *Mythic Worlds, Modern Words: On the Art of James Joyce*. Edited by Edmund L. Epstein. Novato, Calif.: New World Library, 2003.

————. *Myths of Light*. Novato, Calif.: New World Library, 2003.

————. *Myths to Live By*. New York: Penguin Group, 1972.

————. *An Open Life: Joseph Campbell in Conversation with Michael Toms*. Foreword by Jean Erdman Campbell. Burdett, N.Y.: Larson Publications, 1988

————. *Pathways to Bliss: Mythology and Personal Transformation*. Novato, Calif.: New World Library, 2004.

————. *Thou Art That: Transforming Religious Metaphor*. Novato, Calif.: New World Library, 2001.

————. *The Way of the Animal Powers*. Vol. 1 of *The Historical Atlas of World Mythology*. San Francisco: Harper and Row, 1983.

Charbonneau-Lassay, Louis. *The Bestiary of Christ*. Translated and abridged by D. M. Dooling. New York: Parabola, 1992.

Chodorow, Joan, ed. *Jung on Active Imagination*. Princeton, N.J.: Princeton University Press, 1997.

Conforti, Michael. *Field, Form, and Fate: Patterns in Mind, Nature and Psyche*. New Orleans: Spring Journal Books, 2003.

Cook, Theodore Andrea. *The Curves of Life*. 1914; repr., New York: Dover, 1979.

Corbett, Lionel. *The Sacred Cauldron: Psychotherapy as a Spiritual Practice*. Wilmette, Ill.: Chiron Publications, 2011.

Cowan, Louise. *The Terrain of Comedy*. Dallas, Tex.: The Dallas Institute of Humanities and Culture, 1984.

Csikszentmihalyi, Mihaly. *Flow: The Psychology of Optimal Experience*. New York: HarperPerennial, 1999.

Damasio, Antonio. *The Feeling of What Happens: Body and Emotion in the Making of Consciousness*. San Diego: Harcourt Brace, 1999.

Deardorf, Daniel. *The Other Within: The Genius of Deformity in Myth, Culture and Psyche*. Intro. by Robert Bly. Ashland: White Cloud Press, 2004.

DeSalvo, Louise. *Writing as a Way of Healing: How Telling Our Stories Transforms Our Lives*. Boston: Beacon Press, 2000.

Dickinson, Emily. *Poems by Emily Dickinson*. Edited by Mabel Loomis Todd and T. W. Higginson. Boston: Little, Brown and Co., 1912.

Doniger, Wendy. *The Implied Spider: Politics and Theology in Myth*. New York: Columbia University Press, 1998.

Eakin, Paul John. *How Our Lives Become Stories: Making Selves.* Ithaca, N.Y.: Cornell University Press, 1999.

Easter, Sandra. "Beyond Biography: Mending the Ancestral Web." (Ph.D. diss., Pacifica Graduate Institute, 2011.

Eliade, Mircea. *The Sacred and the Profane: The Nature of Religion.* Translated by Willard Trask. San Diego: Harvest Books, 1987.

Engard, Charles J. "Introduction." In *Goethe's Botanical Writings.* Translated by Bertha Mueller. Woodbridge, Conn.: Ox Bow Press, 1989.

Feinstein, David, and Stanley Krippner. *The Mythic Path: Discovering the Guiding Stories of Your Past—Creating a Vision for Your Future.* New York: Jeremy Tarcher/Putnam Books, 1997.

Franz, Marie-Louise von. *Projection and Re-Collection in Jungian Psychology: Reflections of the Soul.* Chicago: Open Court Press, 1995.

Freccero, John. *Dante: The Poetics of Conversion.* Edited by Rachel Jacoff. Cambridge, Mass.: Harvard University Press, 1986.

Gallagher, Winifred. *The Power of Place: How Our Surroundings Shape Our Thoughts, Emotions, and Actions.* New York: Poseidon Press, 1993.

Giegerich, Wolfgang. *Soul Violence: Collected English Papers.* Vol. 3. New Orleans, La.: Spring Journal Books, 2008.

Goethe, Johann Wolfgang von. *Goethe's Botanical Writings.* Translated by Bertha Mueller. (Woodbridge, Conn.: Ox Bow Press, 1989.

Haeckel, Ernst. *Art Forms in Nature: The Prints of Ernst Haeckel.* Mineola, N.Y.: Dover Publications, 2004.

Hillman, James. *City and Soul.* Vol. 2 of *The Uniform Edition of the Writings of James Hillman.* Edited by Robert J. Leaver. Putnam, Conn.: Spring Publications, 2006.

———. *Healing Fiction.* Barrytown, N.Y.: Station Hill Press, 1983.

———. *Re-Visioning Psychology.* 1975; repr., New York: HarperPerennial, 1992.

Jacobs, Jane. *Dark Age Ahead.* New York: Random House, 2004.

Johnson, Robert A. *Owning Your Own Shadow: Understanding the Dark Side of the Psyche.* San Francisco: HarperSanFrancisco, 1991.

Joyce, James. *Dubliners, A Portrait of the Artist as a Young Man, Chamber Music.* New York: Random House, 1992.

Jung, C. G. *Aion: Researches into the Phenomenology of the Self.* Vol. 9, part II of *The Collected Works of C. G. Jung.* Translated by R. F. C. Hull. 2nd ed. Princeton, N.J.: Princeton University Press, 1970.

————. *Alchemical Studies.* Vol. 13 of *The Collected Works of C. G. Jung.* Translated by R. F. C. Hull. Princeton, N.J.: Princeton University Press, 1983.

————. *Archetypes and the Collective Unconscious.* Vol. 9, part I of *The Collected Works of C. G. Jung.* Edited by and translated by R. F. C. Hull and Gerhard Adler. 2nd ed. Princeton, N.J.: Princeton University Press, 1971.

————. "Depth Psychology and Self-Knowledge." In *The Symbolic Life: Miscellaneous Writings.* Vol. 18 of *The Collected Works of C. G. Jung.* Translated by R. F. C. Hull. Princeton, N.J.: Princeton University Press, 1976.

————. *Dream Analysis: Notes of the Seminar Given in 1928-1930.* Edited by William McGuire. Bollingen Series XCIX. Princeton, N.J.: Princeton University Press, 1984.

————. *Memories, Dreams, Reflections.* Edited by Aniela Jaffé. Translated by Richard and Clara Winston. New York: Pantheon Books, 1963.

————. *Mysterium Coniunctionis.* Vol. 14 of *The Collected Works of C. G. Jung.* Edited and translated by R. F. C. Hull and Gerhard Adler. Princeton, N.J.: Princeton University Press, 1970.

————. "The Origin of Myth." In *Jung on Mythology,* edited by Robert A. Segal. Princeton, N.J.: Princeton University Press, 1998.

————. "On Psychic Energy." In *The Structure and Dynamics of the Psyche.* Vol. 8 of *The Collected Works of C. G. Jung.* Translated by R. F. C. Hull. New York: Pantheon Books, 1960.

————. *Psychology and Alchemy.* Vol. 12 of *The Collected Works of C. G. Jung.* Edited by Herbert Read, Michael Fordham, and Gerhard Adler. Translated by R. F. C. Hull. Princeton, N.J.: Princeton University Press, 1968.

————. *Psychology and Religion: West and East.* Vol. 11 of *The Collected Works of C. G. Jung.* Edited and translated by Gerhard Adler and R. F. C. Hull. Princeton, N.J.: Princeton University Press, 1977.

————. *The Red Book: Liber Novus.* Edited by Sonu Shamdasani. Translated by Mark Kyburz, John Peck, and Sonu Shamdasani. New York: W. W. Norton, 2009.

————. *Two Essays in Analytical Psychology.* Vol. 7 of *The Collected Works of C. G. Jung.* Translated by R. F. C Hull. New York: Pantheon Books, 1966.

Kafka, Franz. "The Metamorphosis." In Kafka, *The Metamorphosis and Other Stories.* New York: Oxford University Press, 2009.

Karen, Robert. *The Forgiving Self: The Road from Resentment to Connection.* New York: Anchor Books, 2003.

Keen, Sam, and Anne Valley-Fox. *Your Mythic Journey: Finding Meaning in Your Life through Writing and Storytelling.* New York: Jeremy Tarcher/Putnam, 1989.

Keleman, Stanley. *Myth & the Body: A Colloquy with Joseph Campbell.* Berkeley: Center Press, 1999.

Keller, David G. R. *Oasis of Wisdom: The Worlds of the Desert Fathers and Mothers.* Collegeville, Minn.: Liturgical Press, 1993.

Kendall, R. T. *Total Forgiveness.* Lake Mary, Fla.: Charisma House, 2002.

Kinnell, Galway. "Flower Herding on Mount Monadnock." In Kinnell, *A New Selected Poems.* Boston: Houghton Mifflin, 2001.

Kinsella, W. P. *Shoeless Joe: A Novel.* Boston: Houghton Mifflin, 1982.

Luke, Helen. *Dark Wood to White Rose: Journey and Transformation in Dante's Divine Comedy.* 4th ed. New York: Parabola Books, 2001.

Lynch, Philip. Interview with Dennis Patrick Slattery. *InTouch with Carl Jung,* blogtalkradio.com/carljung. November 3, 2009.

Maritain, Jacques. "Poetic Experience." *Review of Politics* 6, no. 4 (1944): 387-402. Available at http://maritain.nd.edu/jmc/jm3301.htm.

May, Gerald G. *The Awakened Heart: Opening Yourself to the Love You Need.* New York: HarperCollins, 1993.

———. *Will and Spirit: A Contemplative Psychology.* San Francisco: Harper and Row, 1982.

May, Rollo. *The Cry for Myth.* New York: Bantam Doubleday, 1991.

McTaggart, Lynne. *The Field: The Quest for the Secret Force of the Universe.* New York: HarperCollins, 2002.

Meade, Michael. *The World Behind the World: Living at the Ends of Time.* Seattle: Greenfire Press, 2008.

Mellon, Nancy. *Body Eloquence: The Power of Myth and Story to Awaken the Body's Energies.* Santa Rosa, Calif.: Energy Psychology Press, 2008.

Mogenson, Greg. *Northern Gnosis: Thor, Balor, and the Volsungs in the Thought of Freud and Jung.* New Orleans: Spring Journal Books, 2005.

Monaghan, Patricia. "Foreword." In Frank MacEowen, *The Spiral of Memory and Belonging: A Celtic Path of Soul and Kinship.* Novato, Calif.: New World Library, 2004.

Nietzsche, Friedrich. *Thus Spoke Zarathustra.* Translated by Clancy Martin. New York: Barnes and Noble Classics, 2005.

Ovid. *The Metamorphoses.* Translated by Allen Mandelbaum. San Diego: Harcourt, Brace, 1993.

Parker, Lois. *Mythopoesis and the Crisis of Postmodernism: Toward Integrating Image and Story.* New York: Brandon House, 1988.

Pearson, Carol. *The Hero Within: Six Archetypes We Live By.* New York: HarperCollins, 1998.

Plotinus. *The Enneads.* Translated by Stephen MacKenna. Burdett, N.Y.: Larson Publications, 1992.

Pope, Stephanie. "Pandora's Cabala." *A Hudson View Poetry Digest* 1, no. 3 (2007): 21-22.

Purce, Jill. *The Mystic Spiral: The Journey of the Soul.* London: Thames and Hudson, 1980.

Randour, Mary Lou. *Animal Grace: Entering a Spiritual Relationship with Our Fellow Creatures.* Novato, California: New World Library, 2000.

Richards, Mary C. *Centering in Pottery, Poetry, and the Person.* Middleton, Conn.: Wesleyan University Press, 1964.

Ricoeur, Paul. *Figuring the Sacred: Religion, Narrative, and Imagination.* Translated by David Pellauer. Minneapolis: Fortress Press, 1995.

———. *Oneself as Another.* Translated by Kathleen Blamey. Chicago: University of Chicago Press, 1992.

Rilke, Rainer Maria. "Sometimes a Man Stands Up During Supper." In *A Rag and Bone Shop of the Heart*, edited by Robert Bly, James Hillman, and Michael Meade. New York: HarperCollins, 1992.

Ronnberg, Ami, and Kathleen Martin. *The Book of Symbols: Reflections on Archetypal Images.* Cologne, Germany: Taschen Publishers, 2010.

Rowland, Susan. *C. G. Jung in the Humanities: Taking the Soul's Path.* New Orleans, La.: Spring Journal Books, 2010.

———. *Jung as a Writer.* New York: Routledge, 2005.

Scarry, Elaine. *On Beauty and On Being Just.* Princeton, N.J.: Princeton University Press, 1999.

Schoop, Trudi. "Motion and Emotion." *American Journal of Dance Therapy* 22, no. 2 (2000): 91.

Selzer, Richard. "Raccoon." In Selzer, *Confessions of a Knife.* New York: Simon and Schuster, 1979.

Shakespeare, William. *The Tempest.* Edited by Robert Langbaum. New York: Signet Classic, 1987.

———. *The Tragedy of Hamlet, Prince of Denmark.* Edited by Sylvan Barnet. New York: Signet Classic, 1986.

Sheldrake, Rupert. "Mind Memory and Archetype: Morphic Resonance and Collective Unconscious." *Psychological Perspectives* 18, no. 1 (1987): 9. Also available at

http://www.sheldrake.org/Articles&Papers/papers/morphic/morphic1_paper.html.

Slattery, Dennis Patrick. *Casting the Shadows: Selected Poems.* Kearney, Neb.: Morris Publishing, 2001.

———. "Dante's *Terza Rima* in *The Divine Comedy:* The Road of Therapy." *International Journal of Transpersonal Studies* 27 (2008): 85.

———. *Day-to-Day Dante: Exploring Personal Myth through the Divine Comedy.* Bloomington, Ind.: iUniverse, 2011.

———. *Grace in the Desert: Awakening to the Gifts of Monastic Life.* San Francisco: Jossey-Bass, 2004.

———. "Introduction." In Slattery, *The Wounded Body: Remembering the Markings of Flesh*. Albany: State University of New York Press, 2000.

———. *Just Below the Water Line: Selected Poems*. Winchester Canyon Press, 2004.

———. "Narcissus, Echo and Irony's Resonance." In Slattery, *Harvesting Darkness: Essays on Literature, Myth, Film and Culture*. New York: iUniverse, 2006.

———. "Nature and Narratives: Feeding the Fictions of the Body in Homer's *Odyssey*." In Slattery, *The Wounded Body: Remembering the Markings of Flesh*. Albany: State University of New York Press, 2000.

———. "Poem's Pressure." In Dennis P. Slattery and Chris Paris, *The Beauty between Words: Selected Poems*. Stormville, N.Y.: Water Forest Press, 2010.

———. "Psychic Energy's Portal to Presence in Myth, Poetry and Culture." In *Eranos Yearbook: 2006/2007/2008*, edited by John van Praag and Riccardo Bernardini. Einsiedeln, Switzerland: Daimon Verlag, 2010.

———. "Toward an Aesthetic Psychology: A Review of James Hillman's *City and Soul*." *Jung Journal: Culture and Psyche* 2, no. 1 (2008): 49-56.

———. "The Voice of Violence: Its Afflicted Utterance." In Slattery, *Harvesting Darkness: Essays on Literature, Myth, Film and Culture*. New York: iUniverse, 2006.

———. "What You Tell Me In the Dark." In Dennis P. Slattery and Chris Paris, *The Beauty between Words: Selected Poems*. Stormville, N.Y.: Water Forest Press, 2010.

———. *The Wounded Body: Remembering the Markings of Flesh*. Albany: State University of New York Press, 2000.

———, and Glen Slater, eds. *Varieties of Mythic Experience: Essays on Religion, Psyche and Culture*. Einsiedeln, Switzerland: Daimon Verlag, 2008.

Smiley, Jane. "Taking It All Back." In *The Writing Life: Writers on How They Think and Work*, edited by Marie Arana. New York: Public Affairs, 2003.

Somé, Malidoma Patrice. *Of Water and the Spirit: Ritual, Magic, and Initiation in the Life of an African Shaman*. New York: Penguin Books, 1994.

Stevens, Wallace. "The Creation of Sound." In *Wallace Stevens: Collected Poetry and Prose*. New York: The Library of America, 1997.

Taylor, James. *Poetic Knowledge: The Recovery of Education*. Albany: State University of New York Press, 1998.

Tresidder, Jack. *The Complete Dictionary of Symbols*. San Francisco: Chronicle Books, 2005.

Turner, Victor. *The Ritual Process: Structure and Anti-Structure*. New York: Aldine de Gruyter, 1995.

Ulanov, Anne and Barry. *Primary Speech: A Psychology of Prayer*. Atlanta: John Knox Press, 1982.

Underhill, Evelyn. *Mysticism: A Study in the Nature and Development of Man's Spiritual Consciousness.* 12th ed. 1922; repr., London: Methuen and Co., 1930.

———. *Practical Mysticism: A Little Book for Normal People and Abba: Meditations on the Lord's Prayer.* New York: Random House, 2003.

Wentworth, D'Arcy. *On Growth and Form.* Cambridge: Cambridge University Press, 1992.

Whitehouse, Mary Starks. "The Tao of the Body." In *Aesthetic Movement,* edited by Patrizia Pallaro. London: Jessica Kingsley Publishers, 1999.

Whitmont, Edward C. *The Alchemy of Healing: Psyche and Soma.* Berkeley, Calif.: North Atlantic Books, 1993.

Willis, Peter, Timothy Leonard, Anne Morrison, and Steven Hodge, eds. *Spirituality, Mythopoesis & Learning.* Mt. Gravatt, Queensland: Post Pressed, 2009.

Young, Dudley. *Origins of the Sacred: The Ecstasies of Love and War.* New York: Harper, 1992.

ABOUT THE AUTHOR

Dennis Patrick Slattery, Ph.D., has been teaching for 42 years, the last 17 in the Mythological Studies and Depth Psychology and Depth Psychotherapy programs at Pacifica Graduate Institute in Carpinteria, California. He is the author, co-author, or co-editor of 18 books and over 300 essays on scholarly and cultural topics as well as book and film reviews that have appeared in books, magazine, journals and newspapers.

His works include *The Idiot: Dostoevsky's Fantastic Prince*; *The Wounded Body: Remembering the Markings of Flesh*; and *Grace in the Desert: Awakening to the Gifts of Monastic Life*. With Lionel Corbett he co-edited *Depth Psychology: Meditations in the Field* and *Psychology at the Threshold*. He co-edited with Glen Slater *Varieties of Mythic Experience: Essays on Religion, Psyche and Culture*; with Jennifer Selig he co-edited *Reimaging Education: Essays on Reviving the Soul of Learning*. He has published four volumes of poetry: *Casting the Shadows: Selected Poems* and *Just Below the Water Line: Selected Poems* (both with accompanying CDs); *Twisted Sky: Selected Poems*; and *The Beauty Between Words*, co-authored with Chris Paris. With Charles Asher he co-authored his first novel, *Simon's Crossing*. His latest book is *Day-to-Day Dante: Exploring Personal Myth through The Divine Comedy*. With Jennifer Selig he is finishing a collection of co-edited essays on the importance of the humanities in education: *The Soul Does Not Specialize: Revaluing the Humanities and the Polyvalent Imagination*. He offers writing retreats on personal myth through the work of Joseph Campbell in the United States and Europe. When not writing and teaching, Slattery and his wife ride their Harley-Davidson Electra Glide Classic through the ranch roads of Texas.

Contact:

dslattery@pacifica.edu — www.dennispslattery.com

You might also enjoy reading these fine Jungian publications

Re-Imagining Mary: A Journey Through Art to the Feminine Self
by Mariann Burke — ISBN 978-0-9810344-1-6

Threshold Experiences: The Archetype of Beginnings
by Michael Conforti— ISBN 978-0-944187-99-9

Marked By Fire: Stories of the Jungian Way
edited by Patricia Damery & Naomi Ruth Lowinsky
— ISBN 978-1-926715-68-1

Farming Soul: A Tale of Initiation
by Patricia Damery — ISBN 978-1-926715-01-8

Transforming Body and Soul:
Therapeutic Wisdom in the Gospel Healing Stories
by Steven Galipeau — ISBN 978-1-926715-62-9

Lifting the Veil
by Fred Gustafson & Jane Kamerling
— ISBN 978-1-926715-75-9

Resurrecting the Unicorn: Masculinity in the 21st Century
by Bud Harris — ISBN 978-0-9810344-0-9

The Father Quest: Rediscovering an Elemental Force
by Bud Harris — ISBN 978-0-9810344-9-2

Like Gold Through Fire: The Transforming Power of Suffering
by Massimilla & Bud Harris — ISBN 978-0-9810344-5-4

The Art of Love: The Craft of Relationship
by Massimilla and Bud Harris — ISBN 978-1-926715-02-5

Divine Madness: Archetypes of Romantic Love
by John R. Haule — ISBN 978-1-926715-04-9

Eros and the Shattering Gaze: Transcending Narcissism
by Ken Kimmel — ISBN 978-1-926715-49-0

The Sister From Below: When the Muse Gets Her Way
by Naomi Ruth Lowinsky — ISBN 978-0-9810344-2-3

The Motherline: Every Woman's Journey to find her Female Roots
by Naomi Ruth Lowinsky — ISBN 978-0-9810344-6-1

The Dairy Farmers Guide to the Universe: Jung and Ecopsychology
by Dennis Merritt
Volume 1 ISBN 978-1-926715-42-1   Volume 2 ISBN 978-1-926715-43-8
Volume 3 ISBN 978-1-926715-44-5   Volume 4 ISBN 978-1-926715-45-2

Becoming: An Introduction to Jung's Concept of Individuation
by Deldon Anne McNeely — ISBN 978-1-926715-12-4

Animus Aeternus: Exploring the Inner Masculine
by Deldon Anne McNeely — ISBN 978-1-926715-37-7

Mercury Rising: Women, Evil, and the Trickster Gods
by Deldon Anne McNeely — ISBN 978-1-926715-54-4

Four Eternal Women: Toni Wolff Revisited—A Study In Opposites
by Mary Dian Molton & Lucy Anne Sikes — ISBN 978-1-926715-31-5

Gathering the Light: A Jungian View of Meditation
by V. Walter Odajnyk — ISBN 978-1-926715-55-1

The Promiscuity Papers
by Matjaz Regovec — ISBN 978-1-926715-38-4

Enemy, Cripple, Beggar: Shadows in the Hero's Path
by Erel Shalit — ISBN 978-0-9776076-7-9

The Cycle of Life: Themes and Tales of the Journey
by Erel Shalit — ISBN 978-1-926715-50-6

The Hero and His Shadow:
Psychopolitical Aspects of Myth and Reality in Israel
by Erel Shalit — ISBN 978-1-926715-69-8

The Guilt Cure
by Nancy Carter Pennington & Lawrence H. Staples
— ISBN 978-1-926715-53-7

Guilt with a Twist: The Promethean Way
by Lawrence H. Staples — ISBN 978-0-9776076-4-8

The Creative Soul: Art and the Quest for Wholeness
by Lawrence H. Staples — ISBN 978-0-9810344-4-7

Deep Blues: Human Soundscapes for the Archetypal Journey
by Mark Winborn — ISBN 978-1-926715-52-0

Fisher King Press publishes an eclectic mix of worthy books including Jungian Psychological Perspectives, Cutting-Edge Fiction, Poetry, and a growing list of Alternative titles.

Phone Orders Welcomed — Credit Cards Accepted
In Canada & the U.S. call 1-800-228-9316
International call +1-831-238-7799
www.fisherkingpress.com

17276770R00122

Made in the USA
Lexington, KY
05 September 2012